Generalship in the Ancient World

Books by the same author

Applied Thinking for Intelligence Analysis: A Guide for Practitioners, Canberra: Air Power Development Centre (2014)

Generalship in the Ancient World

Timeless Insights on Command from the Greeks and Romans

Charles Vandepeer

Pen & Sword
MILITARY

First published in Great Britain in 2026 by
Pen & Sword Military
An imprint of Pen & Sword Books Limited
Yorkshire – Philadelphia

ISBN 978 1 03618 480 3

A CIP catalogue record for this book is available from the British Library.

Typeset by Mac Style
Printed in the UK by CPI Group (UK) Ltd, Croydon, CR0 4YY.

FSC
www.fsc.org
MIX
Paper | Supporting responsible forestry
FSC® C013604

The Publisher's authorised representative in the EU for product safety is Authorised Rep Compliance Ltd., Ground Floor, 71 Lower Baggot Street, Dublin D02 P593, Ireland.
www.arccompliance.com

For a complete list of Pen & Sword titles please contact:

PEN & SWORD BOOKS LIMITED
47 Church Street, Barnsley, South Yorkshire, S70 2AS, England
E-mail: enquiries@pen-and-sword.co.uk
Website: www.pen-and-sword.co.uk
or
PEN AND SWORD BOOKS
1950 Lawrence Road, Havertown, PA 19083, USA
E-mail: uspen-and-sword@casematepublishers.com
Website: www.penandswordbooks.com

To you, the reader.

Contents

Acknowledgements

This book has come out of years of research and writing, supported along the way by numerous people I wish to acknowledge and who are included here (excusing ranks and titles). My thanks to Larry Regens for the suggestion very early on in the project to present each chapter as an enduring question of warfare, and for your years of support and mentorship. To the initial team who were such great supporters of the concept, gave feedback on the first rough draft, then followed up again with the complete manuscript, providing valuable insights, suggestions and recommendations: Richard Trotman-Dickenson, Troy Whitford, Aleem Hossain, Ashlynn Vandepeer and Bruce.

To the reviewers across the world, drawing on their invaluable mixture of experiences and insights as military, academic, and military-interested peers and colleagues, my great thanks and appreciation for your detailed and considered feedback, comments and suggestions on the manuscript: John Admire, Greg Allen, Stu Armour, Nandor Balogh, Rod Barton, Mick Burgess, Joji Domonatani, Amy Erickson, James Findlay, Ian Gibson, Andrew Hoffmann, Dirk Maclean, Michael O'Byrne, Joe Piers, Matt Rainbow, Larry Regens, and Will Trotman-Dickenson. Thanks also to Mitch Mott for helping with the book pitch, and to the family and friends who assisted with the initial design. I have been genuinely humbled and grateful to each of you for your time and efforts.

My appreciation to the entire team at Pen and Sword UK for your work and assistance, firstly in recognizing the value of the book and then taking it all the way through to final publication. To Jan Chamier, my appreciation for your professionalism and deft touch with editing the manuscript.

Finally, to my family who have been with me throughout the research and writing process, supporting me from the initial idea to the final publication, and beyond. I will be forever grateful.

As ever, any mistakes or errors are mine alone.

Preface

This book emerged out of my practical, professional, and research interest in warfare. As a military intelligence officer, later a defence operations researcher, and now an academic, what has always interested me is the human aspect of conflict. While the technologies, tactics and weapons of warfare have changed immensely throughout history, it is people who have remained the central and constant factor across the ages. The result is that every epoch of history remains relevant when approached from the perspective of humans in conflict. Therefore, whether Thucydides' account of the Peloponnesian War, Polybius' descriptions of the First and Second Punic Wars, or the myriad of ancient accounts of warfare included in this book, these ancient sources still have much to offer in terms of their enduring relevance to those who fight and those who lead others in wartime.

A key lesson I learned as an intelligence officer was to get as close to the original source of information as possible. In the case of these ancient texts, a great deal has survived across the millennia and is accessible to a modern reader, usually with multiple translations against which to compare and contrast. There are certainly differences between the ancient authors' accounts and debates about the accuracy and reliability of their works will long continue. Consequently, in engaging with these early accounts of conflicts, battles, soldiers and generals, the approach I have adopted is a questioning one, deliberately considering 'Is it logical?', 'Is it credible?', 'Is it consistent?', 'Does it accord with more recent military history?' and, ultimately, 'Does this address an enduring challenge in warfare?'. It was in the positive answers to these questions that this book emerged.

We all have much to learn from those who have gone before us, both in terms of the generals and soldiers who fought the battles, won victories or suffered defeats and from the writers who dedicated their time and effort (for some it was a lifelong endeavour) to capturing these accounts. It would be remiss of us to waste those hard-earned lessons and insights which have survived down the ages. The wisdom of the ancients is available to us, we have only to reach out and take hold of it.

Sapientia omnia vincit – Wisdom conquers all

Introduction

Iphicrates used to [compare] an army marshalled for action to the human body. The phalanx he called the breast, the light-armed troops the hands, the cavalry the feet, and the general the head. If any of the inferior parts were wanting, the army he said was defective: but if it wanted a general it wanted everything.

Polyaenus

The ancient Greeks and Romans understood war. Their knowledge was hard-earned and grounded in the reality of battle. They knew what it took to be victorious on the battlefield and they knew the costs of defeat. Fortunately for us, much remains of the writings of these early Greek and Roman observers on what it took to win in battle, to overcome the enemy in combat, and even how defeats could be reversed. This book draws on these accounts.

What is evident is that these ancient authors wrote to provide their readers with knowledge and insights from history. They recognized that their accounts of these campaigns and battles, and of the leaders and armies who fought them, contained lessons which could be learned and applied. Writing over 2,000 years ago, Greek historian and statesman Polybius (*c.* 200–118 BC) argued there were two ways that people can learn: either through their own mistakes, or through those of others. Learning from our own mistakes is certainly more memorable but learning from the mistakes of others is a far less painful way to acquire knowledge, and consequently the latter is the better approach in life. Polybius made it clear that as no one can claim omniscience, historical knowledge of past events is not just an asset but absolutely essential for sound decision making, as it provides the best opportunity to determine the most favourable approach to take in any situation, at least risk to ourselves. Polybius was not alone in this argument, particularly when it came to capturing the history of battles.

Why did so many of these Greek and Roman authors focus heavily on accounts of war, military campaigns and battles? Why did they often emphasize that they were writing to impart lessons and knowledge on why and how armies and navies were victorious or suffered defeats? Because they saw such knowledge of and insights into warfare as critical to the success and survival of their nations. Further, they clearly believed that in chronicling such events they were enabling others to learn the lessons evident in these battlefield successes and failures and to apply them to achieve future victories.

Generals themselves recognized the importance of capturing these events in writing for the purpose of enabling learning. In his treatise on the Roman army (*De re militari*), Roman author Vegetius (fourth century AD) observes, 'Cato the Elder, who was often Consul and always victorious at the head of the armies, believed he should do his country more essential service by writing on military affairs, than by all his exploits in the field. For the consequences of brave action are only temporary, while whatever is committed to writing for public good is of lasting utility.'

Failure on the battlefield matters in a way that most other aspects of life do not. Reflecting again on the observations of Roman general, senator and historian, Cato the Elder, Vegetius states:

> misconduct in the common affairs of life may be retrieved, but … it is quite otherwise in war, where errors are fatal and without remedy, and are followed by immediate punishment. For the consequences of engaging an enemy, without conduct or courage, is that part of the army is left on the field of battle, and those who remain receive such an impression from their defeat that they dare not afterwards look the enemy in the face.

Military success was crucial to the survival of cities, nations, and empires. It was not enough to be respected by one's neighbours, a state also had to be feared. As Vegetius further argued, 'No state can either be happy or secure that is remiss and negligent in the discipline of its troops. For it is not profusion of riches or excess of luxury that can influence our enemies to court or respect us. This can only be affected by the terror of our arms'. Who ensured the state's terror of arms? The generals.

As the senior military commanders of armies, it was ultimately these fighting generals who knew of war through experience and who exercised this terror of arms on the battlefield. To these we can also add admirals as the senior commanders of the early naval forces also included in this book.* The ultimate responsibility for either victory or defeat on land and sea was laid at the feet of a nation's generals and admirals. Unsurprisingly then, ancient accounts of wars, campaigns and battles were written largely with the focus on the generals. Both Greek and Roman authors had much to say about senior military commanders and less to say about the soldiers and sailors. Consequently, it is generals who are a central and consistent feature of these early accounts of war, and it is on these generals that we shall focus our attention. Generals are (and remain) central to the decision-making, the preparation and planning, and the execution of a nation's military actions. The ancients saw them as the crucial factor in any army, reflected in General Iphicrates' opening description of the general as the 'head' of the army.

But in Iphicrates' analogy another crucial aspect is apparent, namely that a general might be the head, but without soldiers and subordinate commanders there is no body, no means of putting plans into action, no means of fighting a battle, no means of achieving victory. The Roman general Germanicus understood this when he disguised himself and walked around his camp at night, listening into his soldiers' unguarded conversations prior to battle. Only once Germanicus heard from his soldiers' own mouths that they were confident in themselves, the plan, and his leadership, was he assured that they would succeed in the upcoming battle.

When generals such as Julius Caesar physically threw themselves into the fight, it was to rally their soldiers, to lift the spirits of those men in the battle, to ensure that each soldier did his part, because only the fighting soldiers could ensure victory. Even Alexander the Great clearly understood that his campaign and conquests rested on his army's fighting spirit, military skills, and physical endurance. It was not Alexander or his enemies who

* The term 'general' is used in this book to collectively refer to ancient admirals and generals, though admiral is used when recounting specific naval battles and discussions. For broader discussions relating to enduring insights, the term 'general' refers to the collective of star-ranking officers, regardless of nation or service (sea, land, air). This broader use to describe star-ranking officers across military services often appears in discussions on modern militaries and that is the approach adopted in this book.

ultimately determined the limits of his empire, but his own army. Despite achieving battlefield victories from Greece to the Indian subcontinent, and having survived crossing the formidable Hindu Kush, when the Macedonian soldiers determined that they would go no further despite their general's ambitions for ever more battles and conquests, Alexander recognized that his campaign was at its end. He turned his army around and marched them homewards, since a fighting general without fighting soldiers is merely a figurehead. Consequently, while the focus of this book is on these ancient generals, because it was largely the perspective that the ancient authors wrote from, the ultimate foundation of warfare is the warrior – no warriors, no armies, no generals. Generals, both ancient and modern, either recognize this or ignore it at their own peril.

What Iphicrates' description also serves to underscore is a fundamental and enduring aspect of warfare: war is ultimately a human activity. Wars are led and fought by humans. Despite the centuries and sometimes millennia between these accounts and ourselves, and the enormous changes and developments in weapons, technologies, and tactics, warfare remains fundamentally and irrevocably a human activity. In distinguishing these aspects of conflict, we can draw on the Prussian military officer and theorist Carl von Clausewitz who saw a difference between the constantly changing *character* of war (how wars are fought) and the enduring *nature* of war (the more human aspects of war).

Both the character and nature of war matter, but too often it appears that modern analysis of warfare favours understanding the weapons and technologies used to fight without a similarly detailed effort at understanding the humans doing the fighting. Perhaps this is because weapons and technology are relatively easier to understand than the complexity of human behaviour in combat. If the primary focus of analysis of warfare becomes the weapons and technologies, then we lose sight of the fact that it is people who use, employ and fight with them. Further, it is against humans and their will to fight that any such technology is ultimately aimed. Whatever the characteristics of battles and wars, whether state-based conflicts, insurgencies, guerrilla warfare, high- or low-tech, and any combination or adaptation of these, regardless of how battles are fought or the weapons and technologies used, it is the *human* who occupies the central role in warfare.

Modern military historian John Keegan captures this effectively in his classic *The Face of Battle*. Examining warfare across the ages, from ancient to modern times, Keegan makes the point that it is humans who represent the common and consistent aspect of conflict. For Keegan, any study of conflict must, therefore, be based on an understanding of the very human behaviours and emotions, of fear and courage in the face of violence and uncertainty, of those who lead and fight, and of the cohesion and disintegration of fighting forces. British Army officer and military theorist, Liddell Hart, writing in the twentieth century, reflected on the consistency of human nature, particularly under the stressful and dangerous conditions of warfare. Across millennia, the human element in warfare remains constant meaning that to focus on humans in battle is always timely and appropriate.

Just as the human has continued to be the central actor in conflict there are also enduring themes which generals and their forces need to address to achieve success in the field. These themes appear consistently within ancient and modern accounts of battle and can be framed as a series of enduring questions about warfare. The questions themselves remain relevant across ages and wars, requiring deliberate effort to answer for every new conflict, though we can gain insights from what the Greek and Roman accounts revealed about the answers to them. These questions include: *How do you understand yourself? How do you understand the enemy? How do you choose a battlefield? How do you deceive and surprise an enemy? How do you exploit a victory?* and *How do you recover from defeat?*

While each question is addressed as a separate chapter in this book, the discussions, insights, examples and answers are interrelated. Indeed, it will be evident how comfortably individual accounts of generals and battles could fit within multiple chapters, and occasionally an event is deliberately included in more than one chapter as it provides insights from different angles. The questions are answered by drawing widely from the writings of Greek and Roman authors over a period of some 868 years (Battle of Marathon 490 BC to the Battle of Adrianople AD 378). The chapters present a mixture of short and longer accounts, some quoted directly to allow the reader to hear the voices of these historic authors themselves, other times retold, but always analysed with the purpose of answering these enduring questions. Included at the beginning of each chapter is a series of short, more modern, attributed quotes on warfare, highlighting the ongoing relevance of these topics to conflict. For ease of reading, all references and sources for the quotes and accounts are provided at the end of the book. The overlapping nature of the topic of generals and warfare is ultimately drawn together in the final chapter *What makes a good general?* reflecting multiple factors which, often combined, have helped leaders achieve battlefield success.

Who were these generals? Some in this book are well known – Alexander the Great, Julius Caesar, Hannibal and Scipio Africanus. Others less so for many readers today, such as Philopoemen, Iphicrates and Fabius Maximus. How did they achieve their rank? It very much depended upon their society and circumstances. There were similarities and differences in how military generals were chosen, in the span of their authority and levels of accountability, depending on the society, era and context in which they lived. For Greeks and Romans, the rank of *general* (e.g. *strategos, legate*) was a formal designation of senior military command. Further, for both Greeks and Romans it was not unusual to have multiple generals on a battlefield, sometimes with one recognized as having overall command, whereas at other times the chain of command is not so clear from the historical record. As regards their battlefield opponents the title of general was usually applied to them also, by classical writers detailing the events. These senior military commanders leading armed forces against the Greeks and Romans across hundreds of years of recorded history included emperors, kings and queens, tribal chiefs, rulers of cities and provinces (one rebellion was even led by a gladiator). Therefore, in the context of this book, the term *general* is applied broadly but appropriately, aligning with the Greek and Roman chroniclers and enabling a greater insight by including so many often formidable military leaders and their forces.

Even amongst classical Greek states, there were differences in how generals were selected and appointed. In Athens, a general (*strategos*) was elected to the position and needed to be re-elected at regular intervals. Athenian generals and admirals had scope for military decisions and actions but were notably at risk of sacking, exile and even death if they were judged to have failed in effectively conducting their duties. For the Spartans, they had the unusual situation of being ruled concurrently by two kings. In conflict, one of the kings would be chosen by a select Spartan assembly as the supreme general to lead the campaign. Spartan generals had total decision-making authority once they were beyond Sparta's borders. They were celebrated when successful but could also be put on trial on return from campaign if their decisions and actions were considered to have failed.

For kings like Philip II of Macedonia and his son, Alexander the Great, their generalship came from their royal position, having absolute authority over decision-making and answerable only to themselves. Such was the situation too for Persian kings such as Xerxes and Darius, military leaders with no authority above them. Of course, as history shows us, the risk for such dynastic kings and generals was that a loss on the battlefield could be the loss of their position (even if they survived), which then passed to other family members or opened the path for others to fill the new gap in power, a point not lost on these leaders in their decision-making.

Under the Romans, the selection of a general was a formal process, though the power and scope of authority could change given that the emperor himself could take the field as the supreme general. For much of Rome's history generals were chosen by the Senate and usually from amongst the members of the Senate, to either head a specific campaign or as a consul or praetor with overall military command of a region. A designated leader could also be appointed as a *legate* (general) with military command over an individual Roman legion (typically some 4,000–5,000 soldiers). Roman generals, at the consul level in particular, had significant scope of decision-making and actions while still very much being answerable and accountable to the Senate. Of course, it depended on circumstances and the situation and desperation of the state, particularly in wartime. Following the loss of a general on the battlefield, there were instances of surviving soldiers electing a new general on the spot, reflecting the desperation of the situation and the need for an army to have a recognized leader making ultimate decisions.

While there were differences in how generals obtained the position, there is a common theme for these early Greek and Roman military commanders. Almost without exception, generals who were selected, elected or who acquired the rank by some orthodox route, came primarily from aristocratic, wealthy and powerful families. Rarely if ever did anyone 'rise through the ranks' to the top position. While aristocratic origins were usually a necessity for selection or election, there was also a requirement for military skill and experience. Aristotle, tutor to Alexander the Great, argued that in selecting a general the focus should be on military ability rather than virtue, 'as there are fewer capable of conducting an army than there are good men.' There are sound historical reasons for this. The cost of selecting privileged but incapable generals is counted in lives lost. As Aristotle also observed, reflecting on early Greek history, 'as the generals were men of no military experience, who owed their position solely to their family standing, it continually happened that some two or three thousand of the troops perished on an expedition; and in this way the best men alike of the lower and the upper classes were exhausted.' Therefore, military capability and skill was important in the selection of a nation's generals.

How was such military knowledge acquired? Usually from a very young age. Many of these generals had grown up around armies led by relatives, allowing them to gain first-hand insight of military command, soldiers, camp life and even battle. Indeed, many subsequently achieved the position of general while they were still young, certainly by modern standards. Alexander the Great was leading a military campaign in Macedonia at 16 when his father, Phillip II, was fighting beyond the borders. Roman general Pompey was commanding an army at 23, the Carthaginian Hannibal achieved the rank of general at 26, and Scipio Africanus was leading the Roman army in Spain at just 27. For many, military knowledge and senior command came to them very early in life, while they were young enough to rapidly learn and adapt.

If the risks of failure, including death on the battlefield, were clear then so was the glory, honour and recognition (even riches) that victory could bring. Indeed, it was clearly the desire for glory and honour that drove many of these generals. Such honours and awards, ambition for success, praise and adoration, played a significant role and was a very human aspect of generalship. Ego mattered. Public honours for victorious generals were particularly apparent in Roman society in the form of the 'triumph', a formal parade through the streets of Rome and the highest recognition and acknowledgement for a general who had achieved success in a foreign military campaign.

While debate continues over the triumph as an event, what is evident from the ancient accounts is that generals actively desired, sought and lobbied the Senate to approve the awarding of a triumph for their battlefield successes. Across hundreds of years, such victory parades were a feature of Roman society. Ancient authors describe triumphant generals riding in a chariot led by four horses, resplendent in a purple toga and wearing a laurel crown. Accompanying the general were his officers on horses and his soldiers marching, and sometimes even his family sharing his chariot and his glory. Featured too were prisoners from the defeated nation or tribe, surviving enemy commanders, surrendered nobility and their families, as undeniable evidence of Roman military might and conquest. Carts filled with captured treasure and enemy weaponry were part of the parade, along with imagery depicting the general's victorious battles and achievements, with musicians and exotic animals from the conquered lands adding to the incredible spectacle.

The public recognition, adoration and even worship of such victorious warleaders further encouraged the consolidation and expansion of the empire. In 71 BC, four Roman generals (Metellus, Lucullus, Pompey, and Crassus) were awarded triumphs, highlighting that these were more frequent events than we might have otherwise thought. Certainly, populations followed closely the successes and failures of their military commanders, upon whom so much depended. Their actions were central to the power, wealth, and security of their nations. Not long before General Germanicus' death, when news spread in Rome that the commander was recovering from illness, the Emperor was woken to the sound of citizens singing, 'Rome is safe, our country safe, for our Germanicus is safe'. Security relied on successful generals and populations were well aware of this fact.

For both generals and admirals of course there was that crucial relationship with their armies and soldiers, their navies and sailors. Generals needed their soldiers to achieve battlefield victories, and the soldiers relied on the generals for their own survival, both in wartime and out of it, for sustenance and pay – even wealth. A general who was successful on campaign could amass significant riches, attracting greater loyalty by selective distribution of wealth to their men as, for example, Julius Caesar did. Generals were also physically present, sharing conditions and dangers with the ordinary soldiers. Xenophon, Alexander the Great, Hannibal and Scipio Africanus, among many ancient generals, lived and fought alongside their troops. This was how battles were contested, with entire opposing armies each within sight of the other, all ranks on the one battlefield, each led by their general. Consequently, these commanders had to lead by example – all eyes were on the generals and their conduct.

There are many differences between modern generals and their ancient counterparts. There are no 16- or 23-year-old generals today, nor is the rank now the province of the privileged, selected or elected based on wealth and power. Whereas all Greek and Roman generals and their armies were entirely composed of men, today women increasingly serve in armed forces, occupying all ranks up to and including that of general. Warfare itself has changed as well. Whether or not these enduring questions remain primarily the preserve of generals in today's era is certainly open to debate. How is military leadership exercised in today's era with the breadth, complexities and challenges of a dispersed modern battlefield? Is battlefield command now exercised at lower levels? Is greater battlefield initiative required at the level of the soldier, sailor or aviator? Is there greater delegation and reliance on decision-making throughout all rank levels within armed forces? Such questions will continue to be debated, with insights and answers based on ongoing experiences of conflict and the continuing changes in how wars are fought. For all the differences, however, there are key similarities.

The rank of general remains firmly established as a feature of all armed forces (land, sea and air). The generals are ultimately responsible for understanding and addressing the enduring military challenges which their predecessors faced; they are expected to be able to prepare for, plan, execute and lead armed forces in battles and campaigns, to defeat an enemy and be victorious. Today's generals still take ultimate command and authority, as well as remaining accountable for their actions and decision-making, and their appointments are usually subject to political approval.

It is also fair to argue that a general's personal behaviour and example still matters greatly, and those they lead draw confidence or otherwise based on the professional conduct of their leaders. General Dwight Eisenhower, Supreme Commander of the Allied Forces in Western Europe during the final stages of the Second World War, argued that the greatest factor in success in war is human morale. Good morale relies heavily on soldiers' perceptions of the quality and capabilities of those leading them in war, in particular the generals in overall command. Like their early counterparts, generals today are usually adorned with rank and insignia (stars, red tabs, gold braid), deliberately designed to make them stand out from those they lead. Despite standing apart, just like their predecessors the generals are still human beings with all their strengths and frailties, and those they lead are human beings as well. War, for all its changes and technological development, still comes down to humans fighting humans.

There are certainly differences between the various ancient Greek and Roman texts and their authors. We can recognize the brilliance of Thucydides' epic account of the war between the Peloponnesian and Delian leagues, as well as the more self-promoting works of Julius Caesar detailing his successes against the Gauls and the mixed perspectives on Herodotus' accuracy as a historian. For some events there are multiple ancient authors and accounts while for many others the historical record is based entirely or largely on a single source. Recognizing that debates over the accuracy and reliability of these texts will long continue, it is on the surviving Greek and Roman texts that much of our historical knowledge rests and it is on these ancient texts that this book draws.

What is clear in reading these texts is that much that was written thousands of years ago echoes across the entire historical record of humans in conflict, up to and including the modern era. The early accounts provide timeless insights into the challenges facing military leaders in war. Ultimately, the best understanding of warcraft comes from the study of warfare itself. Polyaenus, a Macedonian author (second century AD) who wrote a wide-ranging account of military stratagems, argues that, 'generals cannot form themselves to victory by surer means, than by studying the arts by which ancient generals obtained it.' This is sound advice and one which has informed the writing of this book.

Chapter 1

How Do You Understand Yourself?

That victory may with much certainty be expected by the party taking the offensive when the general in command possesses the talent of taking his troops into action in good order and of boldly attacking the enemy, adopting the system of formation best adapted to the ground, to the spirit and quality of his troops, and to his own character.

General Antoine-Henri Jomini

The good quality of troops will more than ever secure victory.

Colonel Ardant du Picq

It is not the big armies that win battles, it is the good ones.

Maurice de Saxe

A general who wants to be victorious in war needs to understand both their own armed force and that of the enemy. Vegetius observes, 'A general is not easily overcome who can form a true judgement of his own and the enemy's forces.' He develops the point further: 'Thus a vigilant and prudent general will carefully weigh in his council the state of his own forces and those of the enemy, as a civil magistrate judging between two contending parties.' The fundamental importance of a general understanding their own forces and those of the enemy is echoed across Greek and Roman accounts of individual battles and discussions of warfare in general.

Famously, a similar point is highlighted by the Chinese military theorist Sun Tzu in the maxim, 'If you know the enemy and know yourself, you need not fear the result of a hundred battles. If you know yourself but not the enemy, for every victory gained you will also suffer a defeat. If you know neither the enemy nor yourself, you will succumb in every battle.' Why is it that such a seemingly obvious point is constantly emphasized across different cultures' reflections on warfare? At least two good reasons are evident. First, for a general such knowledge is crucial and could be the difference between victory and defeat, glory and humiliation. Second, because achieving and maintaining such knowledge and understanding of one's own forces and the enemy is difficult in practice. Ancient accounts of campaigns and battles reveal to us the challenges in knowing the fighting ability of one's own army, particularly when it came to actual combat, let alone the fighting abilities, plans and intention of the opposing forces. The picture is often partial and fleeting, depending upon the vicissitudes of war. Regardless, it is upon such knowledge that generals base their plans, decisions and actions, so there is a clear priority in achieving as good an understanding as is possible.

In this chapter the focus is on a general's understanding of their own forces and soldiers, while in the next chapter the challenges of understanding the enemy are explored. Although these two aspects of warfighting are considered in separate chapters, there is a clear overlap. A general who understands their own fighting force is in a good position to evaluate the enemy's; knowledge of both oneself and the enemy requires the ability to compare and contrast.

Understanding of military command

As we have said, a general needs a good knowledge of their own armed forces and personnel. However, they also need to understand their own qualities as a military commander, capable of making plans, identifying and selecting strategies, giving orders and coordinating actions. Generals are required to develop their own skills in commanding and controlling their forces before, during and after battle. The development of an understanding of generalship often began very early in leaders of antiquity, as indicated by the many known to have been still in their teens and twenties. Even at such early ages, these commanders would usually already have had experience in military encampments, on campaigns, and even on the battlefield, allowing them to witness first hand the exercise of command in their senior officers.

Alexander the Great, Hannibal and Scipio Africanus, for example, were themselves the sons of generals, and witnessed their fathers exercising military command at the highest level. Conduct in camp, planning, issuing orders, executing strategies, commanding in battle, all would have been closely observed by these future generals as they grew up around armies and the men who led them. There is no doubt that such experiences shaped the generals they became. Even if youthful when achieving the highest rank, a general would have ideally already experienced command of smaller elements (e.g. cavalry) within an army before taking on the most senior role. Aristotle himself noted that a general (indeed all ranks in the army) needed to learn by being commanded, because 'no one knows how to command who has not himself been under the command of another.'

These insights would have provided early learning in effective leadership and command of armies and soldiers in warfare, invaluable military knowledge which they could apply to their own generalship. Such lessons could illuminate both the positive and negative aspects. As a young Roman commander serving in his father's army (General Strabo), Pompey witnessed the effects of Strabo's poor command and leadership skills, having to intervene himself and plead with the men not to kill or abandon their general. Pompey's efforts proved successful and shortly after, following General Strabo's death (from natural causes), the young man quickly became a highly respected general, esteemed both by his soldiers and the populace of Rome.

Even during this ancient period, there were already written accounts of still earlier generals and their battles and campaigns, which the Romans (and also their enemies) would take the time to study, learn from and apply the lessons to their own generalship. Scipio Africanus and Hannibal both reflected on and learned from the actions and examples of previous successful generals. There is also a story of Julius Caesar, before his campaign in Gaul, reported to have openly wept after reading of Alexander the Great's battlefield successes and comparing them to his own, then-modest, achievements.

Of course, whatever the individual circumstances and context behind achieving the highest rank, to truly understand themselves, every general needs to learn from experience in the role. Generals need to learn about themselves *as generals*, while actually bearing the weight of accountability, responsibility and decision-making as the ultimate military commander. Knowledge of generalship then comes from the definitive insight and measure of how they command in battle. What is more, that knowledge is cumulative; with every battle fought and won, generals can learn more about themselves as senior commander, about their forces and personnel, the way to fight and win. As Plato asked in his dialogues, 'Does not the general aim at victory and superiority in war?', before concluding that 'a general who knows not victory' cannot be said to have gained understanding.

Active leader, not passive observer

Knowledge is not about some casual awareness or passing interest. A general is responsible for ensuring that their forces are prepared, ready and ultimately victorious on the battlefield. A general might struggle to exert constant influence over their military forces during the chaos of battle, but they have no excuse for not exercising effective command and control over the forces assigned to them outside of conflict. Generals hold the authority and the position to *make things happen*, to build their military units into the fighting forces that they want, and the nation needs. Certainly, a general has subordinate commanders to execute their orders, senior soldiers to conduct training and maintain discipline directly, but it is the general who has ultimate responsibility for ensuring that the armed forces they lead are a formidable and cohesive fighting entity. As Roman author Florus (possibly *c.* AD 74–130) in his work *Epitome of Roman History* observes, 'It is a true proverb which says that a general has the army which he deserves.' It is on the shoulders of the generals that the responsibility for the army rests, both in understanding and getting the best out of the forces they lead. Ultimately, the most effective way for a general to learn, understand and influence their forces is through their physical presence.

Few generals achieved this better than Alexander the Great, Hannibal and Julius Caesar. They understood their armies and the soldiers they led because they campaigned, lived and fought alongside their men for years. These generals actively developed their armies by exercising direct control; seeing with their own eyes, knowing what their soldiers could achieve, and getting the behaviour they wanted, on and off the battlefield. For the Roman generals, their tent was physically positioned in the very centre of their camp, providing the perfect situation to see, understand and know their soldiers and the army that they led. They developed invaluable knowledge and understanding by being 'on the ground' with their men.

At times generals are sent to take over command of an existing army, following a failure, death, or simply a change of command. Under these circumstances there is a more limited opportunity to develop an understanding of the force under their command and its associated fighting abilities. Regardless of similarities in weapons, training and organization, every army is made up of individual soldiers, people with their own motivations, fears and idiosyncrasies, experiences and expectations. Consequently, no two armies are identical and the general needs to understand the nature of the army and the soldiers they will lead. For example, it would be a mistake to assume that all Roman armies were efficient, effective and formidable simply because they were Roman, as history demonstrates. In 109 BC, General Metellus was sent to North Africa to take command of Rome's forces in their ongoing war against the Namibian general Jugurtha, a formidable opponent who had himself previously served as a respected commander with the Roman armies fighting in Spain. The Roman author Sallust (Gaius Sallustius Crispus *c.* 86–35 BC), a contemporary of Julius Caesar, allegedly a highly corrupt governor and later an influential historian, provided an insight into Metellus' challenges on arriving in Africa. The army he took command of:

> was an army spiritless and unwarlike; incapable of encountering either danger or fatigue; more ready with the tongue than with the sword; accustomed to plunder our allies, while itself was the prey of the enemy; unchecked by discipline, and void of all regard to its character.

The new general, accordingly, felt more anxiety from the corrupt morals of the men, than confidence or hope from their numbers.

Metellus was handed an army which stole from the locals, made up of soldiers who were consistently absent from duty, sold their own rations and were lazy. In terms of security, the army rarely moved camp and, when it did, failed to fortify the new camp or even establish watches. Recognizing the state of the army he had inherited, Metellus refused to accept them as they were and determined to reinforce drill and training, to bring the soldiers back into a war-ready state before they took the field against Jugurtha's forces. He turned an ill-disciplined rabble into an army, banning the selling of food and the owning of slaves and pack animals, and ensuring his soldiers trained for war. Now the army broke camp every day, to engage in raids across the country, fortifying each new camp and setting sufficient guards, whom Metellus personally inspected accompanied by his officers. In this way Metellus not only restored the army, he also came to *know* his army because he had trained them, tested them, observed them and led them.

It was a long campaign, but Rome was ultimately successful over Jugurtha. However, if Metellus had gone into battle with the army as it was when he arrived, it would have proved disastrous. Metellus dealt in reality, recognizing the weaknesses of the force he had taken over and proactively building it into the army he needed to fight Jugurtha. The Roman general understood what his army was and what it could be, and made it a reality. As Metellus demonstrated, a good general is no passive observer, simply accepting the state of the army he is given, but one who takes swift and appropriate action to turn his soldiers into a capable force with the best chance of victory on the battlefield.

How many soldiers

The number of soldiers available to a general is a reflection of the military capability which can be deployed against the enemy. Numbers are a crucial element of any effort at knowing yourself and the opposing side. But if there is one consistent theme within Greek and Roman writings when considering a fighting force, it is that superiority in numbers does not equate to military capability. Quintus Curtius Rufus, a first-century AD Roman author who wrote a history of Alexander the Great, describes the scene as Alexander's Macedonians face the enormous Persian force just before the Battle of Gaugamela (331 BC). Looking out at the massed Persian forces, Alexander makes the point to his officers that there is a key difference between the two armies – the Persians had more men in the ranks of their army but the Macedonians would have more men who would fight in the upcoming battle. This recognition that numbers alone usually do not decide victory in the field is even more pertinent given the nature of combat in ancient warfare: close, physical, hand-to-hand fighting. Numbers of military personnel under arms matter but are, on their own, an insufficient basis for a general's understanding of either their own armed forces or those of the enemy.

The Spartans' reputation as excellent soldiers and warriors was hard-earned and well-deserved. As a society built around developing warriors almost from birth, an entire culture built to fight and win, the Spartans' reputation remains well-known to this day. When questioned on why it was that the city of Sparta had no walls, Spartan king and General Agesilaus responded by pointing at their soldiers, saying: 'Here are Sparta's walls.' Not an unjustified claim and one that kept the city of Sparta safe from direct attack for hundreds of years. The Spartans' reputation as formidable warriors is best remembered and captured in Greek historian Herodotus' account of the Spartan general Leonidas and the Greek soldiers at the Battle of Thermopylae, when they stood against the might of Persian King Xerxes' enormous army at the start of its invasion of the Greek states in 480 BC.

Herodotus (*c.* 490–425 BC) wrote about the wars between Greece and Persia (fifth century BC) in the *Histories*. The Greek historian put the number of Xerxes' forces in the millions (which appears improbable, though it was likely in the hundreds of thousands), against a combined Greek force of possibly some 5,000-plus soldiers from across the Greek states, including 300 Spartan hoplites. Leonidas selected the narrow pass at Thermopylae as providing the best geography to hinder the movement of the Persian forces into Greece with the small numbers of men available to him. But a good geographic position still requires an effective armed force. Leonidas knew the fighting abilities of the Spartans and the other Greek soldiers under his command; he understood what they were capable of. In contrast, King Xerxes demonstrates a leader's dawning realization of the poor fighting abilities of his own soldiers, despite their formidable numbers.

After waiting four days for the Greeks to surrender or flee Thermopylae, Xerxes finally launched his enormous army against Leonidas' small force defending the pass. To Xerxes' astonishment, the initial results were devastating. Despite deploying wave after wave of soldiers, including Xerxes' own 'King's Immortals', the Persians were unable to break through or destroy the Spartan general's forces. Herodotus observes Xerxes' growing recognition of the poor capabilities of his own soldiers, noting that it was clear to everyone, including the king, that he had a lot of people in his army, but very few soldiers who could fight. The breakthrough came not from Xerxes' soldiers but when the king was provided with information about a path through the surrounding mountains, which offered a means of getting around the Greeks and attacking them from behind.

Early on the morning of the third day of battle, a Persian force caught the Greek forces guarding the alternative pathway by surprise and overwhelmed them. When Leonidas became aware that the Persians were on their way down the mountain to attack his Greek forces, he recognized the inevitable defeat of his army was at hand. The Spartan general called a war council and, realizing many of the other Greek soldiers had lost heart at the hopelessness of the situation, he sent them away before the final attack. The 300 Spartan soldiers remained to fight to the death, alongside their Peloponnesian allies and a contingent of 700 Thespian hoplites, while Leonidas appeared to keep 400 Theban soldiers as hostages, due to their apparent Persian sympathies. Leonidas then led out the remaining Greek forces to engage with the Persians, taking the fight to the enemy in front of them before the approaching Persian forces had the chance to attack the Greeks from behind. Leonidas, the Spartans and the Thespians died in this final battle at Thermopylae though at a heavy cost to Persian soldiers' lives. The Thebans apparently surrendered to the Persians when they were able.

While the result was a Greek defeat and the deaths of Leonidas and his warriors, after Thermopylae Xerxes was clearly shaken by the disastrous start to his campaign and the fighting abilities of the Greeks, in particular the Spartans. According to Herodotus, the Persian king summoned his Greek advisor, Demaratus, and asked him directly how many more Spartans there were and were they as good as the soldiers who fought here? Demaratus' answer was that there were 8,000 more in the city of Sparta and they were just as good as the 300 who had fought and died at Thermopylae.

The Persians were not the only ones to learn that Sparta's military capability went beyond the simple question of numbers. Even Sparta's own allies were provided with such a lesson. Spartan general Agesilaus is recorded as leading a group of soldiers to join a coalition army. Seeing the apparently modest size of the Spartan contribution, his allies were initially not happy:

> Upon a complaint of the allies, that the Lacedaemonians [Spartans] had brought into the field fewer forces than themselves, Agesilaus commanded them to sit down by themselves; and the Spartans to do the same, so that the matter might be brought to a proof. Thus seated, a herald made proclamation for all the potters to rise: of the allies a great number did so. Upon the second

> proclamation, which was for the smiths to rise, many more stood up. All the carpenters, who were a large body, were next ordered to rise, And, in the same manner, all other handicraftmen and mechanics, in their order. So that amongst the allies, there were scarce any left seated. But of the Lacedaemonians, not a man was seen standing; for they are by their laws restricted from practising any mechanic employment. Thus were the allies taught, that though they contributed towards carrying on the war, more men, yet the Lacedaemonians brought into the field more soldiers.

A good general understands that the quality and calibre of individual soldiers is crucial. But it goes further. While high-calibre individuals offer the general a fighting capability, a cohesive fighting force will achieve far more than soldiers fighting as individuals ever can.

Discipline and Training

Discipline and training are constant themes of the Greek and Roman literature in terms of what makes an army of individual soldiers into a cohesive and formidable fighting force. Vegetius makes this point clear: 'The ancients, taught by experience, preferred discipline to numbers.' A highly organized, disciplined and coordinated force, presented a particularly difficult problem for an enemy. As Alexander emphasized to his officers, each of them had to make sure 'to preserve discipline in the critical moment of action… to take care to obey his orders as quickly as possible, and to transmit the orders they had received to the ranks with all rapidity'; his army's success depended upon the collective efforts of individual officers and soldiers. Discipline, training and coordination ensure that generals have a capable army, ready to operate cohesively on the day of battle. Athenian general Iphicrates provided such an example:

> At Corinth he commanded the army with so much strictness, that no troops in Greece were ever better disciplined, or more obedient to the orders of their leader; and he brought them to such a habit, that when the signal for battle was given them by their general, they would stand so regularly drawn up, without any trouble on the part of the commander, that they seemed to have been severally posted by the most skilful captain.

Iphicrates had a disciplined and trained army because that is how he had prepared them. He knew that they would be battle-ready because he had trained and exercised them that way.

It was the Romans who developed permanent standing armies – a force of trained and disciplined soldiers always at the ready. Such forces were foundational to Rome's conquest, expansion and maintenance of the Empire against her many enemies. During Rome's outward expansion, the army became progressively proficient and professional; a disciplined, well-trained, efficient and effective military, capable of overcoming numerous adversaries across Europe, Africa, and the Middle East. The professionalization of the military produced better soldiers and a stronger army:

> The courage of a soldier is heightened by his knowledge of his profession, and he only wants but an opportunity to execute what he is convinced he has been perfectly taught. A handful of men, inured to war, proceed, as it were, to certain victory, while on the contrary numerous armies of raw and undisciplined troops are but multitudes of men dragged to slaughter.

Discipline and a profession of arms offers a massive advantage over part-time soldiery. Full-time, well prepared, and highly disciplined soldiers trained to fight as a collective are a known capability for their general, commanders and themselves. Regardless, a general still needs to ensure that discipline and training are *constantly* enforced. As was evident when General Metellus arrived in North Africa and took command of the Roman army there, it was an ill-disciplined force entirely unready for combat. It might once have been an effective unit but by the time Metellus arrived the long neglect of military discipline and warfighting training had made them weak. Vegetius captured this very point when arguing 'if that discipline is neglected, there is no longer any difference between the soldier and the peasant.' An ill-disciplined force reflects a general's poor leadership and failings, but more than this it represents a diminished military capability. A general who allows such poor discipline clearly does not understand the consequences of their own inaction. Such a general knows neither themself nor their personnel.

Tactics

An important part of discipline and training is the ability to cohesively execute coordinated and well-rehearsed tactics. A general needs to bring individual personnel together, combining them into a formidable fighting unit where organization and synchronization increases their strength as an armed force. Improvements in how groups of warriors fought were developed by generals in antiquity, with a view to defeating the enemy on the battlefield through better use of the resources available to them.

The development of the phalanx by the Greeks is an example of a formation designed to maximize the fighting abilities of individual soldiers by having them operate as a coordinated armed group. The phalanx was a formation of tightly packed lines of soldiers, with shields to protect them in the front, and using lengthy spears to engage with the enemy at a distance. The phalanx formation enabled spears from multiple ranks of soldiers to engage with the enemy, not just those of the front rank.

The use of the phalanx by Alexander the Great reflected tactical formation of soldiers designed to fight as a collective and overpower opponents. This formation was a feature of Greek fighting well before Alexander incorporated and further adapted the phalanx. This particular method of organization proved effective against many enemies, and endured over centuries, including Alexander's use of it against the Persians as a crucial tactical formation within his army. However, such formations have their limitations – for example when a general faces a force using the identical formation, as was often the case in battles between the Greek states.

Alternative formations and options would naturally be developed as generals sought advantage. The Macedonian phalanx was defeated by the Romans at the Battle of Cynoscephalae (197 BC) when the Macedonian king, Philip V, took on the Roman general Quinctius Flamininus. Greek historian Polybius, who wrote an extensive Roman history covering the period 264–146 BC, contrasts the superiority of the Roman formation over the Macedonian phalanx. According to the writer, the phalanx was suitable only for flat, open terrain where there were no features or obstacles to impede it. However, in warfare the locations for battle are many and various. As a result, the phalanx had many limitations on where it could be used and risked being unable to adapt if it was successfully broken up. Rather than attempting to match the Greek formation, to meet them head on with equal forces or a similar front, the Romans adopted entirely different tactics.

Writing in the second century BC, Polybius describes a Roman formation in which each soldier kept space around them (3 feet on each side) to fight with their swords, spears and shields, usually in maniples (multiple lines of 120 soldiers), which enabled these soldiers and lines to adapt to any terrain and situation. Gaps between soldiers in the maniples enabled soldiers to advance through ranks in front of them or allowed them to retreat into the ranks behind, as well as closing ranks into a tighter formation when the need arose. This formation allowed more flexibility and, once the phalanx had charged and lost its shape in fighting and moving, the Romans were able to occupy the areas around the phalanx and to attack the flanks and rear of the Greek formation where it was least protected.

A Roman legion usually consisted of some 4,000–5,000 soldiers (legionnaires), including 300 cavalry, under overall command of the general, with subordinate command exercised by tribunes (officers) and centurions (senior soldiers). The youngest soldiers were usually assigned to the *Velites*, who fought as skirmishers (armed with a sword, javelin and small shield) and whose numbers varied. Immediately behind the Velites came the first of the formally arranged infantry ranks, the slightly older *Hastati* with their long shields, swords and two javelins, some 1,200 soldiers in total arrayed in maniples. Behind the Hastati were ranks of 1,200 similarly armed, but more experienced, *Principes*. Finally, 600 of the most skilled and battle-proven *Triarii* formed the rear ranks, armed with long shields, swords and long thrusting spears. In this way, even if an enemy had success against the first rank, they found themselves facing multiple ranks of increasingly capable soldiers, in addition to the challenge of protecting themselves from the mobile Roman cavalry.

This Roman tactical formation proved superior to the Greek phalanx as well as numerous other enemy tactics and formations, but did not remain static. Roman tactics adapted over time in response to new challenges and enemies as well as ongoing improvements and developments in weaponry and military thinking, such as the well-known testudo (tortoise) in which soldiers join together with interlocking shields for protection and strength.

But Roman tactics were not infallible and could be defeated on the battlefield by enemies who were equally determined to achieve victory. The key point is that no single military tactic can guarantee success in all situations and against all enemies. Consequently, generals not only have to ensure their military units' tactics are effectively coordinated for the fight, but also ensure their forces are ready and able to adapt, to counter and defeat superior enemy tactical formations whenever and wherever these arise.

Weapons

Superior weapons also help make an armed force more capable than their enemies. At the Battle of Granicus (334 BC) between Alexander's army and Persian forces, the role of weaponry clearly helped to make the Macedonians a stronger force on the day. Despite difficulties, according to Greek historian Arrian (*c.* AD 86–160), who wrote an extensive account of Alexander's campaigns, 'At last Alexander's men began to gain the advantage, both through their superior strength and military discipline, and because they fought with spear-shafts made of cornel-wood, whereas the Persians only used darts.' The Macedonian spears were simply longer and stronger, providing Alexander's army with a clear superiority of weaponry over the Persians. A soldier's weapons and armaments are a fundamental extension of their fighting capabilities and strengths. For any general, analysis of their own personnel's weaponry compared to those of the enemy is essential in understanding their armed force's strengths and weaknesses. Consequently, judgements about the effectiveness of an armed force's weapons do not occur in a vacuum, but are *in comparison* with the adversary's weapons.

This type of analysis was undertaken by Julius Caesar in *The Gallic War*, his own account of his campaign in Gaul (58–50 BC), reflecting a general who clearly understood how to measure his own army's weapons against the enemy's. Caesar describes how during fighting a single Roman spear would often pierce through the Gauls' overlapping shields and pin them together. As the iron of the spears then bent, the Gauls were unable to pull them out and instead threw away their shields to fight unprotected. This is the observation of a general well aware of the effectiveness of his soldiers' weapons on the battlefield and the corresponding problems created for the Gauls and their ability to defend themselves. To be forced to fight without a shield and with usually inferior weapons would clearly prove disastrous, something Caesar recognized and exploited.

The quality of steel used in the Roman swords meant they were mostly superior to those of the enemies they faced and helped the Roman soldiers to be successful in close combat. During engagements with Gallic tribes this was very apparent, the Gallic swords being observed to bend and lose their strength and shape in the heat of battle. In fact most Roman armour, shields and weapons were on the whole stronger and more effective than those of their opponents, giving them a clear advantage. However, this was not always the case, as when General Crassus and his Roman army were annihilated at the battle of Carrhae (53 BC), where the definite superiority of Parthian steel arrow heads was demonstrated, piercing the Roman shields and armour. Thus confidence in the superiority of their weapons and armaments might only be justified in certain circumstances and against certain enemies, underscoring the need for generals to consistently evaluate the strengths and capabilities of their own armed forces against an array of potential and known enemies.

The will to fight

A general needs to nurture the will to fight in their armed forces: to fight harder, to fight longer, and to push onwards to victory regardless of cost. The importance of the human will to fight, the desire to win, and the determination of both generals and personnel to defeat and destroy the enemy while refusing to countenance defeat themselves often proves crucial. These intangible factors are well captured in Greek and Roman accounts of warfare.

Sextus Julius Frontinus (*c.* AD 35–103), a Roman military commander and author of *The Stratagems*, provided military leaders with guidance on instilling 'determination' and the drive to win within their soldiers, the will to conquer and not be defeated, to want victory more than their enemies and to fight harder to achieve it. This requires an attitude and mindset to push through all difficulties and ultimately to outfight and outlast the enemy. The will to fight, the resolve to overcome and defeat the enemy is foundational to an army's strength, and it is ultimately the general who is responsible for developing this determination in their soldiers. General Scipio Africanus set out to instil this drive to win in his own soldiers, urging them to adopt a winning mindset in battle by focusing on just two options:

> Go, therefore, to meet the foe with two objects before you, either victory or death. For men animated by such a spirit must always overcome their adversaries, since they go into battle ready to throw their lives away.

A formidable fighting force is a reflection of both physical capability and mental strength. Before the Battle of Thermopylae, Xerxes asked his Greek adviser Demaratus whether the Greeks would dare to take up arms against his massive army. Demaratus explained the Spartan mindset to the Persian king – that regardless of the size of their enemy the Spartans would fight with whatever soldiers they had, whether it was a thousand in the field, or any number greater or smaller. Greek biographer Plutarch (*c.* AD 45–120), who wrote extensively on the lives of famous Greeks and Romans as well as morals, customs and sayings, depicted the Spartan mindset similarly, noting that when it came to an enemy the Spartan way was not to ask what the enemy numbers were, but simply where were they.

The expression, 'It's not the size of the dog in the fight, but the size of the fight in the dog that counts' is reflected in warfare; the size of the fight in the soldiers often counts for more than the size of the army facing them. Taking the battle to the enemy, maintaining the initiative and bringing destruction upon one's opponent, relentlessly and despite many challenges, all matter. Vegetius argues that, 'it is indispensably necessary for those engaged in war not only to instruct [soldiers] in the means of preserving their own lives, but how to gain the victory over their enemies.' It is the general who should know whether or not their soldiers have such a will to conquer and, if not, it is they who must instil such determination within their army.

In ancient battles, soldiers fought at close quarters, face-to-face, in brutal and deadly combat. For both general and soldiers, their enemy on the field was usually within visual range. Victory mostly went to the side who refused to break ranks, whose confidence and determination to battle on remained strong, and who fought until the other side broke ranks and fled. The willingness to fight and face the risk of death reveals a stronger mindset over those who will hesitate, particularly in the face of such resilience. The often-quoted phrase that 'the best form of defence is attack' captures the benefit of an offensive approach, reflecting how a general and his soldiers' fighting spirit and willingness to take the battle to the adversary and put *them* on the backfoot will gain the initiative, regardless of circumstances.

Not all soldiers are equal

Knowing one's own forces requires a general to see beyond the massed ranks and recognize soldiers as individuals. Despite all the similarities of training and weaponry, actual combat experience is still a crucial means of understanding a soldier's ability. Indeed, simply assessing time in uniform is not the best indicator of individual skill or capability; some soldiers are experienced in warfighting, others have just spent a long time in the army. Vegetius reinforces the point, arguing, 'Length of service or age alone will never form a military man, for after serving many years an undisciplined soldier is still a novice in his profession.' Roman general Corbulo experienced this with the Roman soldiers sent from Syria to support his campaign against the Parthians. Roman historian Tacitus (*c.* AD 56–120), who gives us detailed accounts, particularly of Rome's first-century history, argues that these newly arriving soldiers were as much a challenge to the general as the enemy. The legions Corbulo was sent consisted of soldiers who had no combat experience and, though they had spent years in uniform, their base had mostly been in the comfort of towns. These troops knew little of military camp life or discipline, had never been on night watch, and even lacked their own armour; they were soldiers in name only.

In essence, what a general needs is to ensure they are developing and leading experienced *warfighters*. Inexperience is clearly a weakness on any field of battle, whereas familiarity with the reality of conflict has proven time and again to be critical to an army's strength and success. The capability gap between veterans and soldiers inexperienced in battle was apparent on many occasions during Roman civil wars. As a general, Julius Caesar recognized the capability of his own soldiers in the civil war against General Pompey's armies. Reflecting on Caesar's strategy in the campaign which ultimately brought him to power, Roman author Frontinus argues that, Caesar, in the civil war, always tried to engage in battle knowing that his adversary had recruits whereas he had an army of veterans. Until he faced Caesar, Pompey had always been a victorious general. But Caesar had a battle-tested army, returning from a long, brutal and successful campaign in Gaul. In comparison with Pompey's recent recruits, Caesar knew his hardened veterans were much more capable as a fighting force.

Discipline and drill will help turn soldiers into a cohesive fighting unit, but the best training is actual combat, because the ultimate measure of an armed force is the ability to fight and win on the battlefield. Polybius reflected on the strength of Hannibal's army as it made its way towards Rome, noting that the Carthaginian force was powerful not just in numbers but because of experience, having fought a series of campaigns in Spain. Hannibal had trained his army in war; he and his soldiers knew how to fight and how to win. As Polybius highlights, this training had been a continuing process:

> For the enemy's forces had been trained in actual warfare constantly from their earliest youth, they had a general who had been brought up together with them and was accustomed from childhood to operations in the field, they had won many battles in Spain and had twice in succession beaten the Romans and their allies, and what was most important, they had cast to the winds everything else, and their only hope of safety lay in victory.

Here was a general who truly *knew* his soldiers. Hannibal understood his men because he had led them and fought alongside them in battle. The African general and his soldiers had learned their craft in the field and this formidable, battle-hardened army went on to march into Italy with devastating effect.

But the story of Hannibal offers another aspect of a general's knowledge of his soldiers. As Hannibal recognized, once-formidable warriors could, after a break in fighting, be diminished in terms of their fighting skills and motivation. After resting his soldiers during a winter in Italy, Hannibal expressed concern at the state of his own force, saying, 'he recognized the arms and standards which he had seen and employed at Trebia and Trasimenus, and lastly at Cannae; but that he had indeed led one sort of troops into winter quarters at Capua, and brought another out.' Vegetius similarly provides guidance that 'soldiers [unused] to fighting for a length of time must be considered in the same light as recruits.' Thus, even an experienced troop could, after a break from battle, lose their edge.

Soldiers are human

Armed forces consist of humans, who need water and food, sleep and rest, clothing and shelter – a general or commander who fails to take these into account risks making disastrous decisions. Roman general Longus failed to do so when fighting in northern Italy against Hannibal's army, at the battle of Trebia river (218 BC). Polybius explains how Longus was goaded into battle with Hannibal before his soldiers had properly readied themselves for the fight. Hannibal sent forward his Numidian cavalry early in the morning, to harass the Romans. In response, Longus deployed his cavalry to engage the Numidians, but then rashly followed up by sending out his entire army, before they had eaten or warmed up against the bitterly cold December day. The bulk of the Carthaginian army, on the other hand, had taken time to eat and drink, resting in the warmth of their tents and preparing for battle around their campfires. As the day's fighting wore on the Roman troops suffered from both cold and hunger, whereas most of the Carthaginian forces were rested, fed and prepared for the elements before they took the field. These were two very different armies in terms of their preparation and comparative fighting abilities on the battlefield. Unsurprisingly, the outcome of the battle was disaster for Longus and the Romans and a clear victory for Hannibal and his forces.

Perhaps the best known example of an exhausted force taking on a well-rested army was at Gaugamela (331 BC), a battle between Alexander the Great's 47,000 soldiers and Persian King Darius' force of some one million infantry and 40,000 cavalry, according to Arrian. While this is likely an exaggeration of the Persian numbers, it appears reasonable to assume there were several hundred thousand on the Persian side, significantly outnumbering the Macedonians. After months of the Macedonians seeking to engage with Darius and his forces, the two armies were at last camped opposite each other with no doubt that a battle would occur.

The Macedonian king determined he would fight Darius on the plain of Gaugamela the following day. Alexander had rejected advice from one of his commanders to attack the Persians during the night as he wanted there to be no doubt that victory would be credited to Macedonian military superiority. Darius, not knowing Alexander's intentions and fearful of being attacked in the darkness, ordered his army to stand in their ranks all night. Too focused on his fear of Alexander, Darius failed to consider his soldiers and the consequence was that he himself thoroughly exhausted the men before the battle had even begun. When morning came, Alexander's much smaller but well-rested and refreshed army drew up opposite Darius' massive force and in his own time, in full daylight, Alexander launched his attack. Describing the lead up to the ensuing battle, Arrian reflects on the impact of Darius' decision on the by then exhausted and demoralized Persian soldiers:

> The success of the Persians, on this occasion, was impeded especially by this long standing on watch with their arms, and by the fear which usually springs up before great dangers; which, however, was not then suddenly aroused by a momentary panic, but had been experienced for a long time, and had thoroughly cowed their spirits.

Alexander's victory at Gaugamela was in no small part assisted by this mistake on the part of Darius. As Vegetius notes: 'Two armies, one tired and spent, the other fresh and in full vigour, are by no means an equal match.'

Military capabilities take time to develop

A general also needs to allow for the fact that developing a military capability takes time, effort and deliberate focus. The *intention* of doing something is very different to the *action* of doing it, words versus deeds. Such a situation is depicted in accounts by the Athenian Admiral Thucydides (*c.* 460–404 BC) who gave us one of the definitive histories of warfare in his writings on the Peloponnesian War. The conflict between Sparta and Athens and their corresponding allies would last some 27 years (431–404 BC) and eventually see Sparta prevail, though more because of Athenian over-reach than Spartan brilliance.

Thucydides himself commanded during the early years of the conflict but was put on trial and exiled from Athens after failing to reach a besieged Athenian army at Amphipolis (northern Greece) in time to prevent the Spartan capture of the city. The exiled admiral subsequently invested his time researching and writing about the war in which he had previously fought. While the Spartan soldiery exemplified well-honed fighting abilities, this same warrior culture demonstrates that developing a new military capability takes time and effort. The original Spartan method was designed to build boys into warriors, but within the context of fighting on land. When attempting to develop a navy capable of taking on the well-established and proficient Athenian naval force, the Spartans discovered just how difficult it was to build up a new military capability, particularly during a war that was already well underway. What is apparent from Thucydides' account is that the Spartans struggled throughout the war to transfer their land-based fighting skills to create a similarly formidable naval expertise. In contrast, the Athenians did have a good understanding of both their own naval capabilities and those of the fledgeling Spartan navy.

At the outset of the conflict, Athenian Admiral Pericles' reflections on the challenges of developing a military capability emphasized the benefit of knowing one's own abilities and the difficulties an enemy was likely to face. Pericles observed that the Spartans were not sailors and lacked the naval skills and experience needed to build a maritime force. In the coming conflict, Pericles argued, the Athenian navy would not allow the Spartans either time or space to freely develop a naval capability. Their enemy's lack of understanding of sailing and fighting at sea would lead to mistakes that the Athenian naval forces could exploit, further diminishing the Spartans' confidence. Pericles observed that a maritime capability could not be wished into existence but needed constant focus and dedicated effort, which the Spartans would be unable to achieve during a war. The admiral knew from the Athenian naval experience exactly what was required to develop an effective naval force and just how difficult it would be for the Spartans to establish one themselves.

This was precisely what happened in practice. Despite their aim to build a navy able to defeat the Athenians at sea, throughout the conflict the Spartans more often than not struggled simply to survive naval engagements.

Maritime victories by the Spartans over the Athenians were few and usually only achieved with the assistance of allies such as the Corinthians, and later Syracusans, who already had well developed naval capabilities before the start of the Peloponnesian War.

Miscalculation is always a risk

Accurate understanding of one's own forces is a crucial requirement for any general and there is always the risk of a general miscalculating their strength, resulting in failure and defeat. Even the most proficient and respected of military leaders can make such mistakes and err in their judgements of their own capabilities against an enemy. A good example of this is the Battle of Pylos (425 BC) between the Spartans and Athenians, in the early stages of the Peloponnesian War.

Following a successful lodgement by the Athenians on Pylos (not far from Sparta), the Spartans launched a campaign under Admiral Thrasymelidas to retake the location. Despite their undoubted fighting abilities, the Spartans overestimated themselves and underestimated the Athenians, finding themselves on the verge of defeat in the land and naval engagement. As a consequence, they were forced to send a delegation to negotiate a truce with the Athenians in an attempt to rescue their soldiers trapped at Pylos. The Spartans openly admitted that despite their military reputation they had simply miscalculated their existing capabilities in the current battle, arguing that such a mistake could be made by anyone in war. That such expert warriors could still misjudge their own military abilities in fighting a particular battle should highlight just how difficult such calculations are in practice. If the Spartans could make mistakes in their pre-battle judgements so could anybody. A general's understanding of their own force's strength and capability is context dependent. It requires consideration of the situation, the timing and location of the battle and, critically, a sound knowledge of the enemy.

Chapter 2

How Do You Understand the Enemy?

Great advantage is drawn from knowledge of your adversary, and when you know the measure of his intelligence and character, you can use it to play on his weakness.

Frederick the Great

Decide what will hurt the enemy most within the limits of your capabilities to harm him and then do it.

General George Patton

There is a clear motivation for a general to know their enemy; such knowledge can prove the difference between victory or defeat, glory or shame, survival or death. Greek and Roman generals usually had a distinct advantage in understanding their enemies because their societies had lengthy experience in fighting one another; they knew their adversaries in practice, not just in theory. Consequently, knowing both one's own forces and those of the enemy is, for a general, an inherently practical matter and one into which the leaders of the ancient world provide valuable insights.

Know the enemy commander

Knowing *who* is leading an enemy into battle will often provide an understanding of how the enemy will be likely to fight and, therefore, how they can be countered on the battlefield. Vegetius advised, 'It is essential to know the character of the enemy and of their principal officers; whether they are rash or cautious, enterprising or timid, whether they fight on principle or from chance, and whether the nations they have been engaged with were brave or cowardly.' It all matters, to know the enemy one must understand the character of the soldiers *and* that of the general leading them.

With this knowledge, a general can anticipate how an opposing commander will plan, think, act and react. Without such understanding, much of a general's efforts will be guessing and hoping, neither of which presents a good basis for fighting a campaign or battle. We see the benefits of knowing the enemy commander and the difficulties when such knowledge is lacking in the case of Hannibal's early campaign in Italy (218 BC). In these first battles Hannibal used intelligence to gain insights into Roman generals opposing him. In Roman accounts of Hannibal (the only ones that we have), the Carthaginian is credited with investing time and effort, drawing on spies and defectors, to understand the Roman generals he would fight against. Such preparation was intended to achieve success on the battlefield by goading his opponent into a disadvantageous fight or by circumventing an unfavourable set of circumstances himself.

In General Gaius Flaminius, Hannibal identified an opponent he would be able to provoke into committing his forces to fight under conditions highly unfavourable to the inexperienced Roman commander. Polybius notes that the Carthaginian general had gathered intelligence to develop a solid appreciation of Flaminius as an individual and as a military leader. The Roman commander had little understanding of the practical aspects of warfighting but, despite this, was over-confident in his own abilities. As a leader he was always trying to be popular with the masses, meaning that if Hannibal began devastating the country around him, the Roman would be unable to resist his own soldiers' demands to attack the Carthaginians. Additionally, Flaminius would want the glory of victory all to himself, so would avoid waiting to join forces with a fellow Roman army in the region. Hannibal recognized that the character of the Roman general would result in the Carthaginian army finding plenty of opportunities to attack.

Having established this knowledge of his opponent, Hannibal mobilized his own army and began attacking the territory in front of Flaminius. Despite the Roman general being warned by his own commanders to avoid engaging Hannibal before they could combine forces with General Gnaeus Servilius and his army, who were heading towards them, Flaminius rejected all advice and immediately marched his men out to attack Hannibal. But Flaminius was also careless, following Hannibal's army without taking necessary precautions, entirely focused on what he imagined would be his impending victory over the African general. What followed was the annihilation of Flaminius and his forces at the Battle of Lake Trasimene (217 BC), in which Hannibal and his army were able to use the terrain and a mist covering the area to conceal their forces and ambush the Roman general and his army, catching them in a confined space with hills on one side and a lake on the other. The result was the death of Flaminius and some 15,000 Roman soldiers.

Reflecting on Hannibal's forward thinking, Polybius describes the Carthaginian general's planning as wise and well considered precisely because it was based on a solid appreciation of his Roman opponent. Indeed Polybius goes further, arguing, 'There is no denying that he who thinks that there is anything more essential to a general than the knowledge of his opponent's principles and character, is both ignorant and foolish.' While Hannibal proved able to anticipate the thinking and actions of numerous Roman generals opposing him, the reverse was not the case.

In the early stages of Hannibal's Italian campaign, the Roman commanders struggled to gain a corresponding understanding of the Carthaginian general – how he thought, what he was planning, how he would fight. Their lack of success in this meant that the Roman leaders were less able to anticipate, prepare and plan appropriately against the African leader. General Quintus Fabius Maximus, recognizing this dearth of knowledge, did best by avoiding conflict and shadowing Hannibal's army with his own, avoiding unfavourable tactical situations which would otherwise have provided Hannibal with the opportunity to engage and destroy him. Possible chances to defeat Hannibal were arguably lost, and Fabius was initially heavily criticized, but in the circumstances and in the face of the slaughter of entire Roman armies, General Fabius arguably pursued the most logical option. He denied Hannibal freedom of movement, gave Rome time to regroup, and provided the Roman commanders with more opportunity to develop some insight into this formidable Carthaginian. Fabius would later be recognized and honoured as having saved the Roman Republic from Hannibal through judicious delay (earning him the name the 'Great Delayer') and denying the Carthaginian the opportunity to land a decisive final blow against the Romans.

Indeed, reflecting on Hannibal's failure to take the Italian city of Nola (216 BC) we see Roman forces celebrate not simply surviving, but claiming a victory against the Carthaginians. This was despite the fact that the Roman forces at Nola did not come close to thoroughly defeating, let alone destroying, Hannibal's army. The Roman historian, Livy (59 BC–AD 17), who wrote an extensive *History of Rome*, observes, 'Whether the victory was so great or not; it is certain that a very important advantage, and perhaps the greatest during the war, was gained on that day: for not to be vanquished by Hannibal was then a more difficult task to the victorious troops, than to conquer him afterwards.'

Such was the Romans' initial challenge – to understand Hannibal – that to avoid being defeated by him was considered a great success. However, even in such successes (and even in victories), without an understanding of the opposing commander or the opposition forces, there remained a risk of serious miscalculation. How does the enemy commander see the situation? What are their intentions? What are their aims and goals? How do they plan, lead and fight? Outside of knowing this, a general is merely guessing, which is always a risky basis for making decisions in war. In addition to understanding the commander, good generals would also seek knowledge of the soldiers, the culture and the nation that they are fighting against. Such insights may prove critical to battlefield success.

Julius Caesar – to know and to conquer

Julius Caesar was a general who knew that knowledge of his adversary could be used to his battlefield advantage. A reading of Caesar's own account of his campaign against the Gauls reveals a general who actively sought to understand his enemy; to identify how the Gauls thought and how they fought. There were various tribes in the Gallic regions (modern day Western Europe including France and Belgium, also some areas in Germany, Switzerland, the Netherlands, and even Northern Italy), with similarities and differences between tribes, and they had varying levels of military success against the Romans throughout Rome's history.

Caesar knew that the Gauls were dismissive of the Romans' relatively smaller physical stature, noting this commonality in Gaulish thinking, 'for our shortness of stature, in comparison with the great size of their bodies, is generally a subject of much contempt to the men of Gaul.' This was, of course, something Caesar could turn to his benefit.

In contrast, Caesar was not contemptuous of the Gauls or overconfident in his outlook. As a commander he recognized and credited the enemy's fighting abilities and strengths, seeking to understand them for the sole purpose of defeating them. As noted:

> Caesar at first determined to decline a battle, as well on account of the great number of the enemy as their distinguished reputation for valour: daily, however, in cavalry actions, he strove to ascertain by frequent trials what the enemy could effect by their prowess and what our men would dare.

Here we see Caesar's deliberate use of small skirmishes to build up his knowledge, both of the enemy and of his own soldiers. Once he determined that his Roman troops were a match for the Belgic forces opposing him, Caesar was prepared to engage them in a major battle.

The enemy's tactics and ways of fighting were also considered in detail. For example, in analysing how the Belgae tribe attacked fortifications, Caesar gives a detailed explanation of their approach, noting that their soldiers will surround the fortification, attack the wall with stones to clear away the defenders upon it and then, locking their shields above their heads, advance to the walls and undermine them. Caesar shows the breadth of his knowledge by noting that this was the same approach as the other Gaulish tribes used to attack fortifications. Knowing how the enemy fought informed the development of his plans to effectively defeat his enemies.

Beyond tactics, Caesar also sought to understand how his enemy thought, what motivated them, and even what their religious beliefs were. No detail was disregarded if it enabled insight into how the Roman general could defeat his enemy. We see this in practice when Caesar was fighting against German tribes. Despite setting up an armed camp opposite the massed forces led by Ariovistus, Caesar could not convince the German commander to engage him in battle. Caesar looked for answers by asking German prisoners why Ariovistus would not come out of his camp and fight, and discovered:

> that among the Germans it was the custom for their matrons to pronounce from lots and divination whether it were expedient that the battle should be

> engaged in or not; that they had said, 'that it was not the will of heaven that the Germans should conquer, if they engaged in battle before the new moon.'

So what did Caesar do with this information? He attacked the Germans in force before the new moon, and won decisively. Knowledge really was power in this case and Caesar used what he had learnt as the basis for defeating his enemy.

Knowledge of the enemy can be achieved and applied with success by any general willing to make the effort, and was certainly not limited to Julius Caesar. Roman general Fabius, who conquered the Samnites and Gauls at Sentinum (295 BC), developed a battleplan based on knowing how the enemy fought: 'The Romans, under Fabius, rather repelled than offered assault, and the contest was protracted until very late in the day, for their general knew very well, that both Samnites and Gauls were furious in the first onset, so that to withstand them would be sufficient.' Fabius was armed with the understanding that his adversary would fight fiercely at first but would subsequently lose momentum. Accordingly, he selected the best tactics to destroy them – to withstand the initial onslaught and then attack in full strength when the Samnites and Gauls had tired. Such an informed strategy certainly offered a better chance of success and demonstrates that knowledge of the enemy can provide a general with a solid basis on which to achieve victory.

Xerxes – the king who never understood his enemy

Returning to Xerxes' campaign against Greece (480–479 BC), we see a leader who assembled what was described as the greatest military force the world had ever seen up to that point in history, a Persian army and navy amassed for the total conquest of the Greek states who had refused his demands that they submit to him as king. But we also see a military commander who never really understood his enemy. Herodotus' account of Xerxes' ultimately disastrous campaign provides us with insight into the battlefield outcomes of such a critical failing.

A foretaste of what was to come is captured in the story of an early effort by Persian governor Hydarnes to convince some visiting Spartans to submit to Xerxes' rule without a fight. The Spartans' refusal should have given Xerxes a better insight into those he would soon be fighting. On being advised of the 'benefits' of recognizing the Persian king, and effectively surrendering their state to him, the Spartan response reflected a very different mindset. They argued that Hydarnes' advice came from a limited perspective, as he had only known what it was to be a slave and had no experience of freedom. If Hydarnes had experienced freedom, they said, then his advice would be quite the opposite – to fight for it 'not with spears only but also with axes'. The Greeks would not cede their sovereignty in peace, and they would not surrender in war, something Xerxes never truly understood right up to his navy's defeat at the Battle of Salamis (480 BC) and his army's defeat at the Battle of Plataea (479 BC). Perhaps not even then.

This absence of insight into his enemy's mind was obvious prior to and during the Battle of Thermopylae. When the Persian forces arrived at the mountain pass to find the Greeks blocking their path, accounts of the Spartan soldiers' behaviour were brought to Xerxes. Instead of retreating in the face of their enemy's obvious numerical superiority, the Spartans appeared unconcerned and were clearly preparing to stand and fight. On receiving these reports, Xerxes simply could not understand what was happening, that the Greeks were going to fight despite being heavily outnumbered and with no realistic prospect of success. Because of his inability to comprehend the Greeks, Xerxes waited four days without attacking, expecting that they would soon recognize the hopelessness of their situation and flee. But the Greeks stayed in place, ready for battle. The Persian king's poor understanding of his enemy led to a delay in acting and only on the fifth day, in a state of rage, did Xerxes finally order his forces to attack Leonidas and his troops.

Even after defeating the Greeks at Thermopylae, Xerxes still seems to have remained blind to the character and mindset of those he sought to conquer. During his campaign, he was told about the Greek Olympic games and the rewards on offer. The athletes competed for the award of a wreath of olive leaves, though the true reward was public recognition and acclaim as a champion throughout the Greek states. On hearing the nature of the prize, a Persian commander exclaimed incredulously to those present at the strangeness of the people they were waging war against – men who fight 'not for money but for honour!' The statement well captures Xerxes' complete inability to understand the people he was fighting.

The irony was that Xerxes actually had numerous Greek advisors serving him before and during the campaign, whose advice was regularly sought and just as regularly disregarded. Xerxes' inability to comprehend a perspective so different from his own and his incapacity to consider things from another culture's viewpoint, illustrate a general's complete failure to understand his enemy. At no time during his campaign did Xerxes ever appear able to appreciate an outlook, mindset and culture so different to his own. This failure cost him dear on the battlefield and, upon return to Persia defeated, most likely cost him his life. But Xerxes was far from the only military leader who appeared unable or unwilling to understand their adversary.

General Crassus, a peer of Julius Caesar and Pompey and member of the triumvirate (a political agreement between the three military leaders), was determined to replicate Caesar's military successes in Gaul. He embarked on a campaign against the Parthians (modern-day Türkiye and Syria). However, in contrast to Caesar's efforts in understanding his enemies, and against the advice of his own commanders, Crassus moved swiftly to engage his enemy in a major clash of arms. Shortly after arriving in the region, and without having a clear understanding of the Parthian military or their tactics, Crassus eagerly launched his 30,000-strong army into battle against a Parthian force of unknown strength at Carrhae (53 BC).

After initially attacking the Roman square formation with spears, the Parthians realized the strength of their enemy's military configuration and rapidly adapted their approach. They broke off the engagement and pretended to retreat, only to begin attacking the pursuing Romans with arrows. They turned their focus on to the remaining compact formation of Roman soldiers, showering them with a fusillade of arrows from a safe distance. The arrows proved far superior to the Romans' defensive equipment, piercing their shields and armour. Whether the Romans attempted to charge or stayed in place, they were killed or wounded without being able to engage the Parthians. Uncertain of how to counter these unfamiliar tactics, Crassus was left simply hoping that the Parthians would run out of arrows. But the Parthians had come well prepared, with camels loaded with extra supplies of arrows, and the result was a bloodbath. The Roman general was killed and beheaded and his army annihilated, with estimates of 20,000 dead and 10,000 captured. Crassus' careless ignorance of his enemy went down in history as one of Rome's greatest military disasters.

Intimate understanding of the enemy

What a general should aim for is a deep and detailed understanding of their enemy. Athenian general Alcibiades made this point when advising the Spartans, after his own exile from Athens during the Peloponnesian War. Alcibiades explained the value of identifying what strategies and tactics their enemies were most anxious about, in order to use those very means against them. To the Spartans, Alcibiades recommended placing armed forces in Decelea, near Athens, arguing it was of this action that 'the Athenians are always most afraid.' The reasoning behind his advice was clear – 'the surest method of harming an enemy being to find out what he most fears, and to choose this means of attacking him, since everyone naturally knows best his own weak points and fears accordingly.' With intimate knowledge of their enemy, the question for a general to ask and answer is simply, 'What does the enemy fear most?' Once identified, he should do exactly that.

Even victory does not necessarily equate to understanding

Without a clear understanding of the enemy's goals, aims and mindset, the risk is that even when victorious, a general might still not really know their enemy, setting the foundation for undoing whatever success has been achieved. Admiral Nicias made this clear to the Athenians who had been surprised by their early victories over the Spartans in the Peloponnesian War. Nicias warned the Athenians that despite this initial success they had not achieved a true understanding of the Spartans. After all their pre-war fears, the Athenians had quickly won a series of victories, with the result that they stopped concentrating on the ongoing threat posed by Sparta and focused instead on launching an attack on far-off Sicily. As highlighted by Nicias, over-confidence based on their enemy's initial misfortunes was a flawed foundation on which to base decisions. The Athenians had by no means broken the spirit of the Spartans but they did not realize it. To Nicias it was obvious what lay ahead – the Spartans would focus their entire efforts on restoring their military reputation by victory on the battlefield against the Athenians. Based on this, the Athenian focus needed to be on defending against Sparta at home rather than sailing away and campaigning in Sicily (415–413 BC).

In their contempt for the Spartan threat, the Athenians disregarded Nicias' advice and launched their fateful Sicilian campaign, a move which would ultimately cost them the war. Admiral Nicias subsequently lost his life in Sicily, having been elected to lead the Athenian campaign that he had forcefully spoken against, though his advice would ultimately prove correct. The Spartans were driven on by their desire to defeat the Athenians, finally achieving victory over their enemies with the surrender of Athens in 404 BC and somewhat restoring their military reputation.

Beyond reputation and appearances

Knowledge of an enemy goes beyond awareness of their reputation and appearance and needs to be based on the reality of their current and actual fighting abilities. Roman general Flamininus made the point to his soldiers when about to engage the once-great Macedonians at Cynoscephalae (197 BC) in Greece. Flamininus argued that, 'the kingdom of Macedonia had been hitherto supported by its reputation, not by real strength; and that even that reputation had, at length, vanished.' The Macedonians had *once* been the regional military power under Alexander, but that had long passed. When Flamininus and his Roman army came to fight them, the Macedonians were great in reputation only – a reputation which the Romans subsequently disproved by defeating them in battle. Strength is not a permanent condition for any military, but involves constant effort. An army is the army of today, not the army of reputation or history and to maintain its strength requires consistently renewing experience, training and effort. Rome herself would eventually go the same way as the Macedonians, when her reputation exceeded her military strength, and the formerly all-powerful Romans found themselves defeated by peoples they had previously conquered.

In addition to warnings about not placing too much store on an enemy's reputation, generals also advised their soldiers to look beyond outward appearances and to judge soldiers by their fighting abilities in the field. When formed up opposite Samnite forces before a battle, the Roman soldiers observed their opponents' ornate, shining armour, plumes in their helmets, and visibly impressive appearance; however, Livy wrote:

> The Romans had been apprised of these splendid accoutrements, and had been taught by their commanders, that 'a soldier ought to be rough; not decorated with gold and silver, but placing his confidence in his sword. That matters of this kind were in reality spoil rather than armour; glittering before action, but soon becoming disfigured amid blood and wounds. That the brightest ornament of a soldier was valour; that all those trinkets would follow victory, and that those rich enemies would be valuable prizes to the conquerors, however poor.'

Elaborate uniforms and immaculate appearance did not necessarily equate to fighting ability and, as the Roman commanders understood, the true measure of a soldier is their ability to fight.

Recognize an enemy's superiority, and use it against them

Where an enemy is recognized as superior in weaponry, armaments or tactics, good generals will acknowledge and adapt to these, including copying their enemy's tactics and capturing and reusing their enemy's weapons and equipment. The superiority of Roman soldiers' weapons and armour was recognized by Hannibal's own forces when fighting against the Romans. Consequently, the Carthaginians simply adopted their enemy's captured equipment as their own. After defeating Roman armies in Italy, the Carthaginians took the weapons and armour from their slain foe to use for themselves. Livy describes the sight soon after: 'One would suppose the Africans were for the most part Romans, they were so equipped with arms captured at the Trebia, and for the greater part at the Trasimenus.' As a result, subsequent Roman armies found themselves fighting against their own weapons and equipment, now wielded by their enemies.

This is not unusual in warfare, ancient or modern. Recognized superior weapons are adopted and even reverse-engineered to counter or copy. One of the earliest recorded instances of reverse engineering of military equipment took place when the Romans realized the superiority of the Carthaginian navy's ships to their own during the First Punic War (264–241 BC). The Carthaginians were a well-established naval power with a formidable fleet of ships, which the Romans were unable to match and indeed they lacked the knowledge to build such capable vessels. But once a Carthaginian ship came too close to a Roman-controlled shore, and inadvertently ran aground, the Romans had what they required – a working model of a Carthaginian warship.

The Romans wasted no time in building an entire fleet of ships based on the captured vessel. The scale and scope of the construction was staggering – they constructed some 120 ships within sixty days. Even while this immense shipbuilding work was being undertaken, the Romans began training the sailors who would crew the vessels. The approach was ingenious: they set out rowing benches on dry land, to the design and scale of the captured vessel, so the men could learn the necessary rowing actions and associated commands. When the ships were ready, the crews took them to sea to finalize their training and adapt their drills to seagoing conditions. As a result of this one captured ship, and the mass construction and concurrent preparation of crews that followed, Rome was able to rapidly field a navy to take on Carthage in an area of warfare in which the Carthaginians had previously been unassailable. Not long after, at the naval battle of Mylae (260 BC), the Romans secured a stunning victory.

The enemy is trying to learn about you

The Roman victory at Mylae highlights another important point, that just as generals and their armed forces are trying to learn and understand their enemies, so their enemies are trying to learn and understand them. Plutarch described a Spartan rule which banned frequent campaigns against the same foes, lest these adversaries should grow used to defending themselves against them and thus become skilled in warfare. Plutarch highlights that the Spartan king and general Agesilaus broke this rule with his frequent campaigns against the neighbouring Thebans. The story goes that when a fellow Spartan saw Agesilaus wounded after one such engagement, he observed, 'The Thebans pay you well for having taught them to fight, which they were neither willing nor able to do before.'

The warning ultimately proved apt. At the Battle of Leuctra (371 BC), General Epaminondas led the Thebans and their allies against the Spartans under General Cleombrotus. According to Greek general and historian Xenophon (*c.* 430–355 BC), the Spartans were no longer at the peak of their military prowess. There were cavalry forces on both sides, but the contrasting nature of phalanxes played a crucial role in the battle. The Spartan phalanx was just twelve men in depth whereas Epaminondas had stacked the Theban phalanx with a strength of some fifty shields deep. The Spartans were eventually forced back by the mass of Thebans and ultimately defeated, with the loss of General Cleombrotus and some 1,000 soldiers, including 400 officers. The battle represented a significant shift in military power in the Greek states and it proved to be a defeat that the Spartans never recovered from, ending Sparta's military dominance just over four decades after their long fought for victory over the Athenians in the Peloponnesian War. By the time of Leuctra, the Thebans were well-versed in fighting the Spartans, and apparently no longer intimidated by them, ultimately proving superior on this key battlefield.

Clearly a general's attempts at learning about the enemy risks that enemy learning about their own forces, tactics, and fighting abilities. This situation has to be managed by a commander but, even then, circumstances might dictate that such knowledge and understanding is already established long before any clash of arms occurs. In the case of Rome and its civil wars, the challenge could be one of facing almost identical forces. During the civil war that followed Julius Caesar's assassination (44 BC), Octavian and Mark Antony's armies fought against Brutus and Cassius' armies, ultimately defeating them at Philippi (42 BC) in Macedonia. But this was no easy victory, precisely because it pitted Roman against Roman:

> never before had such numerous and powerful Roman armies come in conflict with each other. These soldiers were not enlisted from the ordinary conscription, but were picked men. They were not [recruits], but under long drill and arrayed against each other... Speaking the same language and using the same tactics, being of like discipline and power of endurance, they were

> for these reasons what we may call mutually invincible. Nor was there ever such fury and daring in war as here, when citizens contended against citizens, families against families, and fellow-soldiers against each other. The proof of this is that, taking both battles into the account, the number of the slain even among the victors appeared to be not fewer than among the vanquished.

Fighting against such a 'mirror image' proved difficult and highly destructive for Rome, despite Octavian and Antony's ultimate victory. Rome's many civil wars offer an insight into what happens when *both* sides come closest to understanding themselves and their enemy, due to similar mindsets, training, tactics and weaponry. When Romans fought Romans, the result was that both victory and defeat came at an enormous cost.

Experience and understanding of warfare might help fill in the gaps

There is a caveat to this crucial understanding of an enemy. Given that warfare is a fundamentally human undertaking, a good grasp of human nature, of how people are likely to think, behave and react, can also provide a suitable foundation for victory in the absence of specific knowledge. This is apparent in Alexander the Great's campaigns, when the Macedonian general would regularly defeat an armed force because he had planned a battle based on how he understood people were *likely* to act. His knowledge was built up over a series of successes, making him a formidable foe even when engaging opponents he had never before encountered and neither he nor his soldiers had any direct experience in fighting.

As an example, facing the Telmissians (in modern day Türkiye), Alexander was faced with a problem in how to take the town. According to Arrian, the mountains on either side of the road approaching the town provided the Telmissian defenders with a natural choke point, from which they could easily hold off the Macedonian army. The locals accordingly sent their forces into these mountains in readiness against Alexander's approaching army. Seeing the situation, Alexander had his soldiers give the appearance of preparing to rest for the night, figuring the Telmissians would then send most of their own forces home to sleep and leave just a few men to guard the pass. The Telmissians did exactly as Alexander expected and, once the main force had withdrawn to the town, he launched his men against the small number of

Telmissians guarding the road. The Macedonians easily overcame the few defenders and Alexander was free to move his army forward and set up camp close to the town, with no further obstacles in his way and the fall of the town now inevitable. Alexander's experience in fighting and his appreciation of human nature, as well as knowledge of his own forces, enabled him to defeat an adversary he had not previously engaged.

Chapter 3

How Do You Prepare and Plan?

In the last analysis, luck comes only to the well prepared.

Helmuth von Moltke the Elder

In forming the plan of a campaign, it is requisite to foresee everything the enemy may do, and to be prepared with the necessary means to counteract it.

Napoleon

Vegetius delivered a statement which has echoed across the ages, 'He, therefore, who desires peace, should prepare for war.' This first line of Vegetius' guidance is the best known, but the Roman author provided additional important advice, going on, 'He who aspires to victory, should spare no pains to form his soldiers, and he who hopes for success, should fight on principle, not chance.' Vegetius' quote provides a good place to start our examination of what a general needs to consider when preparing and planning campaigns and battles.

Trained soldiers

Preparing for war requires that a nation should, by means of its generals, put its efforts into training personnel for conflict. Even without a specific battle to prepare for, having troops who are trained, ready and available to fight ensures that whenever an enemy emerges, a general (and the nation) has the means to put up a fight. For the Greeks and Romans, this meant developing and practising manoeuvres, formations and tactics during peace time, to ensure that soldiers were ready and knew how to fight, both as individuals and as a coherent fighting force once battle commenced. As Vegetius says, 'These evolutions, often practised in the field of exercise, will be found easy in execution on actual service.'

It is the practice and preparation outside of combat that help to ready an armed force to be able fight when the need arises. The Romans' development of a professional standing army, with a common structure across legions, similar weaponry, tactics, camp life and fortifications, all assisted in ensuring that sufficient soldiers were ready to deploy and fight across the vast empire, and beyond. These developments went on for centuries and, for the most part, Roman armies met with success over their enemies, despite significant differences in the nature, character and locations of their adversaries and subsequent battlefields. The decline of the Roman Empire is certainly well-known, and was brought about by numerous reasons including the decreased capability of the army, however, for centuries Rome proved itself a formidable power based largely on its professional fighting force. But readiness for war was not a peculiarly Roman attribute.

Plutarch described Spartan military training as achieving such a level of preparedness that when their soldiers went on a military campaign the physical exercises and requirements they faced were less daunting than during times of peace, arguing that 'for them alone of all mankind, war was felt as a relief from preparation for war.' Plutarch might have been overplaying the description but what is apparent is that Spartan society did prepare its citizens well for war, and most of their opponents knew it. Such preparation not only ensured their soldiers were trained and ready but could also prove an effective deterrent, with enemies avoiding battle altogether rather than fight the Spartans. And where deterrence failed, Sparta's Greek enemies understood that if they were going to fight the Spartans they would be facing a well-prepared, war-ready force, eager to do battle.

Weapons and armaments

Being prepared is also about ensuring that weapons and armaments necessary for fighting are available and that those who will wield and operate them are already familiar with their use. In the case of Athenian naval power, this originally grew out of deliberate preparation for one conflict but then was employed in an entirely different war. When the Athenians had accumulated significant wealth from their mining operations at Laurium, they had planned to distribute the funds amongst their citizens. Themistocles had another idea and persuaded the Athenians to invest the money in the construction of 200 warships (triremes). The ships were intended for use in a local war, but the decision was to prove decisive in the defence of the Greek states against the Persians.

By the time Xerxes launched his invasion by land and sea, Athens was thus already an experienced naval power, ready to take on the much larger Persian fleet. Before Xerxes' army was defeated at the Battle of Plataea (479 BC), his navy had already been beaten by a combined Greek fleet at the Battle of Salamis (480 BC). The Athenian ships had proved decisive in ensuring that the Greeks had the means of taking on the Persians at sea. While their military preparation had not deterred Xerxes, the readiness of Athenian ships and crews guaranteed that once the campaign was launched, the Persian naval force could be countered and ultimately defeated. The Persians found the Athenians armed and ready with a formidable fleet, manned by trained commanders and sailors. The equation was clear: no Athenian fleet, no ultimate Greek victory over the Persian navy. Circumstances change, but the weapons and tools for fighting need to be available to use against whatever enemy emerges.

Logistics and supplies

Commencing a campaign and ensuring that the armed personnel, weapons and equipment are ready and available is part of the requirement of preparation and planning. Additionally, a general will likely need to move their armed forces to launch a campaign or counter an advancing enemy, adding another factor for consideration.

In 255 BC during the First Punic War, the Romans launched a force of 364 ships towards North Africa, intent on an invasion into the Carthaginian homeland. For the route, the Roman commanders Marcus Aemilius and Servius Fulvius chose to sail down the southern coast of Sicily, a rocky coastline with few safe anchorages, and against multiple warnings from their own pilots about the dangers. While the Roman armada was sailing along the Sicilian coast they were caught in a storm that resulted in the near destruction of the fleet. Of their 364 ships, only 80 survived, with the rugged coastline and shore strewn with the bodies of dead Romans and the wreckage of ships. The disaster was on a scale unheard of at sea until that time, and Polybius made it clear the fault lay entirely with the commanders. The Roman leaders had destroyed their military capability without even making it to Africa.

Byzantine Emperor Maurice (AD 539–602), writing soon after the fall of the Western Roman Empire, made the point that a military commander who did not secure food and supplies for his forces was laying the foundations for their defeat, even in the absence of an enemy. Nearly a thousand years earlier, Xerxes had received similar advice in terms of the land and sea potentially becoming formidable adversaries in his forthcoming Greek campaign. Persian general Artabanus advised the king that the Persian navy was so large that it risked being exposed to the elements, since there was no harbour large enough to protect the fleet, and the Persian army was so enormous that the land itself would be unable to sustain it. Logistics was and is the ultimate constraint for any armed force and campaign and the ultimate leveller, for neither a general nor the most junior-ranking soldier is of any value without adequate food and supplies.

Unsurprisingly, conquering an enemy by starvation rather than force of arms was encouraged as a recognized and efficient strategy. Given this clear risk, it was fundamental that leaders ensured that everything required for the sustenance and survival of their army was available and secured. Forgetting this, a general risked the very survival of their forces, as became evident during the Batavian Revolt in Germany against the Romans (AD 69–70):

> Threatened with this gathering storm, Munius Lupercus and Numisius Rufus, who were in command of the two legions, proceeded to strengthen the rampart and walls. They pulled down the buildings near the military camp, which had grown into a small town during the long years of peace, fearing that the enemy might make use of them. But they omitted to provide a sufficient store of provisions for the camp, and authorised the soldiers to make up the deficiency by looting, with the result that what might have supplied their needs for a long time was consumed in a few days.

Failure to adhere to the guidance of keeping everything in the camp during peacetime led directly to poor decision-making at the outbreak of war, with the securing of available resources being entirely overlooked. Supplies readily available during peace were well within these generals' control, but their lack of even basic forethought condemned them, along with their men, when war came. What kind of generals were these? Military commanders setting themselves and their armies up for inevitable failure. Vegetius highlights this 'too little too late' approach to army supplies, arguing: 'When provisions once begin to fail, [frugality] is ill-timed and comes too late.' In contrast, thinking ahead and ensuring supplies are available and secured is a foundation of military generalship.

Money

The ability to financially support a war or campaign was also critical in making preparations well ahead of time. Plutarch reiterates the earlier observation that money was the sinews of war – to go to war and carry out a campaign is costly, so absence of funds would prove an immediate handicap to any nation attempting to raise and maintain an armed force. When considering Sparta's preparations prior to the outbreak of the Peloponnesian War, Athenian Admiral Pericles highlighted the compounding challenges that lack of money presented. Pericles observed that their enemies would be hampered by absence of funds and would be delayed in their attempts to secure more, 'but the opportunities of war wait for no man.'

We see here strong reasoning for why preparations matter so much – because opportunities in warfare can prove fleeting, and those who are unprepared may waste chances which never offer themselves again. Further, campaigns often prove incredibly costly in terms of 'blood and treasure', lives and money, usually more so than originally anticipated. Certainly, money and treasure could be captured during the campaign to help fund the maintenance of these forces and enrich the general, soldiers and nation. But this was not guaranteed and a general needed to have a plan to ensure that, whether by his own efforts or by ongoing funding from the state, any campaign could be financed.

A clear aim

Planning for a campaign requires a clear aim and actions taken in direct support of achieving it. There is a risk of 'mission creep,' in which the original goal is forgotten as the campaign progresses and is allowed to turn into something very different to what was intended, a point noted throughout military history. With a clear aim, the military commander can confirm that any action taken will directly support achieving this goal; everything else being wasted effort. Admiral Gaius Lutatius gives us one example of how to maintain focus on the aim. In 242 BC, during the First Punic War, the Romans:

> appointed Gaius Lutatius to the command and dispatched him at the beginning of summer. Suddenly appearing off the coast of Sicily, he seized on the harbour of Drepana and the roadsteads near Lilybaeum, the whole Carthaginian navy having retired to their own country. First of all he constructed works round the city of Drepana and made all preparations for its siege, but while continuing to prosecute this by every means in his power, he foresaw that the Carthaginian fleet would arrive, and was not forgetful of the original motive of the expedition, the belief that it was only by a sea battle that the war could be decisively finished. He did not, then, allow the time to pass uselessly and idly, but every day was spent in exercising and practising the crews properly for this purpose. He also paid unremitting attention to the matter of training, so that in a very short time he got his sailors into perfect condition for the anticipated battle.

Such a deliberate focus on maintaining the aim and purpose of the campaign by the Roman admiral is in stark contrast to the Athenian operation on that very same island more than 170 years earlier. Despite effectively still being at war with Sparta, and instead of concentrating all their efforts on defeating this immediate threat to their homeland in Greece, the Athenians decided to launch a military expedition to Sicily, committing significant maritime and land forces to the campaign. This failure to plan and act in accordance with their own principal goal of defeating Sparta proved a ruinous decision for Athens, when the forces sent to Sicily were soundly defeated, most of the men were killed and the ships destroyed or captured. It was a military fiasco that Athens never recovered from and ultimately cost them the war against Sparta. Yet this circumstance was entirely counter to Admiral Pericles' guidance at the outset of the war with Sparta. Pericles had argued that the Athenians would prevail if they were patient, maintained their naval capability, avoided efforts to expand their empire, and kept the city safe. Instead, they wasted much of their military might in a disastrous campaign, having forgotten the primary objective of the war – to defeat Sparta – an aim which they subsequently never achieved.

Planning based in reality

Planning provides a foundation for achieving victory before any actual clash of arms takes place. Consequently, many early authors emphasized planning but with the proviso that a general's plans need to be based on reality. Whether a campaign or an individual battle, planning and forethought grounded in reality provides a general with a solid basis to maximize the chances of their military endeavours meeting with success. Persian commander Artabanus, advisor to King Xerxes, argued that leaders should take counsel and identify all the risks that might occur, which would enable them to act boldly when the time came. Decisive action could be taken precisely because every eventuality had been prepared for. Similarly, Athenian Admiral Themistocles argued that if people made plans with due consideration, they would usually get the outcome that they were seeking. However, taking actions without prior deliberation meant that even the gods were unlikely to support their success. Reflecting on good leadership, Polybius made the point that there are always risks in military operations which require detailed evaluation; however, success is achievable where the steps taken in developing and implementing a plan are well-reasoned and considered.

Athenian Admiral Nicias, in his failed attempt to discourage the Athenians from the disastrous Sicilian campaign (which he himself would ultimately be chosen to lead), observed that success rarely comes from merely wishing something to happen but is achieved when actions are based on sound judgements about the future. Curtius Rufus makes the point that human nature means we tend to invest time and effort into considering our actions and decisions after the event rather than before; humans are better at hindsight than foresight. To plan realistically means deliberate effort and critical thinking *before* the event. Such investment increases the chance of a general being able to look back on a battle with satisfaction rather than regret. Any general can have a plan, but it needs to be based on facts rather than hopes and wishes.

Thucydides provides accounts of debates among the Spartans and their allies in the Peloponnesian League, when considering the best actions to take during the war. Often it was the Corinthians who provided sound insights and guidance to their Spartan allies. The wisdom of much of the Corinthians' advice on military planning stands up very well some 2,400 years on. The Corinthians observed that many ill-conceived plans were successful simply because of the stupidity of the opponent, while even well-laid plans often end in disaster. According to the Corinthians, 'The confidence with which we form our schemes is never completely justified in their execution; speculation is carried on in safety, but, when it comes to action, fear causes failure.'

The planning for combat and combat itself are two very different things. This needs to be taken into account in planning if generals are to give themselves the best chance of victory in battle. Part of planning realistically is recognizing that warfare is a human endeavour and that the reality of human action under stress has to be factored into every campaign or battle plan. To ignore the human aspect is to plan in wilful ignorance.

The future hasn't been written

The future, regardless of how well planned for, has not yet been written. A thinking enemy does not simply adhere to their opponent's plans because their opponent wants or expects them to. A willingness to acknowledge that situations can turn out far differently than expected allows a general to build flexibility into the campaign or battle plan, such that when the unexpected occurs, they are readily able to deal with it. Assuming that the future will simply accord with a planned outcome risks disaster on the battlefield.

Uncertainty is a feature of warfare, not an anomaly. Just as much of life is uncertain, how much more does this apply to armed conflict. The importance of allowing for uncertainty was captured in a discussion between two of the greatest generals of the ancient world. According to Livy, before the battle of Zama (202 BC) Hannibal met with Scipio Africanus, seeking terms for peace and hoping to avoid the impending battle which, given Carthage's then depleted forces, he knew his forces were more than likely to lose. Reflecting on the fickleness of fortune in war, the experienced Carthaginian general observes:

> Rarely does that man consider the uncertainty of events whom fortune hath never deceived. ...But if with prosperity the gods would also bestow upon us sound judgment, we should not only consider those things which have happened, but those also which may occur. ...When you consider your own strength, then also place before your view the power of fortune, and the fluctuating nature of war.

Planning is important but a plan is still a general's *intention* of how a battle will play out. The actual battle, however well planned, still has to be fought and won.

Polybius described a conflict between two Spanish tribes, the Medionians and the Aetolians. The Greek author explained how the Medionians were able to defeat the overconfident Aetolians, who had expected to destroy their enemy easily based on unrealistic judgements of their own fighting prowess. Instead, much to their surprise, the Aetolians found themselves defeated. Ever one to draw broader lessons from these individual events, Polybius made his thinking clear:

> The unlooked-for calamity of the Aetolians was a lesson to mankind never to discuss the future as if it were the present, or to have any confident hope about things that may still turn out quite otherwise. We are but men, and should in every matter assign its share to the unexpected, this being especially true of war.

Acknowledgement of the role of the unexpected in war was a regular theme of these early texts, with the takeaway being that a general needed to avoid hubris and overconfidence in any plan and subsequent action. Even when an enemy looked to be defeated, assuming that the outcome had already been determined could lead to disaster if a general and his army failed to land the final, decisive blow. Roman general Drusus was once saved from defeat by such hubris on the part of his enemy. Fighting against German tribes, Drusus and his army became trapped in a narrow pass. According to Roman historian Cassius Dio (*c* AD 150–235), the Roman army should have been annihilated and would have been if the German forces had not become contemptuous of the trapped Romans, considering them already beaten. The jubilant tribesmen left their formation and attacked their enemy in an uncoordinated manner. General Drusus saw his opportunity, counterattacked and defeated the over-confident German tribe.

Every plan needs to factor in the enemy

In any plan, a general also needs to factor in what the enemy will do – how that enemy will think, act and fight. Alexander the Great stands out as a general who consistently thought about his intended actions through the eyes of his enemy and this careful analysis gave weight to his plans. We could identify Alexander's question as 'How will the enemy interpret my action?' Alexander considered this when planning his battles, his manoeuvres, his choice of the timing and location of battle, even in choosing actions not to take.

This picture of Alexander shows a general clearly thinking through the implications of losses and victories on his overall campaign. Early on during his march into Persian territories, Alexander was encouraged to launch an attack on the Persian navy at sea by one of his senior officers, Parmenio, who argued that a victory would be a great advantage, whereas a loss would not matter much as the Persians were already recognized to be a strong power at sea. But Alexander saw the situation differently. He was clearly keeping the broader context in mind when considering this proposal, showing just how a truly great general considered the possible outcomes of a battle from multiple perspectives. Alexander explained that it would be rash to engage a small and inexperienced Greek fleet against the numerically superior and battle-hardened Cyprian and Phoenician crews. He would not risk his courageous soldiers in such an uncertain endeavour, or hazard the Greek states rising against his rule should they gain news of a Persian victory. The logic here reflects Alexander's willingness to decide when it was best to fight and when it was best not to.

Earlier in his Persian campaign Alexander's decision to push through obstacles and engage the Persians at the Battle of Granicus (334 BC) reflected this deliberate consideration of actions and inactions from the enemy's perspective. Parmenio's advice to Alexander on this occasion was to delay crossing the Granicus river, which lay between the Macedonian forces and the Persian infantry and cavalry waiting on the other side. His reasoning was that the Macedonian army would have to ford the river and then risk being attacked by the Persians while they were still struggling up out of the water and trying to organize themselves. Weighing up these difficulties as well as the opportunities, on this occasion Alexander's decision was nevertheless to immediately cross the river and engage the Persians.

Here, Alexander's rationale was heavily influenced by his understanding of how the enemy would interpret any delay. The Macedonian general acknowledged Parmenio's arguments, but was determined to push on across the Granicus even in the face of a prepared enemy. His argument was that any hesitation in fording the river and engaging the enemy would be detrimental to their fighting reputation and his own willingness to act in the face of danger. Further, Alexander reasoned that the Persians would gain courage from such hesitation and consider themselves equal to the Macedonians. Alexander therefore chose to act boldly and attack immediately, leading his army across the Granicus and defeating the Persians, thus commencing a string of victories against Darius' forces.

This is the mindset of great generals, to constantly think about their own actions from the enemy's perspective and plan accordingly. The ability to consider the other perspective makes a general better able to identify the best action to take, to maximize their own chances and minimize opportunities for their enemy. Even without a clear plan or understanding of what to do, maintaining a focus on the opposition at least grounds any decision in reality; a general cannot go far wrong by observing and countering their enemy's actions.

When the cavalry of Roman general Publius Cornelius Scipio (Scipio Africanus' father) engaged with Hannibal's cavalry prior to the Carthaginian army's traverse of the Alps, the outcome of the skirmish was losses on both sides. After the engagement, unsure what to do next, Scipio deliberately focused on the enemy's likely actions as a basis for determining what option to take. Livy notes, 'Scipio could adopt no fixed plan of proceeding, except that he should form his measures from the plans and undertakings of the enemy.' Though unsure how to deal with Hannibal, at least Scipio was determined to base his own plans on countering the enemy's actions, whatever they would be. Hannibal's subsequent crossing of the Alps remains a well-known historical event, but what is less well-known is that when Hannibal arrived in Italy he was surprised to find Scipio had already moved his Roman forces back there. His shrewd guess at least ensured that Hannibal's army still had Scipio's army to deal with – a force that the Carthaginian general had assumed would have remained in Gaul.

As Vegetius argues, war really is a zero-sum contest:

> It is the nature of war that what is beneficial to you is detrimental to your enemy and what is of service to him always hurts you. It is therefore a maxim never to do, or to omit doing, anything that [is] in consequence of his conduct, but to consult invariably your own interest only. And you depart from this interest whenever you imitate such measures as he pursues for his benefit. For the same reason it would be wrong for him to follow such steps as you take for your advantage.

That a general's own actions or inaction can assist the enemy is another aspect which needs to be factored into planning, particularly if the goal is to defeat the enemy and not to help them. Decisions based on making the enemy's life as difficult as possible is a sound approach. General Lycurgus was asked why his orders were to frequently shift camp. His response was simply, 'So that we can do more harm to our adversaries.' This is warfare, ancient and modern. The aim is to defeat your enemy. Therefore, a general's plans can be readily weighed and considered against these two questions: 'Will this hurt the enemy?' and 'Will this help my own forces?'

This argument that a general always needs to ensure what he does benefits himself and harms the enemy is reflected in Thucydides' earlier accounts of the Spartan King Archidamus. Reflecting on Sparta's decisions before the outbreak of the Peloponnesian War, Archidamus succinctly argued, 'This decision will be the best for yourselves, the most terrible to your opponents.' What is best for you and what is worst for them – a simple formula. Despite the Spartans' ultimate defeat of Athens, Thucydides provides a more sobering summation of Spartan actions for much of the conflict. Considering a specific instance of Sparta's failure to take advantage of a rare naval victory against the Athenians in 411 BC, he observes:

> here, as on so many other occasions, the [Spartans] proved the most convenient people in the world for the Athenians to be at war with. The wide difference between the two characters, the slowness and want of energy of the [Spartans] as contrasted with the dash and enterprise of their opponents, proved of the greatest service, especially to a maritime empire like Athens. Indeed this was shown by the Syracusans, who were most like the Athenians in character, and also most successful in combating them.

King Archidamus would have not been happy to have seen Sparta's performance for much of the war, too often helping the Athenians instead of hurting them.

Secrecy

Greek and Roman guidance to generals that they should always try to discover their enemy's plans was accompanied with a corresponding warning to keep their own well hidden. Secrecy is paramount. Vegetius makes it clear: 'Those designs are best [of] which the enemy are entirely ignorant till the moment of execution.' Where a plan is uncovered by the enemy before a battle (usually by spies or deserters in ancient times), then the result is an informed and prepared enemy. Consequently, if the general's battleplans became known to the enemy, Vegetius concluded that there was no other option but to abandon them and start again. The potential consequences are simply too great to continue with the original scheme.

When weighing up military options, the guidance was for a general to consult widely but, when it came to the final plan, this needed to be kept secret. A general should not be too trusting according to Vegetius, who argues you should 'communicate the designs you intend to put into execution to few, and those of the most assured fidelity or rather trust no one but yourself.' At some stage, the details have to be disclosed to subordinate commanders and personnel so that they are prepared and ready to put the general's plan into action. However, the critical importance of secrecy and catching the enemy by surprise means that the longer you can keep the plan to a chosen few, the better. A general, therefore, must balance secrecy with coordination of their personnel to successfully execute the plan.

Ensuring the enemy is kept unaware of your plans until the moment of attack by limiting access to them in your own camp is an approach that certainly pre-dates Vegetius' advice. A shrewd Carthaginian admiral, Himilco, demonstrates how both secrecy and coordination could be achieved in the days before instantaneous, long-distance communications and despite the risk of separation at sea.

> [Himilco]... with the Carthaginian fleet, weighed anchor in the night from Libya to Sicily: having furnished his masters of the ships with sealed tablets, in which he wrote the place of their destination. That so, in case they should be separated, they might know what port to make, without exposing the secret of his expedition to the information of deserters. And the windows at the heads of the ships he stopped up; that the enemy might not at a distance see his lights, and thereby be apprised of his invasion.

With forethought, Himilco successfully balanced secrecy, planning and coordination to launch his fleet, keeping the enemy in the dark about his intentions, and even disguising the presence of his own forces until the moment of the attack. Himilco's example demonstrates that the planning of a successful attack did not necessarily require enormous details or complexities. Simple plans are often enough, and a little forethought can lay the foundation for victory.

Chapter 4

How Do You Select a Battlefield?

The most material point, is to be able to distinguish at first sight all the advantages of which any given space of ground is capable. This art is to be acquired, and even brought to perfection…

Frederick the Great

Selecting a battlefield is such a crucial aspect of a general's planning and decision making that it warrants specific attention. Good generals understand that the choice of battlefield alone can mean the difference between victory or defeat. Choosing the best place to fight is vital, as it influences how a general is able to use their forces to greatest effect and how to best hinder those of the enemy. In ancient times the selection of the right location and timing for battle was about seeing opportunities and risks, such as how to use terrain to maximize the advantages of a general's own forces and minimize the enemy's.

As discussed earlier, Spartan general Leonidas successfully found the best location to counter the might of the invading Persian army by proactively positioning his Greek forces at the pass of Thermopylae. He chose it based on his recognition that the Persians would not be able to take advantage of their cavalry or large numbers of soldiers in the narrow pass. This ability to anticipate how the battlefield itself can influence the coming clash of arms is an essential skill for a general, so that they can make the most of any opportunity to choose the battlefield rather than have to fight on one selected by the enemy.

Maximize your strengths, diminish the enemy's

Roman forces spread across their vast empire often faced the challenge of being outnumbered on what was really foreign soil, facing forces with far better knowledge of the local terrain. Thus, selection of the right field of battle was crucial. In Britain, the rise of the Iceni queen, General Boudicca and her forces presented a significant challenge to the Romans occupying the nation. Boudicca had raised soldiers from multiple tribes into a formidable army which threatened to destroy the Roman forces in the Islands. Her ability to mobilize tens of thousands of Britons to fight the Romans in a short space of time was impressive. Further, according to Tacitus' account, Boudicca was likely not the first female general in her nation's history, given her observation to her soldiers that the Britons were used to being led by women in war.

Following Boudicca's uprising and the defeat and slaughter of Romans at Camulodunum, General Suetonius, the Roman governor of Britain, recognized that he needed to act immediately and defeat Boudicca in battle (60 or 61 AD). He marched his forces to London but, given his small number of troops, then decided the town was unsuitable for an effective defence. Instead, Suetonius with his 10,000 soldiers selected a location ideally suited to counter Boudicca's vast army:

> He chose a position approached by a narrow defile [gorge], closed in at the rear by a forest, having first ascertained that there was not a soldier of the enemy except in his front, where an open plain extended without any danger from ambuscades. His legions were in close array; round them, the light-armed troops, and the cavalry in dense array on the wings. On the other side, the army of the Britons, with its masses of infantry and cavalry, was confidently exulting, a vaster host than ever had assembled, and so fierce in spirit that they actually brought with them, to witness the victory, their wives riding in wagons, which they had placed on the extreme border of the plain. …At first, the legion kept its position, clinging to the narrow defile as a defence; when they had exhausted their missiles, which they discharged with unerring aim on the closely approaching foe, they rushed out in a wedge-like column. Similar was the onset of the auxiliaries, while the cavalry with extended lances broke through all who offered a strong resistance. The rest turned their back in flight, and flight proved difficult, because the surrounding wagons had blocked retreat.

The result was a slaughter. Boudicca's forces were routed, the Romans reportedly killing around 80,000 Britons for the loss of some 400 of their own soldiers. Whatever the actual figures, it meant the end for Boudicca (who reportedly took her own life), her army and the British uprising against Rome. Key to Suetonius' success was the selection of the battlefield and the tactics to match. In rejecting the obvious location of London, Suetonius highlights the importance of generals deciding not only where to fight but also where *not* to fight.

The advantage of the high ground

A general who could choose and occupy the higher ground on a battlefield was usually in a better position than the enemy they faced. The reason for choosing the high ground was simple: it is easier to fight downhill than up. High ground maximized the fighting strength of a force, even a small one, by making life much more difficult for an enemy forced to start lower down. An armed force fighting uphill, weighed down with weapons and armour and facing an opposing force raining down spears, missiles and sword blows, was at a clear disadvantage.

The compounding impact of problems for an adversary attacking uphill is captured well in Livy's account of Roman general Popillius' engagement with an army of Gauls. Instead of racing into battle against the well-prepared force of Gauls, Popillius selected a hill nea the Gaulish camp and proceeded to set up entrenchments there, taking his time and using the view from the height to evaluate the strength of the enemy and leaving them to initiate an attack. Livy's description of the battle which followed captures the importance of holding the high ground. The Gauls,

> being a fierce people and by nature eager for the combat, on beholding the Roman ensigns in the distance, at once drew out their line, as if for instant battle. But perceiving that the Romans did not descend into the plain, but sought to protect themselves not only by their position but even with a rampart, they supposed them to be panic-stricken and at the same time the more open to attack for being just then taken up with their task. They advanced, therefore, with hideous yells. The Romans without a pause in their work, on which the reserves were engaged, began the action with their troops of the first and second lines, who had been standing alert and armed in front of the working party. Besides their valour, they had an advantage

> from the elevation, for their javelins and spears, instead of falling without effect, as they mostly do when thrown on a level field, were steadied by their own weight and all struck home. The Gauls were burdened with the missiles which had either transfixed their bodies, or, sticking in their shields, had made them very heavy; their dash had carried them almost up the slope, but first they halted, uncertain what to do, and then – for the mere delay had abated their ardour and increased that of their foes – they were thrown back, and falling one upon another wrought greater carnage than even their enemies had done; for so headlong was the rout, that more were trodden under foot than slain with the sword.

Selecting and securing the higher ground usually provided the general and his army with a significant advantage to influence the outcome of the battle – the ground did much of the work for them.

But the high ground is not always the best location

A general had to think carefully about the terrain and geography, how it would impact both their own forces and that of the enemy. Choosing a battlefield which maximized one's own strengths and minimized those of the enemy was the key. Because of this, depending upon one's own forces, the higher ground might not always be the best option, as the Carthaginians discovered at Adys (256 BC). Preparing to engage the Romans near the town of Adys (in modern day Tunisia), the Carthaginians took control of a hill overlooking the enemy, who were camped on the open plain. But their choice was a poor one as the rocky hill proved a hindrance to both the Carthaginian cavalry and elephants. Their obvious difficulty on the rugged terrain, in full view of the Romans, showed their opponents exactly how to defeat them. Rather than wait for the Carthaginians to move down to the flat ground, the Romans launched their attack at daybreak the following day, advancing uphill from both sides and rendering the Carthaginian cavalry and elephants useless on the rough terrain. The result was a Roman victory. Despite having the advantage of being able to choose where to position their forces, by selecting compromised terrain the Carthaginians had undermined their own strengths and revealed to their enemies just how they could be defeated. In this case the high ground had cost them the battle. The Carthaginians chose, and chose wrong.

Allow the enemy an escape route

A point worth acknowledging due to its frequent mentions in early literature is that a general should ensure his enemy has the option to escape the field of battle. The advice is based on concerns that an adversary seeing no chance of escape might well become so desperate and formidable as to turn an impending defeat into unanticipated victory. Rather than face an enemy who has no option but to fight to the death, ensuring that they had some opportunity to flee the battlefield was considered a sound tactic. There was an additional aspect to this. Soldiers are far easier to kill while escaping from the battlefield than when they are fighting in a formation as a cohesive force. Providing an enemy with the option of fleeing was a good factor to consider in selecting a battlefield. But while it was considered logical to ensure that an enemy had the option to escape the battlefield, that did not mean that the fight was necessarily finished.

Where the fighting ends

The battlefield is where the fighting starts but extends to wherever the fighting ends. These might be very different locations. Regardless of where the battle opened, it was not unusual in ancient warfare that an opposing force would sooner or later break formation and attempt to escape, resulting in more soldiers slaughtered during their efforts to flee, as their opponents hunted them down and killed them. An army might be *defeated* at a specific location but *destroyed* on their retreat. During the conflict between Rome and Aequi, Livy describes a battle in which the Romans under General Aemilius destroy the Aequi and Volsci forces. However, it was during the retreat of the defeated Aequi and Volsci that the Romans slaughtered more of the enemy than in the actual 'battle' itself, so tenacious was the Roman cavalry in pursuing and killing the fleeing soldiers. For a general and his soldiers, the battlefield can rightly be argued to extend to wherever the killing finished.

Refusing the enemy's chosen battlefield

At sea and on land, admirals and generals could reject an unfavourable battlefield to select a location more advantageous to their own forces. Refusing an initial offer of battle in order to choose a better location, better timing or more favourable circumstances, can make the difference between defeat and victory, as the Athenians discovered at the hands of the Spartan admiral Lysander:

> At the Aegospotami the Athenians several times put out to sea, and bearing down upon the enemy offered them battle, which Lysander always declined; whereupon they returned to their station, exulting in their success and hymning victory. Lysander at last sent two [ships] to observe them; the captains of which, as soon as they perceived the enemy landing, hoisted a brazen shield as a signal to Lysander, who immediately advanced with the rest of the fleet… and came up with the Athenians, just after the forces were landed. Some of them were gone to rest, and others employed, part on one thing, part on another; when the [Spartans] on a sudden attacking them, a regular force against a confused rout, obtained an easy victory.

There are many lessons here about choosing a battlefield, not the least of which is the need for constant vigilance in war. The battlefield is where the fighting actually takes place, not where it is expected to be. Despite the Athenian attempts to get Lysander to fight where and when they wanted, Lysander eventually chose a time and a place to suit his own force, maximizing the Spartans' strength and minimizing the fighting abilities of the Athenians. The result was the utter destruction of the Athenian fleet.

Sometimes the enemy gets to choose the battlefield

Due to circumstances beyond their control, a general cannot always avoid the battlefield chosen by an enemy. Consequently, they have to be ready to fight at any time or place. During Rome's civil war with Catiline and his forces, the Roman general Quintus Metellus Celer was operating around Pisa, on the lookout for Catiline's escaping forces who had taken to the hills. When Celer learned of Catiline's direction from deserters, 'He immediately broke up his camp, and took his post at the very foot of the hills, at the point where Catiline's descent would be.'

Catiline's attempted escape was thus prevented and he and his forces emerged from the mountains to find Celer's three legions waiting for them. Catiline was now stuck between the mountains and multiple Roman armies ready to take him on. While he initially refused to engage Celer and withdrew, all hopes of escape were gone and Catiline was soon forced to fight against another nearby Roman army in northern Italy. It was at Pistoria (62 BC), that Catiline's troops were attacked by General Marcus Petreius and ultimately destroyed. Though Catiline fought valiantly, he and his soldiers died on a battlefield they had neither expected nor wanted.

Ambushes are another example where a general has the battlefield selected for them. This was well understood in ancient conflict and we see consistent warnings of the risk of ambushes (ambuscades), where an enemy seeks to surprise and attack their opponents when they are least prepared. The occurrence of such ambushes illustrates how the *enemy* may choose the battlefield, and a general and his army had better be ready:

> But on a march the soldier is less on his guard, has not his arms always ready and is thrown into disorder by a sudden attack or ambuscade. A general, therefore, cannot be too careful and diligent in taking necessary precautions to prevent a surprise on the march and in making proper dispositions to repulse the enemy, in case of such accident, without loss.

While far from ideal, sometimes the enemy selects the battlefield and a general needs to ensure that their armed forces are mentally and physically prepared to fight on whatever ground has been chosen for them.

Choosing when to fight

When to fight is another critical decision for a general to make. Whether to engage early in the morning, the middle of the day, afternoon, or even at night is what a general must consider. The choice of timing can influence how to fight and engage the enemy, and has the potential to significantly impact the outcome of battle. Scipio Africanus' fight against Carthaginian general Hasdrubal Gisco at the Battle of Ilipa in Spain (206 BC), demonstrated a masterful use of time to wear down an adversary. Scipio chose a morning attack to catch the Carthaginians before they had eaten, and then he deliberately drew out the fighting, keeping his main attack until later in the day. This clever timing ensured that the Carthaginian forces were exhausted when the major Roman attack finally began:

> as the day was now getting on, Hasdrubal's troops began to grow languid, having been dispirited by the alarm in the morning, and compelled to go out hastily into the field, without refreshing themselves with food. Scipio had designedly spun out the day, in order that the battle might take place at a late hour; for it was not until the seventh hour that the battalions of infantry charged the wings. It was considerably later before the battle reached the centre, so that the heat from the meridian sun, and the fatigue of standing under arms, together with hunger and thirst, enfeebled their bodies before they engaged the enemy.

By the time of the main attack Hasdrubal's army was fatigued 'in body and mind'. Scipio's plan on the timing of the battle appeared so critical and noteworthy to Livy, that the terrain gets no mention in his description of the fight.

Ammianus Marcellinus, a Roman soldier and author, provides us with an account of the Battle of Adrianople (AD 378 in modern-day Türkiye). Emperor Valens and his army had conducted an eight-mile march in the heat and over rough terrain to arrive in front of the Goths' camp, exhausted but eager to engage with the large Goth force opposing them. Instead, the Goth chief Fritigern deliberately delayed the battle with an armistice, allowing time for his cavalry to make their way to the battlefield, as well as to wear down the Roman soldiers in the summer heat, which was made worse by fires the Goths had deliberately lit in the surrounding countryside. The delaying tactic proved effective in permitting the Goth cavalry to arrive before the battle started, so Fritigern had the large, combined force he was aiming for. When some of the Roman soldiers finally began striking out at the Goths in frustration and in a disorganized manner, the Goths launched their attack in force, taking on the already exhausted, dehydrated and hungry Roman forces. Marcellinus describes the scene:

> The sun ...scorched the Romans, who were emaciated by hunger, worn out with toil, and scarcely able to support even the weight of their armour. At last our columns were entirely beaten back by the overpowering weight of the barbarians, and so they took to disorderly flight, which is the only resource in extremity, each man trying to save himself as well as he could.

The result was the death of Emperor Valens and destruction of the Roman army on the battlefield – a significant and lasting setback for the late Roman Empire. By drawing out the time of the battle, Fritigern had successfully out-generalled Valens.

Choosing when not to fight

Perhaps the only general to be recognized and celebrated for *avoiding* battle was the Roman general Fabius. Following Hannibal's crossing of the Alps into Italy and subsequent destruction of Roman armies at Trebia (218 BC) and Lake Trasimene (217 BC), Rome's forces were facing annihilation by the brilliant Carthaginian commander who appeared undefeatable. So Fabius chose not to fight, but to delay, shadowing Hannibal's army wherever they went with his own Roman army, and not allowing Hannibal's forces to manoeuvre without having to factor in the risk of being surprised by Fabius' forces. Initially criticized by the Senate and citizenry for not attacking the Carthaginians, Fabius' strategy was eventually recognized to be brilliant. By breaking Hannibal's string of successes, Fabius gave the Romans the time to rebuild their forces and learn to understand the Carthaginian general. Florus captures this well:

> The first hope of the Empire, as it began to recover and, so to speak, return to life, was Fabius, who devised a new method of defeating Hannibal – by not fighting him. Hence he received a new title, significant of the way in which he saved the State, namely, Cunctator ('the Delayer'); hence too the people paid him the tribute of calling him 'the Shield of the Empire.' And so through the whole of Samnium and the Falernian and Gauran forests he so wore Hannibal down that, since he could not be broken by valour, he was reduced by delay.

By frustrating him and preventing him from delivering a final crushing defeat on the Romans, Fabius increased the pressure on Hannibal. The African general struggled over many years to hold together an army of Carthaginians, mercenaries and Gauls on the foreign soil of Italy, consistently needing to secure shelter, supplies and spoils for his forces. The initial delays and subsequent successes by the Romans against Hannibal, albeit minor at first, gradually diminished Hannibal's perceived invincibility.

Seeing what the enemy does not

The ability to see and interpret the same location more clearly than an opposing commander can prove critical. Even when the enemy has chosen the battle site, a good general might be able to reimagine, or even alter, the physical environment to find some element their opponent has not noticed. Alexander's siege of Tyre provides an example of a military commander who simply altered the terrain to meet his own needs. Despite it being an island just off the coast, Alexander's determination to conquer Tyre saw him adapt the situation to bring the fight to the citizens, who had locked themselves inside their island city. Having offered them the choice to surrender or come out and fight, both of which the Tyrians refused to do, Alexander spoke to a group of the city's representatives, telling them that because they lived on an island they believed they had nothing to fear from his land army, but that he would show them that their city was actually part of the mainland. The choice was clear, surrender their city to him or he would put them under siege.

The Tyrians dismissed Alexander's warning. In response, the Macedonian general commenced a siege of the island city, setting his forces to work building earthworks from the shore to connect the mainland to the island. Through a coordinated series of land and sea attacks, Alexander stormed and conquered Tyre, no more an island city.

Chapter 5

How Do You Employ *Stratagems* Against the Enemy?

The surprised adversary does not defend himself, he tries to flee.

Colonel Ardant du Picq

For such expeditions officers should be selected who are bold and full of stratagems. They ought to inflict upon the enemy all the injury they can without compromising themselves.

General Antoine-Henri Jomini

To win in battle is important, but so is *how* the battle is won. A win at great expense to the lives of a general's own soldiers is still a victory, but at what cost? Defeating the enemy with as few losses to one's own side as possible is clearly better. How did the ancient generals achieve such one-sided victories on the battlefield? Deceptions, surprises, ambushes, feints, subterfuge, misrepresentation, and any other tactics for confusing and fooling an enemy were recognized courses of action that a good general would employ. Such *stratagems* were highly regarded in the ancient world as techniques for a general to achieve victory over their enemies while sparing their own fighting force as much as possible. The famous account of the Greeks' successful deception during the siege of Troy, by feigning retreat and leaving an enormous wooden horse outside the city gates is mentioned in several ancient sources. At night, after the Trojans had taken the giant 'gift' inside their gates, Greek soldiers concealed within the giant wooden beast exited and attacked the city from within, ultimately defeating the Trojans. While debate over the veracity of the story remains, ancient audiences were aware of the account and understood the use of such deception in warfare.

Stratagems are a sign of superior generalship

Polyaenus, Frontinus and Vegetius all wrote about and actively encouraged the use of stratagems in war, drawing on historical examples from the Greeks, Romans and barbarians. These early authors encouraged generals to learn and employ time honoured tactics or develop their own new stratagems. Polyaenus observes that courage conquers with the sword 'while superior conduct by art and stratagem prevails: and the greatest reach of generalship is displayed in those victories that are obtained with the least danger.' Consequently, a general who successfully employed such schemes would also gain the approval and confidence of their soldiers, who recognized a commander who would avoid carelessly wasting their lives. In the brutality of hand-to-hand combat, often with numerical mismatches between clashing forces, any and every advantage was worth pursuing. Indeed, it was precisely where a general faced superior enemy numbers that stratagems were most required. 'Good officers', notes Vegetius, 'decline general engagements where the danger is common, and prefer the employment of stratagem and finesse to destroy the enemy as much as possible in detail and intimidate them without exposing their own forces.'

Stratagems allowed a general to avoid meeting the enemy at their point of greatest strength or on their terms, instead maximizing their own strengths and advantages. A variety of deceptions and surprises could be applied to suit the situation. Frontinus makes this point, providing guidance on a range of stratagems for many pre-engagement conditions, including concealing plans, laying and countering ambushes, travelling through enemy territory, distracting the enemy, quelling a mutiny, arousing enthusiasm for battle and dispelling soldiers' fears of adverse omens. The array of situations described by Frontinus reminds us that generals had to deal with the particular enemy as well as manage their own forces.

To the ancients, the ability to conceive and apply stratagems successfully was evidence of a truly capable general, and history shows that those leaders who were most highly regarded were also those who employed deception and surprise against their enemies. Hannibal, Scipio Africanus, Alexander, Pyrrhus, Iphicrates and Caesar all displayed the ability to conquer enemy forces through forward thinking and the use of stratagems. This was not happenstance, they knew exactly what they were doing. Indeed, Caesar himself was reported as highlighting to his soldiers that the most powerful weapon in warfare was surprise. Of course, not all generals could readily conceive and implement effective ruses on the battlefield. The development and use of stratagems required a flexibility of mind, an ability to identify and disregard the obvious, to recognize unexpected and potentially sound tactics and put them into action without the enemy realizing what was going on, until it was too late for them to react effectively.

That seemingly hazardous enterprises employing surprise and deception were so often successful highlights just how the unexpected, or the tactic disregarded by an enemy as being implausible or unlikely, actually carries the lesser risk. The irony, demonstrated time and again in numerous accounts of battle, is that conventional approaches were often very risky while the employment of good stratagems was usually a safer option. Ultimately, a good general uses stratagems for a very sound reason: stratagems work.

Scipio Africanus and the greatest battle that never was

In Scipio Africanus, Rome found a general who could match Hannibal in cleverness, stratagems and battlefield success. While Hannibal and his army were still based in Italy, some 13 years after crossing the Alps, Scipio was provided with military forces to launch a campaign in Africa (205 BC), to directly threaten Carthage in much the same way that Hannibal had taken the war to Rome's doorstep. So successful did Scipio's efforts in Africa prove that Hannibal was recalled from Italy to defend the city of Carthage at the battle of Zama (202 BC), but even the Carthaginian general proved unequal to Scipio. Hannibal's forces were defeated and Carthage surrendered, ending the Second Punic War (218–201 BC), with Scipio's victorious campaign earning him the title Africanus – conqueror of Africa.

Prior to Hannibal's recall from Italy to defend Carthage, Scipio secured numerous battlefield victories which demonstrated his outstanding generalship through deception, surprise, feints and ambushes. Yet the action most enlightening in terms of Scipio's ability to destroy an enemy and preserve his own forces, was not really portrayed as a battle by those early authors who described his campaign, so much as a wholesale slaughter. It stands as arguably the most extraordinary and one-sided destruction of an army in warfare.

During the early stages of the African campaign, Scipio's army was camped in close proximity to two camps of an allied Carthaginian and Numidian force. Scipio sent out ambassadors to engage with the Numidians, to give the appearance of wanting a truce. Secretly however, Scipio had sent centurions disguised as servants with the ambassadors, who were able to survey the entire Numidian camp, gather intelligence and report back to him. Drawing out the negotiations over days, Scipio ensured that nothing about the enemy camp remained unknown to him, despite never setting foot there himself. Soon Scipio understood the entire camp's layout, its approaches and exits, how and when the enemy watches and outposts were set and maintained and, critically, the nature and design of the camp's huts. It was in these huts that Scipio saw the opportunity he was looking for.

Having lulled both the Numidians and Carthaginians into the expectation of more days of negotiations, Scipio led out his forces at night, surrounding both camps, and then had his soldiers set fire to some of the Numidian huts. The fire took off rapidly, spreading fast due to the close proximity of the huts and the flammable material from which they were constructed. The panic and chaos of the inferno, made worse by the darkness of night, resulted in many Numidian soldiers being killed by the flames, or trampled and crushed by each other in their desperate attempts to escape. Focused on escaping, and assuming that the fire was an accident, most of the soldiers had left behind or forgotten their weapons. Consequently, those who managed to escape through the camp's narrow exits found themselves defenceless and face-to-face with armed Roman soldiers, ready and waiting to slaughter their confused enemies.

While the Carthaginians focused on the fire in the Numidian camp, Scipio next attacked the now unguarded Carthaginian camp gates and set fire to the camp, ensuring the rapid, concurrent and wholesale destruction of both camps and their occupants. Most of the soldiers who died appear never to have realized that they were actually in the middle of a Roman attack. The enemy's losses were staggering. Of the Carthaginian and Numidian soldiers, 40,000 were killed by the fire or slaughtered by the Romans. Another 5,000 were taken prisoner, captured along with multiple Carthaginian nobles and senators, 174 military standards, 2,700 horses and six elephants. While Hannibal was being recalled from Italy to counter Scipio's march on Carthage, these armed forces, who could have proven decisive at the Battle of Zama, had already been annihilated. Later titled the Battle of Utica, the one-sided slaughter was arguably the greatest battle that never was as a result of Scipio's outstanding stratagem.

Hannibal – master of stratagems

While Scipio gives us an insight into how a successful general can use deception and surprise to destroy an army, Hannibal provides a case study of a general using stratagems both offensively to achieve victory and defensively to avoid defeat. We can see Hannibal's destruction of a Roman army at Lake Trasimene (217 BC), in what Roman author Florus described as a 'thunderbolt' in which 'Carthaginian craft devised a new stratagem.'

Hannibal prepared to face Roman general Flaminius at Lake Trasimene, placing part of his army on the plains in front of Flaminius to draw the Roman commander into his trap. At the same time, unseen by Flaminius, Hannibal led the greater part of his army through the mountains. With hills to one side and the lake on the other, Flaminius carelessly led his army through the narrow defile, heavily obscured by morning mist from Lake Trasimene. Marching to meet the visible enemy on the plain, Flaminius remained entirely unaware of the Carthaginian soldiers in the hills above him, and their cavalry, who were approaching the rear of the Roman forces. Hannibal waited until Flaminius was completely hemmed in by the lake, the mountains and the Carthaginian troops, and then he struck. A simultaneous charge by the Carthaginian soldiers and cavalry caught the Roman general and his army entirely by surprise: 'A shout being raised on all sides, the Roman found himself surrounded before he could well see the enemy; and the attack on the front and flank had commenced ere his line could be well formed, his arms prepared for action, or his swords unsheathed.'

In the face of the sudden attack and ensuing chaos, Flaminius' position was hopeless, all his value and influence as commander lost, as 'from the noise and tumult, neither his advice nor command could be caught; and so far were the soldiers from knowing their own standards, and ranks, and position, that they had scarce sufficient courage to take up arms and make them ready for battle.' So great was the confusion, made worse by the mist over the battlefield, that 'there was more use of ears than of eyes' for the Roman soldiers; they were fighting blind.

The battle lasted some three hours, and Flaminius was killed during the fighting. Many of the Roman soldiers met a dreadful fate as, with no means to escape, they jumped into the lake and drowned with all their equipment or struggled back into the shallows exhausted, only to be cut to pieces by the Carthaginian cavalry. The Roman soldiers who had gone through first and engaged the Carthaginians in front had no idea of the ambush in the rear until the mist lifted and the battle was already decided. The estimates are that 15,000 Romans were killed in the battle for the loss of some 1,500 Carthaginians – a 10:1 result which left nobody in any doubt of the outcome. 'We have been defeated in a great battle,' was the message sent back to Rome.

In a separate action, Hannibal showed how deception could be effectively employed to avoid defeat as well. Before his success at the Battle of Cannae (216 BC), where he and his army killed some 50,000–70,000 Roman soldiers, he slowly made his way towards Capua. Camping for several days in nearby plains, Hannibal then moved his forces away from the city, only to find himself trapped in a gorge by Fabius and the Roman army. However, once again devising a clever stratagem to instil fear and confusion into the enemy, Hannibal was able to avert disaster. During the day, the Carthaginian soldiers gathered together a number of cattle. When darkness fell, Hannibal had branches set alight and tied to the horns of the cattle and his men drove the maddened beasts towards the Romans guarding the entrance to the gorge. The resulting chaos of fire, noise and uncertainty saw the Roman soldiers on watch abandon their positions. Fabius, not knowing what was going on but suspecting some deeper design, refused to engage and kept his forces in camp. The result was that Hannibal, his entire army, and all their captured treasure, made it safely out of the gorge. A good deception can save a general from an inglorious defeat.

Outfoxing Hannibal – General Nero's dash across Italy

While Hannibal's forces were in Italy in 207 BC, Rome faced a further escalation of the Carthaginian threat. Hasdrubal Barca, Hannibal's brother and a formidable general who had successfully defeated Roman armies in Spain, now marched towards Italy intending to join his army with his brother's forces. General Hasdrubal repeated Hannibal's crossing of the Alps into Italy, increasing the size of his army en route as he gained recruits from Gallic tribes long hostile to Rome. The combining of the two Carthaginian armies in their territory would have proved devastating to the Romans, particularly led by such formidable generals. Something had to be done to prevent them wreaking havoc on Italy. The Roman general Gaius Claudius Nero – whose army was then encamped at Apulia opposite Hannibal's forces, to hold the Carthaginian in check – now succeeded in implementing a brilliant deception that would prevent the Carthaginian brothers from ever joining forces.

Nero first ensured that there would be no change to his camp's outward appearance, to mislead Hannibal into thinking that he was still opposed by a full-strength Roman army. He then rapidly marched the greater part of his forces across Italy to join Marcus Livius, who was encamped opposite Hasdrubal's forces and whose army was heavily outnumbered. Deliberately arriving at Livius' camp at night, Nero maximized the chance of his army remaining undetected by the enemy. Again, Livius' camp was unchanged to all outward appearances, with Nero's soldiers sharing tents with their Roman colleagues. The next day the combined Roman force took the field and Hasdrubal readied his own army, though the Carthaginian general did observe that the Romans facing him held some unfamiliar shields, leaner horses, and there were apparently greater numbers than expected. Hasdrubal sent out a scout to conduct a reconnaissance of the Roman camp, but the soldier soon returned to advise the Carthaginian general that everything appeared unchanged. On this report, Hasdrubal dismissed his own concerns and continued his preparations for battle. Nero's deception had worked.

In the battle of Metaurus (207 BC) that followed, the Roman army with their unexpectedly superior numbers annihilated the Carthaginians, killing Hasdrubal, some 56,000 of his soldiers and capturing another 5,400. Livy noted that at no other time during the war were so many Carthaginians killed by the Romans in one battle. The victory was considered a suitable payback for the Roman defeat at Cannae. Nero's stratagem had borne out his earlier encouraging remarks to his soldiers, that 'there never was a measure adopted by any general which was in appearance more daring than this, but in reality more safe.'

Only once Nero had returned his forces to full strength opposite Hannibal did the Romans reveal what had occurred. Hasdrubal's severed head was thrown to the Carthaginian guards at Hannibal's camp, and two captives released to tell the general what had happened. Hannibal is claimed to have declared that he recognized the destiny of Carthage in the disaster. General Nero's brilliance in outfoxing both Hannibal and Hasdrubal ensured that Rome would never have to face their combined armies in Italy and, as Hannibal himself recognized, set the foundations for Carthage's defeat in the Second Punic War.

There are many aspects to the types of stratagem employed by generals to help them win on the battlefield. While hundreds of different stratagems are presented across the Greek and Roman literature, there are identifiable patterns. These are worth examining as they provide insight into why particular stratagems were used and how they worked in practice.

Build a pattern and then break it

Recognizing that stratagems are aimed at the mind of the enemy's commander and their force, a consistent tactic evident in these ancient accounts was for a general to establish a pattern and then, when once the enemy was confident the pattern would continue, break it. This enabled a general to attack with their forces at a time, place and disposition entirely different to the enemy's expectations. Establishing an observable pattern of behaviour often required a longer-term effort, perhaps over several days, but usually proved to be a highly effective stratagem.

Fighting the Argives, Spartan King Cleomenes recognized that the enemy were closely observing his every move and order from their encampment opposite. Whenever he ordered his soldiers to arms, the enemy armed themselves; if he prepared to march out, they copied his orders and prepared to march out as well; when Cleomenes ordered his troops to rest, the Argives followed suit. Having noted this, Cleomenes secretly made it known to his troops that they were to do the opposite of his next spoken instruction – they were to take up arms when he publicly ordered them to rest. The result was that when the Argives heard Cleomenes give orders for his troops to rest, they did the same and relaxed. The Spartans, however, quickly took up their arms and launched an attack on the Argives, who were by then unarmed and unprepared for combat, and were thus defeated.

Alexander the Great exploited similar approaches, deliberately establishing patterns of behaviour to deceive an enemy into relaxing their guard and giving him the window of opportunity to exploit. When facing General Porus, in modern day Pakistan, Alexander's forces needed to cross a major river in order to engage Porus' army. But he could find nowhere to cross without risking immediate attack, as Porus' forces were shadowing Alexander's on the opposite bank. Having assessed the problem, Alexander implemented the following stratagem. Every night he would move much of his cavalry up and down the river, making as much noise as possible, including war-cries, to give the appearance of being about to cross. Porus had his cavalry shadow these marches along the river for several nights, but the Macedonians never attempted a crossing. Seeing that the Macedonians never went beyond marching, shouting and yelling, Porus decided it was a false alarm and rested his cavalry, choosing instead to post lookouts along the riverbank. This of course provided Alexander with the opportunity he was looking for. Once Porus' forces were no longer shadowing his, Alexander successfully moved his own army across the river without armed opposition. With his entire force now on the same side of the river as his enemy, Alexander was able to attack, defeating Porus at the battle of the Hydaspes (326 BC). Alexander's repeated actions created a false expectation in Porus' mind that the future would mirror the past and encouraged complacency. And this was Alexander's plan all along; create a pattern in order to break it.

The use of patterns to deceive the enemy also applied to building false expectations about how a future battle would be fought. Roman author, Sextus Julius Frontinus, who also served as a military commander and governor of Britain, provides an account of the battle at Ilipa in Spain (206 BC) between General Scipio, later Scipio Africanus, and Carthaginian general Hasdrubal Gisco. Day after day, Scipio had led out his troops in a specific formation, with his best fighting soldiers placed in the centre. The enemy recognized and mimicked the configuration, placing their own best soldiers in their centre ranks. This went on until the day that Scipio had chosen to fight. On the day of battle, Scipio changed everything, placing his strongest troops on the wings, with his light-armed troops in the centre, but set back. By shifting the formation to a crescent shape, with strength on the wings, Scipio was able to attack the enemy's weakest points with his strongest troops and he thoroughly routed Hasdrubal Gisco's army.

Changing the manner and timing of combat was another useful approach. Roman general Postumius was facing a Carthaginian force in Sicily, his fortified camp being some three miles from the Carthaginians' own camp. Each day the Carthaginians would draw up in front of the Roman fortification, to which Postumius would respond only with minor skirmishes, deploying just a small force outside the entrenchments. The Carthaginian commander had come to regard this as the norm, but one morning Postumius readied his entire force within the camp. He met the Carthaginians with his small force as usual but drew out the engagement much longer than normal. When afternoon came, the Carthaginians began retreating to their own camp, tired and hungry, only for Postumius to release the mass of his army, fresh troops ready for battle, catching the enemy by surprise and defeating them.

This deliberate pattern-building stratagem could turn apparent stalemates into victories, and even supposed retreats into advances. Lusitanian general Viriathus demonstrated a high level of planning and military genius during a conflict with the neighbouring Segobrigenses in Spain. Appearing to retreat from a battle, Viriathus marched his forces away from the field for three days – but then turned the men around and marched them back the entire distance in just one day. Upon arriving at the battlefield site, he immediately attacked and destroyed his enemy who were by then absorbed in sacrificing and celebrating, having assumed the battle was won and Viriathus' forces would by then be some four days' march away. By giving the appearance of fleeing, and setting an expectation of the speed at which his forces would travel, Viriathus had caught his enemy entirely unprepared both mentally and physically. Presenting a pattern of observable behaviour, setting up false expectations, and then taking advantage of the enemy's uncritical acceptance of the situation has consistently proved a successful stratagem in warfare.

Unexpectedness

A general can succeed in throwing an enemy off guard with an unexpected *form* of attack to the one anticipated. Vegetius observed: 'Novelty and surprise throw an enemy into consternation, but common incidents have no effect.' Frontinus supported this point by providing guidance on the tactical value of conducting attacks from unexpected directions. Alexander the Great's attack on the Mallians caught them entirely by surprise simply through his choice of direction:

> Most of them were outside the city and unarmed, supposing that Alexander would never come against them through the waterless country. It was evident that he led his army by this route for this very reason, because it was difficult to lead an army this way, and consequently it appeared incredible to the enemy that he would lead his forces in this direction. He therefore fell upon them unexpectedly, and killed most of them without their even turning to defend themselves…

Even highly trained warriors can be caught out by simple tactics where these are unexpected. In their victory at Pylos, the Athenians demonstrated their ability to defeat Spartan forces on land using a basic stratagem. During the battle, the commander of the Messinians, the Athenians' ally, took a force and moved unseen behind the Spartans, climbing cliffs that the Spartans had assumed were too difficult to attempt and had left unguarded. Without warning the Messinian forces attacked from behind, creating panic in the Spartan lines. At the same time, the surprise attack raised the spirits of the Athenians, who saw their allies joining the fight, and they pressed forward with greater confidence, with the result that the battle was soon over. Attacks from an unanticipated direction, particularly where a force finds itself unexpectedly fighting on two fronts, has proven its effectiveness throughout history.

Hiding the true strength of a force

A common stratagem in early warfare involved generals taking measures to conceal the true strength of their force from their enemies. There were two main reasons for this approach. A general could deliberately make a smaller force appear larger to *dissuade* a stronger enemy from attacking or he could make his superior force look smaller to *encourage* a weaker enemy to attack. Either way, the aim was to deceive an enemy into making decisions against their own best interests.

General Xenophon and his Greek mercenary army were at one point trapped inside Persia, having fought for Cyrus the Younger when he unsuccessfully attempted to overthrow his older brother, Artaxerxes II, king of Persia, at Cunaxa (in modern Iraq) in 401 BC. Cyrus was defeated, meaning that Xenophon's Greek force of some 10,000 soldiers – who had refused to surrender – were then forced to fight their way through hostile territory to make it safely back to Greece. As a foreign force surrounded by adversaries, appearing stronger than they actually were in order to deter engagement proved an invaluable tactic for the Greeks. On one occasion, when the Greeks were facing a Persian force of unknown size and strength, Xenophon devised a plan to make his army look much greater than it was, by burning everything in their path:

> The cavalry, scattering as far in advance as was prudent, wherever they set foot, set fire. The peltasts moving parallel on the high ground were similarly employed, burning everything combustible they could discover. While the main army, wherever they came upon anything which had accidentally escaped, completed the work, so that the whole country looked as if it were ablaze; and the army might easily pass for a larger one.

The plan worked and the Greek force moved forward without being attacked.

When Macedonian general Antigonus found his inferior force encamped opposite a stronger army he took a similar approach to deceive his adversaries. With frequent negotiations taking place between the two armies, Antigonus gave orders that when the next group of enemy ambassadors arrived one of his soldiers 'should abruptly introduce himself, panting, and covered with dust; and inform him, the allies were at hand.' The reality was that no such allied force existed, but the soldier did as ordered and, in full view of the ambassadors, raced up announcing excitedly to the general that their allies were coming. At the news, Antigonus jumped up and immediately dismissed the enemy's ambassadors back to their camp. To reinforce the deception, the following day Antigonus extended the front rank of his army to twice its previous length. The enemy, knowing what their ambassadors had told them and now seeing the increased front of Antigonus' forces, assumed they were seeing a much-expanded force and made a hasty retreat. The stratagem had worked. Antigonus avoided destruction by misleading his enemy with a clever performance and simply rearranging his soldiers – not only avoiding defeat but avoiding a battle altogether.

These types of action often prove effective because given the right cues people's imaginations will fill in the details and arrive at fearful, though inaccurate, conclusions. Julius Caesar used a similar approach in his civil war with Pompey, in one instance securing a strategic location without a fight, despite having a smaller force than his enemy:

> Caesar formed a design to possess himself of Dyrrachium, then in the interests of Pompey, and protected by a powerful body of cavalry. But great as their force was, Caesar found means to baffle it with a handful of men and a happy stratagem. He ordered a small body of cavalry at a handsome gallop to attack them; having detached three companies of foot before them, with orders to regard nothing but to raise as great a dust with their feet as they possibly could. The immense cloud of dust that was raised, and the confidence with which the horse seemed to advance to the attack, impressed the enemy with an opinion that they were in great force: and struck with a sudden and general alarm they immediately fled.

Based on a clever deception supported by an overt display of confidence, the enemy was unnerved, ultimately fleeing an inferior force without a fight out of fear of an imagined larger force bearing down on them.

Where a general had superior forces, stratagems to deceive a numerically inferior enemy into attacking were important. If a general could hide the true strength of his force, he could deceive an inferior adversary into over-confidently attacking or committing to battle with expectations of an easy win. Only then, once the enemy had engaged would they discover their fatal mistake, and that it was they themselves who were being led to the slaughter. This was the case when General Nero used the tactic of keeping his military camp overly small, to fool the Carthaginian general Hasdrubal into expecting an inferior force and therefore willingly engaging the Romans in battle.

There are numerous accounts of similar tactics being successful across hundreds of years and in a variety of conflicts, both by land and sea. When the Athenian admiral Diotimus tried to engage a Spartan fleet of 10 ships with his own 10 vessels, they refused to fight, recognizing Athens' naval superiority. Subsequently, he lashed the ships together in twos, hoisting only one set of sails per pair. To the Spartans, going by the sails, there were just five enemy ships and they immediately sailed to engage them. Only when they were too close to escape, did Diotimus untie the ships and confront the Spartans on equal terms. The result was a disaster for the Spartans – six ships sunk and the remaining four captured. Preventing the enemy from getting an accurate measure of your strength is a proven way for a general to fool them into making poor decisions.

Divide and conquer

A consistent challenge facing these early generals was how to avoid having to fight a strong and united enemy. By dividing an opposing force and then defeating these smaller units, generals could secure their objectives at far less cost to their own side and minimize the risk of defeat. Philip II (Alexander the Great's father) achieved this when in conflict with the Byzantines. Finding that the Byzantines were strongly supported by allies, Philip sent individuals to spread rumours amongst the allies that he had despatched forces into their own countries to attack their cities. He reinforced this by sending out detachments of his army on short marches in different directions, adding credence to the rumours. The result was that the Byzantines' allies abandoned them and quickly brought their forces home to secure their own countries, against a threat which did not exist.

A general did not need to fight an opponent to create divisions and distrust between allies. When Greek general Dionysius was fighting the Carthaginians in Sicily, the Africans employed Greek mercenaries to help them. Dionysius was particularly concerned about fighting against fellow

Greek soldiers, given their military capabilities. Consequently, when Dionysius took prisoners during an engagement, he demanded significant ransoms for the Carthaginians he had captured but deliberately let all the Greeks go free. The result was that the Carthaginians became suspicious of their Greek mercenaries and discharged them all from service. Dionysius' successful deception saw his enemies actively diminish their own fighting strength, sending away the otherwise formidable Greek soldiers they had hired.

Feign fear and retreat

An oft-employed stratagem used by generals of the classical era was to engage in battle and then feign fear and conduct a hasty retreat – only to then turn on the pursuing enemy force and destroy them. This could be very effective if an enemy fell for the deception, left their formation, and recklessly chased after their supposedly fleeing opponents, only to find themselves facing a rapidly reorganized force ready for the fight.

Soon after the slaughter of General Crassus and his army by the Parthians, the Romans returned in force to retake Syria. General Ventidius successfully defeated an army of 20,000 Parthian soldiers and cavalry at Mount Gindarus (38 BC), employing just such a false retreat stratagem to overcome the Parthians' use of arrows at distance which had devastated Crassus' army. Pretending to fear combat, Ventidius allowed the over-confident Parthians to approach so close to the Roman camp that they had no room for effective use of their bows. In the fighting that followed the Romans, having nullified the Parthians' long-range weapons, defeated them in close combat.

Appear disorganized or incompetent

A military commander could also fool his enemy into thinking his force was unready for battle or even incompetent, providing another stratagem for winning on the battlefield. Livy recounts how, when a Roman force found itself blocked on both sides of a valley by an army of the Ligures (Ligurians), a plan was made to break through at one end using 800 Numidian cavalry who were fighting with the Romans. Numidians were noted to be exceptional and formidable horsemen, so when they appeared opposite one of the blockading

Ligures forces in an apparent state of incompetence, falling off their horses and riding poorly, the Ligures soldiers grew careless, relaxed and put aside their weapons to watch the spectacle. Once the enemy had dropped their guard, the Numidians turned on them, broke through their defences and set about attacking a nearby town to draw the blockading forces away. In response, the whole Ligures army abandoned their camp and the remainder of the trapped Roman forces escaped the blockade. Creating conditions for an enemy to underestimate their opponents, and then making them pay for it, could prove a highly effective ruse.

Create confusion over friend or foe

Another useful deception was to create confusion and uncertainty over which forces were one's own and which were the enemy. To carry this through usually required forethought and the right circumstances, but often proved effective, on land and at sea. Admiral Nicon managed to take his ship safely through an alien fleet by disguising it to look like the enemy's vessels, even singing salutes to their opponents as they approached, and then sailing right through the enemy force, successfully making their escape.

In contrast, when the Athenian forces had been defeated in battle at Syracuse but still presented a significant threat, Syracusan general Hermocrates, fearful of the Athenians escaping, had his cavalry ride up to the Athenian camp at night. Pretending to be Athens' allies, the Syracusan soldiers advised the Athenians that they should remain where they were at night, because the roads were guarded, and instead organize their retreat during the day. On the strength of this information from, as it seemed, friendly forces, the Athenian generals delayed their escape. The result was a disaster. Instead of the Athenians moving at night when the paths were clear, the delay allowed the Syracusans time to organize and move armed forces into position, to prevent the Athenians escaping. The opportunity to flee passed and the Athenian army was captured almost to a man. Their fate was terrible. The Athenian soldiers ended up as prisoners, and lost their lives to starvation in their thousands after surrendering to the well-organized Syracusans; an Athenian army deceived into capture and death.

Minimal resources for maximum return

Effective stratagems do not necessarily require a massive effort or resources. Indeed, a good deception can be relatively cheap with the smallest of effort used to achieve victory or avoid defeat. When besieging the city of Prinassus in Persia, Philip V of Macedon found the walls exceedingly strong, so decided to undermine them by digging out their foundations from the outside, a common tactic during sieges. However, finding that the city was built on rock prevented this approach, so Philip had a screen erected to hide the futility of his army's efforts from those inside the walls. At night, he had his soldiers bring in dirt from the surrounding area and pile it up around where the supposed mining was occurring. Seeing these mounds of dirt growing every day, the city's garrison feared the worst and surrendered to Philip; a pile of dirt for a city.

When Xenophon and his army were retreating out of Persia, he conducted a raid against locals to secure provisions, using a number of Greek soldiers. During the retreat, they were followed by a sizeable enemy force threatening to attack and overwhelm them. Recognizing the real threat posed by this group, as they pursued the Greeks over difficult and wooded terrain, Xenophon sent eleven soldiers to the rear of his troop. The soldiers were told to pretend to hide from the oncoming enemy, while deliberately flashing their shields in the sunlight to make it appear that the Greeks had set a large-scale ambush for their pursuers. As intended, the enemy saw the flashes from the shields and assumed a real ambush with significant forces was awaiting them, with the result that they decided against attacking and let the Greeks escape. With a simple and low-cost stratagem, Xenophon had avoided his forces being assaulted in a difficult and unfamiliar location, and all the Greeks safely returned to camp, including the eleven soldiers, who rapidly retreated once their deception had succeeded.

Deception through openness

A final double deception by the Spartan general Agesilaus against the Persian general Tissaphernes is worth reflecting on both in terms of its success, and also in terms of capturing the thinking and planning that goes into such a successful stratagem of deceit. Cornelius Nepos gives an account of King Agesilaus of Sparta, one of a number of eminent commanders that he wrote about. According to Nepos, General Agesilaus had launched a successful campaign into Asia, because he was worried that the Persian King Artaxerxes was mobilizing a fleet and army to attack Greece. Agesilaus' attack had surprised the Persians who, under General Tissaphernes, successfully argued for a three-month truce. When the truce expired, Tissaphernes assumed that Agesilaus would attack Caria, the richest province, so that was where he gathered his forces together. Agesilaus did initially march towards Caria, reinforcing Tissaphernes' expectations, but then turned east to Phrygia, laying waste to the country before Tissaphernes could respond. Following this success, Agesilaus led his army to winter quarters in Ephesus and spent the time preparing his troops for war come the spring.

When winter ended, Agesilaus drew up his army and openly declared that he would march on Sardis, knowing that Tissaphernes would not believe a word he said. As anticipated, Tissaphernes remained with his forces in Caria, assuming that Agesilaus was trying to fool him again and that Caria would be the Spartan's true target. Agesilaus, however, now did exactly as he had said he would and marched on Sardis, taking numerous places and an abundance of spoil. Tissaphernes was forced to respond and send out his forces from Caria. But in the subsequent disorganization, Tissaphernes' cavalry attacked the Greeks before their own infantry had arrived, whereas Agesilaus had his entire army together as one force and they immediately retaliated and destroyed Tissaphernes' disjointed army. In this case, having been misled originally by Agesilaus' initial march towards Caria, Tissaphernes was then fooled by Agesilaus' openness. Honesty proved to be the best form of deception.

Chapter 6

How Do You Minimize Surprise, Shock and Fear?

It is pardonable to be defeated, but never to be surprised.

Frederick the Great

Battle of course always furnishes surprises. But it furnishes less in proportion as good sense and the recognition of the truth have had their effect on the training of the fighting man.

Colonel Ardant du Picq

If the benefit of inflicting surprise, shock and fear on the enemy is clear, then a general needs to prevent an adversary creating such emotions in his own forces. The first step is for the general to recognize that they *can* be surprised, that they can be caught out by an enemy whose sole purpose is to defeat them. A general who recognizes this and takes appropriate action to minimize the risk of surprise is in a better position to diminish the shock and fear of an unanticipated and unexpected attack. Preparedness is crucial.

Basic precautions

There are clear and consistent actions which the early writers highlighted as helping a general and his army avoid being surprised. Maintaining an awareness of what else was happening or likely to happen was critical for a general and his army. Engaging scouts and conducting reconnaissance helped to avoid surprises by ensuring that the commander knew what lay ahead, behind and around them at any time. Another requirement, particularly emphasized during the Roman era, was to properly fortify camps against armed attack. Enemy attacks were usually foreseeable and ensuring that a military camp was appropriately secured was an obvious defence, coupled with the use of soldiers to maintain a watch throughout the day and night.

At the end of a march and outside established forts, a good general would ensure that their soldiers did not rest until their location had been fortified. While these were seemingly obvious precautions to prevent surprise attack, a consistent feature of Greek and Roman literature is examples of generals who failed to enforce these basic precautions, often at the expense of the lives of their soldiers and even themselves. Further, it is not just that these precautions need to be taken, but that they need to be consistently enforced. To avoid surprise, therefore, requires preparation, a recognition of the possibility of being surprised, and constant vigilance.

Mental and physical preparation

This ability to prepare oneself and one's army is crucial in countering an enemy's stratagems. Vegetius captures the risk of unpreparedness and the impact on soldiers, arguing 'Men are frightened and thrown into disorder by sudden accidents and surprises of no consequence when foreseen.' As the head of the army, it was the role of the general to foresee such occurrences and ensure that his soldiers were prepared and ready, thus minimizing surprise, shock and fear. Even if a specific attack had not been identified, a well-prepared army would be in a far better position, both mentally and physically, to counter whatever an enemy threw at them. A good example is General Metellus and his Roman army during a campaign in Spain. Evaluating the situation before they broke camp for a new location, Metellus knew his soldiers needed to maintain awareness and discipline in case of attack during the transit. Accordingly, Metellus announced he had received intelligence that the enemy was preparing to ambush them during their march. He urged the soldiers to maintain their ranks, keep near their standards, and be ready to counter the anticipated attack. In truth there was no such intelligence, yet as it happened the enemy did actually launch an ambush on the Romans while they were marching. Thanks to the general's warning, the soldiers were ready and easily repelled the attack. The threat might have been made up, but their vigilance and readiness to counter it was real and swiftly put into action. Metellus used a stratagem against his own soldiers to ensure they were mentally and physically prepared for a fight on the march. Questions about the morality of fooling one's own men might be raised, but an ambush in contested territory is entirely plausible and by ensuring his soldiers were in formation and battle-ready, Metellus actually saved their lives. Recognizing where and how an army was vulnerable also allowed a general to appropriately prepare his forces. Thus, a general who understood warfare would (and should) be better able to avoid enemy stratagems:

> It is asserted by those who have made the profession their study that an army is exposed to more danger on marches than in battles. In an engagement the men are properly armed, they see their enemies before them and are prepared to fight: but on a march the soldier is less on his guard, has not his arms always ready and is thrown into disorder by a sudden attack or ambuscade. A general, therefore, cannot be too careful and diligent in taking necessary precautions to prevent a surprise on the march and in making proper dispositions to repulse the enemy, in case of such accident, without loss.

To attack an enemy when they were on the march and unprepared was a recognized stratagem for a general to use against the enemy and, therefore, a logical tactic for an enemy to use as well. This also highlights that ancient battles were often more than simply drawing up strict formations of organized ranks of soldiers opposite a clearly visible and formed-up enemy force. Such formation-fighting was common, but the risks of ambushes and surprise assaults highlights how a general needed to ensure that his soldiers were mentally and physically ready for all kinds of attacks and circumstances.

Train and exercise for the unexpected

Athenian general Iphicrates provides a study in readiness and preparedness. The Athenian commander used to train and exercise his soldiers in all manner of actions that could occur in war, such as ambushes, surprises, sudden attacks and deceptions. Iphicrates ensured that his soldiers were trained and prepared to counter the enemy's unexpected attacks and to employ these tactics themselves against the enemy. This was no accident. As is clear in accounts of his life, the general was always on his guard. Even when seemingly safe in the palace of his father-in-law, Iphicrates revealed a coat of mail hidden under his clothing, saying, 'I am always in exercise and on my guard.' An interesting insight into their relationship perhaps, but also an indication that this general thought and acted to mitigate his chances of being surprised. It is also difficult to imagine Iphicrates ever being caught out by a stratagem such as that exercised by Scipio Africanus, in his surprise attack on the Carthaginian camp while pretending to negotiate a truce. Why? Polyaenus wrote that on such occasions, the Athenian general remained deeply suspicious of his enemy, and 'during truces always fortified his camp: observing, that it was not the part of a good general, to say: "I could not have thought it."' Iphicrates did not take situations at face value but adopted a questioning approach. He actively prepared himself and his soldiers to deny the enemy the opportunity to catch him or the men off their guard. Such a well-prepared general and army presented their enemies with a formidable challenge.

Effective generals were able to prepare their soldiers with realistic expectations to minimize surprise and shock, but these exceptional military commanders were able to make the unexpected *expected*, with appropriate preparations and precautions. Anticipating potential enemy actions, they had plans in place and had exercised their soldiers to ensure their readiness and confidence to rapidly adjust to a variety of situations. This preparedness also made it easier for the general and their soldiers to recognize when changes were occurring on the battlefield. For example, knowing that his force could be attacked from behind, Commander Appius Claudius actively prepared for such an event. When the situation did occur, Claudius and his soldiers were ready. As Livy explains, 'The rear was commanded by Appius Claudius, who having beforehand prepared his men to expect such an event, that it might not come upon them unawares, instantly made his troops face about, and presented an entire front to the enemy.' The enemy's tactic proved ineffectual as a direct result of Claudius' forethought and his soldiers' training ensured the rapid response to counter this precise tactic. A good general took care that his force was prepared, thus neutralizing the enemy's surprise tactics and minimizing their effects.

Make the unfamiliar familiar

While many of these classical generals and their soldiers were often familiar with their enemies in terms of how they thought and how they fought, this was not always the case, particularly in expanding empires such as Rome's. Where an army was facing a new and unfamiliar opponent there was obviously the risk of being surprised and even defeated in a major battle. Generals such as Julius Caesar would act tactically to minimize such risks by initially engaging these new opponents in minor skirmishes. This had a number of benefits. Through minor engagements a general could learn how this new enemy fought, their preferred weapons and tactics and what fighting spirit they had, as well testing how their own soldiers fared against these particular opponents. For the soldiers, they could become familiar with fighting the previously unknown warriors, reducing their fear of the unexpected and learning how to counter new tactics and weaponry. Such small battles therefore risked little, but provided much needed insights, diminished fear of an unfamiliar enemy, and increased the confidence of both generals and soldiers alike in their ability to meet and defeat these adversaries in major battles.

Recognize stratagems

Being a student of stratagems, a good leader should be well prepared to defend against such deceptions and surprises. A cautious general, aware of the possible use of stratagems against them, is in a better position to recognize many subterfuges that the enemy might try, and thus avoid falling into traps.

Roman general Gnaeus Fulvius, fighting the Etruscans, was brought word of cattle-herders engaging with his soldiers and offering guidance on the best path for his army to take. But both he and his soldiers were observant and suspicious. The herdsmen's accents, their manner and appearance did not align with those of common cattle herders. Fulvius' response to his soldiers' reports was clear, 'Tell them that they may uncover the ambush which they vainly conceal, that the Romans understand all their devices, and can now be no more taken by stratagem than they can be conquered by arms.' A general on the alert for stratagems being used against him was in a good place to recognize the warning signs and not be caught out.

Using surprise to one's own advantage

Despite the often-severe consequences of being surprised in war, if they are not fatal or disastrous, a general can turn such shocks to their advantage.

Where an armed force caught out by an ambush, unexpected tactic, or unfamiliar situation can not only survive but recover, it will be better prepared in future. The experience of being surprised by the enemy is more powerful than any verbal warning. The commander can harness such a confronting experience to help avoid similar events.

At a national level, we see an example in the surprise that Hannibal achieved when crossing the Alps and marching his army into Italy. So unexpected was the event, and so much did Hannibal's sudden arrival catch the Roman public and the authorities completely off guard, that they were shocked into immediately dealing with the threat. All efforts became focused on countering this unexpected peril. The last information on the Carthaginians had been of their capture of Sagnuntum in Spain. Now the Romans received the unwelcome news that Hannibal was actually in Italy and had begun laying siege to cities.

The seriousness of the threat prompted General Longus and his forces to be immediately recalled from Sicily and all Roman soldiers given orders to assemble rapidly, while other military plans were put on hold – the highest priority was the defence of Italy. There was a single-minded focus, rapid reprioritization, quick coordination and expansion of their military forces. The arrival of the Carthaginians resulted in Rome going onto an immediate war footing. There were many years of challenge ahead for the Romans, but Hannibal's crossing of the Alps had shaken them out of their complacency.

Just as Hannibal surprised Rome with his crossing of the Alps into Italy, he had his own surprise on arrival there. As described earlier (see Chapter 3), Hannibal's forces had clashed with Publius Scipio's cavalry in Gaul prior to his ascent into the Alps. On descending from the Alps into Italy, Hannibal received word that Publius Scipio had already moved his army back into Italy and was close at hand. So unexpected was the news that Hannibal at first refused to believe it. In spite of his own rapid movement into Italy, Hannibal had believed Publius Scipio and his forces would have taken longer to get back to Italy. As more reports came in confirming the presence of the Roman general nearby Hannibal was stunned by Scipio's speed and achievement. As we see, even those conducting surprises can themselves be surprised.

Lead by example – an assured general

Soldiers under generals with the foresight to prepare them against surprise tactics are more likely to adapt and thrive as a cohesive fighting force. These efforts at preparing and training to avoid and counter surprises take the advantage away from the enemy. Instead of psychologically breaking in the face of the unexpected, well-prepared soldiers have shown themselves able to adapt and fight on. Further, even in the face of uncertainty and fear, in these ancient accounts it is apparent that good generals were able to restore confidence in their soldiers and allay their fears. When the army of Greeks began to make their escape from Persia, isolated in hostile territory and fearing for their lives, General Clearchus (who was succeeded by Xenophon after Clearchus' later capture by the Persians during negotiations) demonstrated an ability to restore courage amongst his soldiers against baseless fears. During nighttime in their own camp, the Greek soldiers:

> had their turn of scare – a panic seized them, and there was a noise and clatter, hardly to be explained except by the visitation of some sudden terror. But Clearchus had with him the Eleian Tolmides, the best herald of his time; him he ordered to proclaim silence, and then to give out this proclamation of the generals: 'Whoever will give any information as to who let an ass into the camp shall receive a talent of silver in reward.' On hearing this proclamation the soldiers made up their minds that their fear was baseless, and their generals safe and sound. At break of day Clearchus gave the order to the [Greeks] to get under arms in line of battle, and take up exactly the same position as they held on the day of the battle.

Clearchus showed the men he was not panicking and used humour to calm them. He followed this up the next day by returning them to a familiar formation for the march. Even in hostile territory, he minimized the unexpected and restored confidence to the army.

Chapter 7

How Do You Read the Situation and How Do You Adapt in Battle?

My centre is giving way, my right is in retreat, situation excellent. I attack.

General Ferdinand Foch

Plans of campaign may be modified, ad infinitum, according to circumstances – the genius of the general, the character of the troops, and the topography of the theatre of action.

Napoleon

In ancient warfare, generals were present and part of the fight – to see, to act, and to be in a position to maximize their ability to influence the battle. In the chaos of the clash of arms this was not easy and as much as possible needed to be prepared for; but even a prepared force had to be able to quickly change tactics to blunt an enemy's unanticipated tactics, adapt to the terrain and conditions, or exploit unexpected opportunities. The flexibility to adapt to changing circumstances required a leader who was best situated to see and influence the fight. Sometimes this meant being forward, to observe and rally forces, other times it meant being on a point of elevation or in a central location. Whatever the particulars, generals needed to be where they could witness the fight, be seen by their own forces, and be near enough to pass new orders and get them acted on swiftly.

A good general could not be merely an informed or insightful bystander; a general needed to understand the situation on the ground and act to influence the battle accordingly. There is much that has been said by the ancient writers on good planning and selection of the battlefield helping to determine the outcome even prior to fighting, but there is also much said about generals who adapted in battle and exploited opportunities to achieve victory in the field.

See, Understand, Act

Good generals appear to be able to rapidly interpret the reality, risks and opportunities presented by a situation, and act to better their own position and increase their adversary's difficulties. The ability to accurately perceive the situation, comprehend what can or will happen, and act appropriately and at speed, is as critical for a modern general as it was for the ancients: see, understand and act. Further, given the difficulty of issuing orders on the battlefield in all the noise and chaos, a general also needs to identify changing circumstances and adapt their plan in enough time for it to be communicated and acted upon by their commanders and soldiers. It is apparent that this ability to observe, comprehend and take appropriate action is not simply a given and many generals have failed in this regard, whether through a lack of skill, experience or simply in the chaos and confusion of battle. In contrast, notable commanders did demonstrate this ability, even at an early age and irrespective of rank.

Greek general Philopoemen became a highly successful and well-regarded senior commander, but even early in his career his ability to read a situation and adapt his tactics gained him recognition as somebody already possessing the skills of a general. His ability to see, interpret and act appropriately as a junior officer is reflected in a successful battle between the Macedonian king Antigonus III and his Achaean allies against the Spartan king, Cleomenes III. Under the leadership of Antigonus, the allied force moved to engage the Spartans at the battle of Sellasia (222 BC). Signals had been arranged for various forces to join the battle at the appropriate time, including the cavalry under the command of a General Alexander. As Antigonus launched his forces against the Spartans, the cavalry awaited their assigned signal to attack. However, the junior cavalry officer Philopoemen suddenly saw some Spartan troops launch a surprise attack on the Achaean infantry, threatening to overwhelm them:

> At this critical moment Philopoemen of Megalopolis, who saw what was happening and foresaw what was likely to happen, first attempted to call the attention of the commanding officers to it, but as no one paid any attention to him, since he had never held any command and was quite a young man, he called on his own fellow citizens to follow him and boldly fell upon the enemy.

Philopoemen's initiative and action proved crucial in the subsequent victory over the Spartans. After the battle, Antigonus asked General Alexander why he had launched his cavalry before the signal had been given. Alexander said that it was not him but a boy who had ordered the attack against his orders. Antigonus responded that it was the child who had understood the situation and acted like a good general, whereas Alexander, who was the general, had acted like a child.

This ability to read the situation, rapidly alter the plan, and act decisively and effectively, is evidently the mark of a good general. What today is described as 'situational awareness' or 'situational understanding' is apparent in these early accounts of leadership on the battlefield. Whether prior to or during a battle a general needs to understand what the enemy is doing, what their own forces are doing, and how best to take advantage of the real situation. Having a plan is crucial; unquestioningly applying that plan when the reality differs from the expectation is foolhardy. Indeed, as the first-century AD Greek philosopher Onasander argues in his book on generalship (*Strategikos*), there are times when actions and strategies rapidly developed in response to the reality of battle could prove preferable to those developed prior to it. It is in view of the specific circumstances, rather than from experience, that a general might make the most appropriate and effective response. Therefore, a good general will adapt to events rather than stick to an outdated plan.

Using your own eyes

For the early generals, seeing the situation for themselves in order to select the best course of action was often key to success. Arrian reflects on Alexander's strength of both insight and action, 'He was very clever in recognizing what was necessary to be done, even when it was still a matter unnoticed by others; and very successful in conjecturing from the observation of facts what was likely to occur.' Alexander made sound battlefield decisions based on what he saw firsthand. According to Livy, Scipio Africanus, early on in his career during the siege of New Carthage (Spain) in 209 BC, demonstrated the importance of a general seeing the situation with his own eyes in order to act appropriately and quickly: 'Scipio, who had gone out to an eminence called Mercury's hill, perceiving that the walls were abandoned by their defenders in many parts, ordered all his men to be called out of his camp and advance to take the city, and ordered them to bring the scaling-ladders.' Scipio's speedy recognition of the enemy's weakness, timing of the issuing of the order and execution of the action ensured that the Romans took the city.

Identify and use trusted sources

Given that a military commander can only be in one place at a time, there are instances when they need to rely on information beyond what they can see for themselves. In ancient warfare this entailed the use of scouts for reconnaissance in order that the general could understand what (and who) lay ahead and around him and his forces at any time. The challenge was that without seeing firsthand, the general would need to assess and judge the credibility of information and the reliability of those providing it. The safest way to make this work was to use only people in whom they had complete trust to conduct reconnaissance and provide accurate and reliable intelligence.

Xenophon's account of the Greek army's escape out of Persia shows the necessity of accurate information, which clearly made the difference between successful escape and death in a foreign country. In the case of Xenophon, he faced the challenge of leading an army through hostile and entirely unfamiliar territory. Information gathered on what lay ahead, behind and around them formed the basis for important decisions on which way was safest for the army to proceed. Xenophon's decisions would ultimately determine whether or not the army would make it safely back to Greece or be captured or killed in Persian territory.

In one case, Xenophon described the rationale for the selection of Democrates, who was sent to lead a group of soldiers to surveil the mountains following reports of watchfires having been seen, with the concern that these could indicate an enemy force nearby. Democrates was chosen for the task because he had previously proved himself entirely reliable and trustworthy in his reporting. Following the mission, Democrates returned to state that no fires had been located but he had used the opportunity to take a prisoner. This initiative proved invaluable as when questioned the prisoner revealed the enemy's actual location, as well as where they were planning to ambush the

Greeks. Democrates was certainly the type of person that a general needed to identify and use, particularly in the days before maps, satellite imagery and real-time footage.

While those selected to provide reconnaissance for a general need to be entirely reliable and accurate in their information, the reality is of course that this does not always happen. Even good generals can be mistaken in their trust. Julius Caesar himself notes problems with a commander who failed in such circumstances. Hearing that an army of Gauls (Helvetii tribesmen) had massed not far from Caesar's camp, the Roman general immediately sent out a force under his second-in-command Labienus, with orders to take a hill close to the enemy camp and wait there until Caesar arrived with the main force the next day so they could attack the Gauls simultaneously. The following day, as Caesar marched his army towards the Helvetii, he received word from a reconnaissance patrol commanded by Considius, that it was the Gauls who were in command of the hill, while Labienus and the Romans were nowhere to be seen. The attack was delayed due to this information, only for Caesar to discover later that day that the force on the hill, reported to him as Gauls, were in fact the Romans under Labienus awaiting Caesar's arrival to launch the attack. To Caesar's frustration, Considius had entirely misinterpreted what he had seen. In the meantime, the Helvetii force had safely withdrawn. As Caesar's own account illustrates, getting accurate information in war is difficult.

Lack of awareness can prove disastrous

In warfare, both ancient and modern, constant vigilance is key. The early use of advance scouts when on the move, as well as sentries and observation posts around military camps, were designed to ensure generals and their soldiers knew what was happening around them at all times. In contrast, a lack of such awareness could prove deadly and even seasoned soldiers could be caught out not paying close attention to their surroundings. An example occurred with Caesar's own soldiers who were exposed by their lack of vigilance during the establishment of a new Roman camp in Britain during Caesar's second invasion (54 BC, a year after his first invasion in 55 BC).

After defeating a force of charioteers in a skirmish, the Romans turned their attention to fortifying their camp. However, there were still enemy warriors hiding and watching from nearby woods who swiftly took advantage of this opportunity and launched a surprise attack while the Roman soldiers were off their guard. Caesar was forced to send reinforcements to help counter the attack, but the Romans were disconcerted by the Britons' unfamiliar fighting tactics and the enemy were able to escape. This encounter did not prove disastrous for the Roman force but was noted and highlighted by Caesar as an important lesson to be learned. The incident reinforced that in war the absence of awareness can easily be exploited. The unfamiliarity of the enemy and their tactics also put the Romans at an initial disadvantage and created uncertainty exploited by the enemy to escape.

Not every Roman general was able to get away with such a lapse. The example of Caius Oppius demonstrates how a lack of awareness can prove disastrous:

> having pitched on a place near a fort called Mutilum, convenient enough for cutting down the corn (for the crops were now ripe), and setting out without having reconnoitred around, and without establishing armed posts of sufficient strength to protect those who were unarmed and intent on their work, he was suddenly surrounded, together with his foragers, by an unexpected invasion of the Gauls. On this, panic and flight seized even on those who were furnished with weapons. Seven thousand men, dispersed through the corn fields, were put to the sword, among whom was the commander himself, Caius Oppius.

Here, poor awareness and lack of basic protection resulted in a slaughter of the Roman forces. In this instance, ignorance proved deadly. In war, reality has a way of imposing itself on the situation, and a general who lacked a link with reality could be easily destroyed by a motivated and aware adversary. For a general, seeing what is occurring is essential, but seeing alone is not sufficient, a general also needs to *understand* what it means.

Misinterpreting with one's own eyes

Even when a general had 'eyes on' the battle, understanding what was happening and what it meant could prove elusive in the confusion of fighting. Indeed, a general might witness the combat but misinterpret the situation, leading to deadly consequences, even all-out defeat. Following the assassination of Julius Caesar (44 BC), Rome descended into another civil war. On one side was Octavian and Mark Antony and their armies and on the other, Cassius and Brutus and their forces. The decisive engagement between them occurred at the battle of Philippi (42 BC). Florus' account of General Cassius' final moments shows how even with eyes on the battlefield the inability of a military commander to accurately interpret what they have witnessed can lead to disastrous decision making. Florus imakes it clear just how significant Cassius' misunderstanding proved when he declares, 'A mistake decided the victory in this battle.'

During the early stages of the combat, Cassius and Brutus were actually winning. Their armies had achieved an early advantage over the allied forces of Octavian and Antony and were set to press home their position. However, in the heat and chaos of battle, Cassius misinterpreted what he saw in the actions and movement of his own forces:

> [Cassius,] on seeing the cavalry returning at full speed after the capture of [Octavian's] camp, thought that they were in flight and made his way to some higher ground. Here, when the dust and confusion and the approaching darkness prevented him from seeing what had happened, and a scout whom he had sent out to obtain news was slow in bringing it, thinking that his cause was lost, he made one of those who were standing by cut off his head.

Cassius' fears clouded his judgement and, rather than wait and clarify the situation he rushed to judgement and a flawed decision, to end his life. The fatal mistake did not just cost Cassius his life but spelled the end for Brutus too, and both their armies. Prior to the battle, Brutus and Cassius had agreed that they would either be victorious or neither would survive the fight, and such was ultimately the outcome. On seeing Cassius' dead body, Brutus wept. In the absence of his fellow general, Brutus did attempt to fight on, taking charge of Cassius' army, reorganizing it, and making an effort to rebuild confidence and fighting spirit amongst the now combined forces. However, in the end the loss of his fellow general was too great a blow to overcome in terms of leading and commanding his own and Cassius' army, the latter well aware of their general's fate.

Despite putting up a desperate fight against Antony and Octavian's armies over several weeks, Brutus and his combined forces were ultimately routed, and he fled into the mountains with a sizeable force. Shortly after, on seeing his enemies approaching in great numbers and with escape routes cut off to him, Brutus recognized the inevitability of defeat and had one of his companions run him through with a sword. The campaign was over. The battle of Philippi was determined by simply misunderstanding the real state of affairs, an initial success interpreted as failure, leading to the decisions of both Cassius and Brutus to 'fall on their swords', one through his error of judgement and the other as a result of recognition of the impending loss of the conflict. As the saying goes, it was 'defeat snatched from the jaws of victory.'

In battle, such uncertainty and want of accurate information can result in the rapid collapse of even a professional fighting force. Consequently, for a general, correct interpretation of events even in the chaos of battle is crucial. Better still is to create confusion amongst the enemy, to deny them understanding. One of the best ways for a general to achieve this was by taking the initiative on the battlefield and implementing their own plan. This would give a better grasp of the situation because the action would be likely to reflect the execution of the general's own plan. In contrast, the enemy commander and soldiers would be compelled to try to interpret and understand events that were being forced upon them.

In his account of the Peloponnesian War, Thucydides provides an account of an attack by Athenians at Megara against the Spartans and Megarians. The Athenians gained entrance to the town of Megara by night and immediately attacked the walls where the Spartan garrison was. In the confusion and shouting, the Spartans mistakenly thought they were fighting a combined force of Athenians and Megarians – that the Megarians had switched their allegiance and were now fighting with the Athenians. The result was that the Spartan garrison's resistance collapsed and they fled, taking refuge in Nisaea, a nearby town. In the confusion of battle, made more difficult due to the darkness, the Spartans had assumed the worst whereas the Athenians, who initiated the attack, were always abreast of the situation and exploited their enemy's confusion to take the town.

Know the enemy, know yourself

Situational understanding clearly requires an appreciation of the enemy and a recognition of where they are and how they are fighting. A military commander without an understanding of the situation is a danger to themselves and their men. General Gnaeus Fulvius, facing Hannibal at the second battle of Herdonia (210 BC) got caught out, along with his soldiers, by fixating on the enemy in front of them with whom they were heavily engaged in fighting. Fulvius and his soldiers understood *part* of the situation but not its totality. Hannibal waited until he was sure that the attention of his Roman enemies was entirely on the battle in front of them. The Carthaginian general then signalled to his cavalry to ride around and surprise the Romans from behind, while sending another section of cavalry to attack the Roman camp to create further chaos. Fulvius was caught entirely unawares. Up until that point of the battle, he and his soldiers had stood their ground and held their ranks. But when the Carthaginian cavalry unexpectedly attacked the rear of the Roman force, the soldiers lost their nerve and fell apart as a cohesive fighting unit, either being killed or fleeing for their lives.

While maintaining an understanding of the enemy is critical, so is a general's constant understanding of their own forces. Roman troops in Armenia were challenged by a Parthian invasion of that country. The Roman general Paetus (who was ultimately relieved of command) not only demonstrated a complete lack of awareness of the enemy, but also erred by overestimating the strength of his own forces:

> Paetus, ignorant of the impending danger, was keeping the 5th legion at a distance in Pontus; the rest he had weakened by indiscriminate furloughs, till it was heard that Vologeses was approaching with a powerful force bent on war. He summoned the 12th legion, and then was discovered the numerical feebleness of the source from which he had hoped for the repute of an augmented army.

Paetus' failure was all the more inexcusable because at any time prior to a battle a general should have a complete knowledge of the numerical and fighting strength of their own forces. This lack of awareness of the status of his own legions was entirely avoidable but Paetus only discovered the weakness of the force under his command when it was far too late to rectify. The result was a humiliating defeat at the hands of General Vologeses, with Paetus being forced to seek peace terms from the Parthian leader.

Adaptable planning

Any battle plan needs to be adaptable to changing circumstances. The ability to rapidly exploit an opportunity or shift quickly to counter enemy action is a requirement of sound military leadership. A good general is not fixed in their approach but able to modify their tactics in response to updated intelligence. As Polybius observed about Hannibal, here was a general willing to change his plans in the light of new information. Such a sound and logical approach evidently helped him achieve his numerous battlefield victories against the Romans. What a good general has to do is keep an eye on the enemy, an eye on their own forces and an eye on the battlefield conditions (yes, three eyes at least), and always be ready to adjust to the reality of the situation.

Reflecting on Alexander the Great's attack on the city of Sangala, Arrian describes the Macedonian leader recognizing the enemy's significant numbers and their defensive position in front of the city, so 'he drew up his forces in the order which seemed to him especially adapted to his present circumstances.' It was not about wishful thinking but about modifying his tactics and available forces to be most effective against the enemy in front of them.

In terms of adaptable plans, a sound tactic is often that of forward movement – taking the fight to the enemy and keeping up the pressure on them. Initiating action and forcing the enemy onto the back foot is usually a reasonable approach and helps to boost an army's morale. Consequently, a general who wants to succeed (even survive) has to find a way, or make one:

> Clearchus, at the head of a numerous army, having advanced to a river in one place so easily fordable that the water would not reach higher than the knees, and in another so deep as to be breast-high, endeavoured first to effect a passage where the water was shallowest. But finding it roughly disputed with slings and arrows, he marched his heavy-armed troops to the spot where the river was deepest. The greatest part of their bodies being there concealed beneath the water, and that which was above covered with their

shields, they crossed it without loss, and forced the enemy to retreat; while the remaining part of the army passed the shallow ford without opposition.

General Clearchus adapted his army's progress to the reality of the enemy and the topography and found a way forward. This ability to be flexible, to select options which accord with reality and maintain the fight, is often critical to battlefield success.

Given the inherent uncertainties around conflict, if opportunities present themselves to more rapidly or effectively defeat an enemy then a military commander needs to be ready to take advantage of those opportunities. While preparing to attack Mark Antony's forces at sea, Agrippa (commanding Octavian's navy) heard that Antony and the Egyptian queen Cleopatra's fleets had been scattered, struck by a violent storm that had resulted in total disorder. Upon receiving this news, Agrippa advised Octavian to abandon the original plan, changed his tactics and reorganized his ships and infantry (onboard the ships) accordingly, updating his orders across the fleet. With the new plan in place, Octavian's navy then awaited Antony and Cleopatra's regrouped naval forces. Antony and Cleopatra were able to escape in the ensuing naval battle, but Agrippa and Octavian were ultimately successful in defeating the majority of their fleets at the battle of Actium (31 BC).

Don't just stand there, do something

A general cannot be a passive bystander but needs to influence the situation whenever and wherever they can. When Athenian general Chares had a suspicion that there were enemy spies inside his camp, he acknowledged the situation, identified a solution, established the conditions for success, and then acted. Chares placed guards surrounding the camp, then ordered each man to engage with the person closest to them and not let anyone pass until they had answered as to who they were, which company they belonged to, their rank, and the code word. In this way the spies were quickly identified and arrested, being unable to accurately identify their company, colleagues or code word. Through forethought and action, Chares tackled the reality of the situation in the camp and removed the enemy threat.

Even in the face of an unfavourable set of circumstances, with quick thinking and decisive action a general can influence events to their own benefit, as Caesar appears to have done when fighting the surviving Pompeian forces at Munda (Spain, 45 BC). As Florus observes, the enemy, now led by Pompey's sons Gnaeus and Sextus, appeared to gain the advantage during the battle, to the extent that Caesar physically threw himself into the fighting in a desperate attempt to prevent his men from retreating. Then, when the Pompeian forces seemed to be moving back across the battlefield, Florus comments that Caesar used this to his full advantage to turn the tide of battle. Whether he genuinely believed his enemy to be retreating or simply made use of the confusion to rally his own forces, Caesar cried out to his men that the enemy were fleeing, giving his soldiers the impression that they were in fact winning the battle. They responded, renewing their attack with increased vigour and shifting the tide of battle in their favour, ultimately defeating the Pompeian troops. Caesar's quick thinking showed that even when things were going wrong, a general could embrace circumstances and use them to his own ends, taking advantage of the chaos and confusion of battle.

The natural elements themselves provided advantages for commanders to adapt to and exploit. Athenian general Alcibiades, during a battle between his forces and the Syracusans, noticed that there was a quantity of dry fern between the two armies and the wind was at the backs of his soldiers. He ordered the fern be set alight. With the wind driving the smoke directly into the Syracusans' eyes they were no longer able to fight effectively, resulting in a rout of the Athenians' blinded enemy. In a similar incident, to avoid being destroyed during an escape, the Spartan general Brasidas ordered his men to cut down great quantities of wood and set them on fire to secure their rear as they retreated. The tactic proved successful, thanks to Brasidas spotting the opportunity, adapting his plan, and putting his soldiers into action.

Recognize and take advantage of the enemy's mistakes

The ability to read the situation and seize the initiative requires the general to be in a position to observe the enemy and their own forces and change tactics at the opportune moment. Identifying the moment is marked by immediate orders and action. Livy provides an example of an engagement between the Romans and Carthaginians, noting, 'When the Roman generals saw that the ranks of the enemy were in confusion, that they were in a state of trepidation and dismay, their standards moving to and fro, they exhorted and implored their men to charge them while thus discomfited, and not allow them to form their line again.' The generals saw the enemy in disorder and acted, ordering their soldiers to seize on the enemy's confusion, and attack before the Carthaginians could regroup. Such fleeting opportunities need to be identified and rapidly exploited by generals and their armies.

Speedy action to take advantage of an enemy's disorganization is a similarly sound tactic at sea. Athenian admiral Phormio with his 30 ships was resolved to fight an enemy with a much larger fleet of 50 ships. Forming his force into five organized lines, Phormio sailed towards them. Excited by their numerical superiority the enemy, Ambraciots from Epirus, rapidly sought to engage, but without proper order came on to Phormio's fleet as a piecemeal and disorganized force. Phormio maintained his lines, quickly destroyed the enemy's fastest ships who attacked first, sank them, and then bore down upon the rest of the enemy vessels which were either similarly destroyed or fled.

Phormio was an experienced commander who understood the challenges of maritime fighting. The Athenian admiral was known to exploit the inexperience of his opponents by waiting until his enemy was entirely taken up with managing their ships in the conditions at sea, and then choosing this moment to launch his attack; exploiting the point of the enemy's maximum confusion and struggle, his own fleet making easy work of an otherwise-engaged opponent.

Building on this principle, exploiting an enemy's mistakes has long been recognized as a successful approach in warfare. Napoleon's attributed remark, 'Never interrupt the enemy when he is making a mistake' echoes the advice of military commanders some 2,000 years earlier. Spartan general Brasidas argued that the successful commander is the one who recognizes when his enemy is making an error and uses his own forces, not in an open or regular manner, but in unexpected approaches to exploit the opportunity. Polybius also makes this point in his reflections on warfare, arguing, 'Therefore the leader who will soonest gain a decisive victory, is he who is able to perceive the faults of others, and to choose that manner and means of attacking the enemy which will take full advantage of the weaknesses of their commander.' When the enemy messes up, a good general takes full advantage.

New tactics for new situations

When faced with new situations, good military commanders demonstrate the readiness to innovate with their strategies and tactics. During his campaign in Gaul, Julius Caesar recognized that he would need to defeat the Gallic king Vercingetorix, but was struggling to achieve a decisive victory due to the guerrilla tactics employed by the Gauls. Caesar decided on a different approach. Identifying Vercingetorix' home in Alesia, Caesar marched his soldiers there and surrounded the village. Unable to draw Vercingetorix into an open battle, Caesar ordered his men to build an 11-mile wooden wall around Alesia, trapping the Gauls inside. Facing starvation, Vercingetorix managed to send a message to his allies to come and lift the siege by attacking the Romans from behind. But having got wind of this new threat, Caesar simply repeated his earlier strategy and had his soldiers build a second wooden wall, longer than the first, surrounding the original and providing a protective barrier for his troops.

Vercingetorix's allies then arrived in strength but could not break through the Romans' newly built outer wall, with the result that they failed to lift the siege of Alesia. Within the village, weakened by a lack of food, Vercingetorix tried one final time to break through the inner wall. The attempt failed and the Roman wall held, ultimately resulting in Vercingetorix' surrender to Caesar. By adapting his strategy and tactics to novel circumstances, Caesar built the foundation for defeating both the Gallic king and his allies. Never having been done before, the double ring of defences showed just what could be achieved by a resourceful, determined Roman general and his army.

Of course, military tactics are subject to alteration and development in the face of a challenging adversary, but it takes military personnel and commanders to make decisions and change the way they fight based on what they see and understand. Successful adaptation is more than just doing things differently or implementing something that sounds like 'a good idea'. The measure of a successful tactic is whether it works on the battlefield against the enemy and can withstand the chaos and confusion of battle. Every tactic is new and untried until it is first attempted.

We can see an example of successful adaptation in Xenophon's campaign in Persia, with the Greek mercenary army. In preparing to face an attack, Xenophon addressed his officers with a plan to keep some companies back from the battle to be used later to support the main force and to pose a further difficulty for the enemy, who would find themselves unexpectedly engaging with fresh reserves of soldiers. Whether or not this represents the first deliberate consideration of the employment of reserves in battle, as has been argued, what is clear is that at some point in early warfare, the tactic of keeping back part of one's force to surprise and overwhelm a fatigued enemy would have been a new approach. While humans remain the constant factor in military battles, the weapons and tactics used do change, and generals, commanders and soldiers all need to respond to and counter the changes in order to survive and be victorious. Adapt or die.

Chapter 8

How Do You Exploit a Victory or Recover from a Defeat?

First gain the victory and then make the best use of it you can.
Admiral Horatio Nelson

Feed your troops on victory.
General John Monash

In war there is no second prize for the runner-up.
General Omar N. Bradley

The ability to exploit a victory in battle or recover from a battlefield defeat is an essential aspect of generalship. Individual battles are often part of broader campaigns and while a single battle might ultimately determine the outcome of a war, it usually comes after a longer campaign. Consequently, whenever a general is successful on the battlefield there is usually an opportunity (even a requirement) to exploit this single victory and turn it into a series of successes. For Alexander it took three major battles and victories against large Persian armies before Darius was ultimately defeated, when the Persian leader finally broke and ran. In contrast, if a defeated general could survive a loss, there was often an opportunity to reflect, regroup and recover. A defeat need not be final and there can be ways of turning a current setback into a future victory.

Rapidly re-engage a defeated enemy

For a battle-winning general, exploiting a victory usually involves rapid manoeuvres to quickly compel a defeated and demoralized enemy back into armed engagement, before they have time to reorganize and recover; the aim being to repeat the initial victory and compound the enemy's losses with further defeats. There is a clear advantage to acting swiftly on the back of a battlefield success, to follow up with a fresh engagement and ruthlessly destroy them. Caesar recognized the value of this approach, as Suetonius observes, 'He never defeated the enemy without driving them from their camp; and giving them no time to rally their forces.' Maintaining momentum, seizing the initiative and exploiting the compound effect of multiple victories helps to build a perception of the inevitability of ultimate victory for a successful general and their armed forces in the minds of their already beaten adversaries.

To take best advantage of a victory requires a general who is confident in their own abilities and those of their armed forces and personnel. It is usually not enough to win one battle and expect the enemy to give up. Even a defeated army can rebuild their confidence, replace losses and reverse their fortunes. Therefore, a general needs to quickly *convince* an enemy that they have been well and truly defeated and that further resistance will only cause them additional deaths and misery without changing the final outcome. Alexander the Great had a deliberate strategy of swift movement, denying a beaten enemy time to regroup and exploiting the initial shock of their battlefield loss. Darius had been pursued by Alexander relentlessly after the Battle of Gaugamela (331 BC). In the final chase, Alexander rode with such speed that only 3,000 of his own cavalry were able to keep up with him, quickly catching up with the escaping Persians. In their shock and panic, and despite heavily outnumbering the Macedonians, the Persian troops immediately surrendered, failing to recognize how great their own numbers were and just how few enemy they faced. It was only then that Alexander discovered Darius had just been assassinated, in part due to the Macedonian's own speed and surprise.

By maintaining momentum and rapidly following up a victory, a general can keep the initiative and ensure the enemy remains unable to reorganize, rally or regain their composure. Over the course of three years (AD 6–9), Roman general Tiberius campaigned against the Illyrians in what Suetonius describes as the most serious foreign conflict since the wars with Carthage. Tiberius' success was aided by the fact that the Roman general consistently applied pressure on his enemies, never allowing them to go on the offensive against his forces and ultimately reducing Illyricum to complete submission. Maintaining the initiative after an early success, then heaping up difficulties for his opponents, and forcing them into a prolonged defensive strategy proved key to exploiting the initial victory.

Failure to make good use of a victory

What we often see in these early accounts is, however, a failure to make use of victories – instances of generals who missed the opportunity to follow up on success and destroy an enemy once they had been defeated. It is on this point that Polybius observes, 'while success in policy and victory in the field are great things, it requires much more skill and caution to make a good use of such success. So that you will find that those who have won victories are far more numerous than those who have used them to advantage.'

Chief amongst these examples is Hannibal. Despite his recognized military genius and his early successes against Roman armies in Italy, Hannibal's failure to make the most of his overwhelming victory at the battle of Cannae, to go on and attack Rome, does remain a matter of debate. There are some doubts as to its feasibility, but even Hannibal himself acknowledged it was a failure not to have exploited his success and marched on to the capital.

Following his defeat of the Roman army at Lake Trasimene (217 BC), Hannibal's forces had again engaged with the Romans in 216, at Cannae. In this battle Hannibal cleverly manoeuvred his troops and effectively surrounded the massive Roman army, preventing his enemy's freedom of movement and trapping them within their own formation. The subsequent slaughter of perhaps 70,000 soldiers remains one of the deadliest single-day battles in human history. His failure to move rapidly on to Rome following the destruction of that great force was of immense frustration to his fellow Carthaginians, according to Plutarch:

> After this immense success, Hannibal was urged by his friends to follow up his victory and enter Rome with the fugitives, promising that five days thereafter he should sup in the Capitol. It is not easy to say what reasons could have deterred him from doing so, and it seems rather as if some divinity prevented his march, and inspired him with the dilatory and timid policy which he followed. It is said that the Carthaginian, Barca, said to him, 'You know how to win a victory, but do not know how to use one.'

This criticism by his friends was devastating and haunts Hannibal's reputation to this day. Instead of marching immediately on Rome, Hannibal spent the time reviewing and releasing the Roman prisoners that he had captured. Livy's conclusion is, 'That day's delay is firmly believed to have been the preservation of the city and the empire.' With Rome within reach and with an air of invincibility created by the immense confidence of his soldiers and the utter despair of the Romans, Hannibal let this opportunity pass, never to be within his grasp again despite years of subsequent campaigning in Italy. When Hannibal was recalled from Italy back to Carthage to defend it against Scipio's forces, Livy provides the following account of a sorrowful commander standing on the ship taking him back to Africa:

> [Hannibal] frequently looked back upon the shores of Italy, and, arraigning both gods and men, cursed himself and his own head that he did not lead his troops, while reeking with blood from the victory at Cannae, to Rome.

Such a failure to exploit a winning position was not confined to Rome's enemies. Roman generals themselves fell short in this regard too. In the case of the civil war between Caesar and Pompey, Pompey defeated Caesar's forces at Dyrrachium (48 BC), but then failed to pursue them into their camp. Julius Caesar clearly recognized the enormity of Pompey's mistake, saying, 'Today the victory would have been with the enemy, if they had had a commander who knew how to conquer.' Pompey's hesitation allowed Caesar time to regroup, reflect and change his entire strategy, ultimately resulting in the defeat and death of Pompey himself.

The contrast between this battle and the battle at Pharsalus (48 BC) soon after is stark and illuminating. When Caesar's forces routed Pompey's, they pursued them all the way to Pompey's camp and then fought their way inside. That action ended the war with Pompey, who fled the camp and escaped to Egypt only to be killed there. Where Pompey hesitated after his own initial victory, Caesar drove forward and delivered the final and decisive defeat, overcoming Pompey and claiming the Roman Republic. It is worth noting that Pompey's son, Sextus Pompeius, would also make war against Caesar after his father's death, but similarly lacked the will to exploit his successes. On Pompeius, Appian notes that despite numerous opportunities to take the fight to his enemies, the commander chose to remain on the defensive. In the end Pompeius was unable to even maintain his own defence, finishing his days with his army defeated and himself captured, finally being executed by his fellow Romans.

Sound decisions after victory

The ability to make sound decisions about what to do following a victory might be difficult because of the surprise and sheer relief of defeating an enemy, particularly a formidable one. Early on when Rome was still establishing itself as a major power in Italy, the Samnites achieved a spectacular victory over their Roman enemies. Livy describes how the Samnites deceived the Romans into marching off to raise a non-existent siege at their allied city of Luceria. As the Romans made their way to Luceria, the Samnites surrounded and trapped two Roman armies in a narrow defile. Surprised by their success, and with these Roman forces entirely at their mercy, the Samnite commander sought advice from retired general Herennius Pontius. The old general's initial advice was to immediately release all the Romans unharmed. The Samnites rejected this suggestion, and he was asked for an alternative. Pontius responded that if they were not to be released unharmed then the entire Roman force should be killed to a man. This idea was also rejected, and the retired commander was brought into the Samnite camp to justify his reasoning.

Pontius explained that the first plan – to release everyone without harm – was designed to establish a lasting peace and friendship with a powerful Rome; the second plan – to kill every soldier – was to put off a major war with Rome by destroying these two armies entirely, thus significantly diminishing the military might of their enemy. The Samnites again rejected both recommendations and decided on a third option, namely, to release the two Roman armies unharmed but make each man pass 'under the yoke' – a ritual in which disarmed soldiers were humiliated in front of their enemies, but physically unharmed. Pontius warned that such a strategy which neither gained friends nor removed enemies would stir up Rome's anger until they avenged the humiliation. The Samnites went ahead and had the Roman soldiers pass under the yoke, then released them unharmed.

Pontius proved correct. The Romans later returned and got their revenge by militarily destroying the Samnites, who had proved they did not know how to exploit a victory.

Confirm that the battle is won

Within the ancient literature there is consistent advice and guidance on ensuring that an enemy is given a means of escaping from the battlefield. The rationale is to prevent placing almost defeated soldiers in a position where they had no other option than to fight to the death, with the risk that such desperation would renew their fighting spirit and they might emerge victorious. This is reinforced by related advice that a general needs to confirm that the victory really has been won. Such views were demonstrated by the Spartans, who would pursue their enemies only far enough to make quite sure that the battle was over. They then ceased following and let the surviving enemy escape, rather than chase and kill them. Plutarch observes that this practice is noble but also practical, as it became known that the Spartans would kill those who fought against them, but allowed those who surrendered or fled the battlefield to survive, ensuring that their enemies knew it was easier to flee than to fight a losing battle. Such a well-known tactic encouraged Spartan successes because an adversary would be constantly weighing up whether to fight on with the risk of death or injury, or flee to safety.

Julius Caesar adopted a similar approach, reflected in his actions after defeating Pompey. Pompey's soldiers, though they had fought against Caesar, were still fellow Romans. Instead of killing these soldiers, Caesar offered them the opportunity to come over to him and serve in his army. In this way Caesar preserved at least some of Rome's military capabilities, taking advantage of victory and replenishing losses in his army with experienced soldiers, fellow Romans who owed their very lives to his mercy – thus laying the foundation for future victories. Caesar's decision proved sound, and he was able to rely on these soldiers to fight with him in later battles.

Avoid victory at too high a cost

An important point regarding triumph on the battlefield is to ensure that victory does not come at such a high cost that it achieves little more than mere survival. The expression 'a Pyrrhic victory' describes a win that comes at such cost it may ultimately lead to defeat (i.e. you can win the battle but lose the war). The term comes from the Greek general Pyrrhus and his battlefield experiences against the Romans. Considered an outstanding commander, reportedly at one time approached by Italian nations to lead their armies, Pyrrhus defeated Roman forces at Heraclea in 280 BC and again at Asculum in 279 BC. But these victories were achieved at terrible cost to his own soldiers' lives, losses which he simply could not afford. In contrast, the Romans were able to absorb their own significant losses and replace their casualties, something Hannibal would later encounter when fighting in Italy.

Pyrrhus himself recognized the disastrous cost of his victories over the Romans. When congratulated on his success following the battle of Asculum, he is said to have replied, 'If we win one more such victory over the Romans, we shall be utterly ruined.' Though Pyrrhus did win these engagements, he lost the war against Rome, his two victories proving so costly that they ultimately led to his defeat. Avoiding such Pyrrhic victories is therefore crucial for any general who wants to achieve lasting success over their enemy.

Learn the right lessons from defeat

Even the greatest of generals suffered battlefield defeats, highlighting that losing was not necessarily final. If he was not killed on the battlefield, a general could use the loss as an opportunity to learn, reflect, adapt and go on to future victories. As we saw, Pompey's failure to destroy Caesar after defeating him at Dyrrachium (48 BC) allowed Caesar to reflect on the defeat, learn from it and adjust his strategy, going on to win the campaign. Caesar reflected and learned the right lessons. However, the ability to honestly review one's failure and draw out the correct lessons is not easy, mainly because of human nature. A defeated general needs to be willing to look reality in the face, to acknowledge his errors, avoid shifting the blame, and take responsibility for his own mistakes. Learning can be difficult, as difficult as being defeated and maybe, for some generals, even harder.

Sparta's first attempt at taking on the experienced and formidable Athenian navy proved to be an utter disaster. Thucydides' account of the naval battle showed how the newly trained Spartan sailors under Admiral Cnemus struggled just to control their ships against the elements, in contrast to the Athenians who were experts in sailing and fighting at sea. Despite outnumbering the Athenian fleet (47 ships to 20), the Spartans and their allies were thoroughly defeated by Admiral Phormio and his fleet. But the Spartans then compounded their loss by failing to learn the right lessons. Following the battle, Sparta sent out a commission of three generals to get the fleet ready for the next encounter, to try to ensure that they would not again be bested by such small numbers of Athenian ships. But, as Thucydides notes, the commissioners were angry, failing to understand what had happened and figuring that there had been misconduct or cowardice on the part of the Spartans.

None of them had any idea of anything being wrong with the newly established Spartan navy and clearly their assumption was that fighting at sea was the same as fighting on land. What the commissioners failed to take into account was that this was Sparta's first naval engagement, and that their newly-trained and inexperienced sailors were up against a well-established and hardened adversary. Without experience or insight, the Spartan commission did not understand enough to form an accurate picture of what had occurred and why the Spartans had actually been defeated. They could not learn the correct lessons because they did not have the necessary insight or experience, and their minds had already fixed on an incorrect rationale. Ultimately the Spartans did prevail in their conflict with Athens, but at a much higher cost than was necessary, and having usually come off second-best in their naval battles.

The Spartan military reputation on land did survive and many of their generals were able to hire themselves out as mercenaries in the ancient world. Indeed, even after her decline as a military power, Sparta's fighting reputation still meant Spartan commanders were listened to for their military understanding and insight. During the First Punic War, after the Carthaginians had suffered a series of defeats at the hands of Roman armies,

Xanthippus, an experienced Spartan general, undertook an evaluation of the Carthaginian military forces and the country's resources. Xanthippus' findings were that the Carthaginians had lost not because of Roman superiority but due to their own commanders' inexperience.

As a result of the crisis facing the Carthaginians, these findings became well known amongst the people and the military and Xanthippus were subsequently questioned by the Carthaginian leadership on his conclusions. Whether out of desperation, or in frank recognition of the sound insights of the Spartan commander, the Carthaginians rather astutely put aside national pride and, in the ultimate case of 'put your money where your mouth is', gave Xanthippus command of their armed forces. Thus, a Spartan general would lead the Carthaginian troops into their next battle with the Romans. Proving equal to his insight, Xanthippus led the Carthaginians to a decisive victory over the Romans at the Bagradas river in 255 BC. The Carthaginians celebrated their reversal of fortune but Xanthippus, perhaps recognizing the risks of having clearly outperformed Carthage's own military hierarchy, chose to retire back to Sparta.

Learn from others' defeats

Even better than learning from their own defeats is a general who will learn from other commanders' defeats or, better still, their enemies' battlefield failures, and will then avoid such mistakes altogether. Certainly, identifying lessons from the defeats of colleagues and adapting their own tactics as a result was a far less costly way of learning, as Polybius notes.

The defeat of General Varus and his Roman legions by the Germans in the Teutoburg Forest in AD 9 shook Rome, and ranked alongside Crassus' destruction by the Parthians in terms of the scale and shock of the disaster – arguably having an even greater psychological impact. The following year, General Tiberius campaigned in Germany, conscious of learning lessons from Varus' failure and applying them to his own operations. Tiberius, recognizing that the disaster had been due to Varus' recklessness and negligence, established a war council to advise him on proposed actions, in contrast to his previous approach of relying on his own independent judgement. He became more cautious and paid close attention to seemingly minor details. When his army crossed the Rhine, Tiberius inspected each wagon to ensure only essential supplies were carried. Once he had crossed over, Tiberius ate his meals on the bare ground, and often slept in the open. All his orders for the following day and guidance for emergencies he put into writing, with the instruction that any officer who was uncertain over any matter was to personally consult him at any hour, day or night. In the aftermath of Varus' destruction, Tiberius changed his own behaviour and tactics to successfully ensure that there would be no repeating his fellow general's mistakes.

Lose small and learn

If defeats must come, the smaller the better, allowing a general to learn and adapt. An ancient strategy was to deliberately engage a new enemy in minor skirmishes initially, so the general and his soldiers could learn how the enemy fought and he could see how his soldiers fared against these new opponents, while ensuring that any defeats would be minor and large-scale surprises and disasters could be avoided. The logic is sound – small defeats are far preferable to major ones. When Xenophon's forces were attacked by Persian allied commander Mithridates' cavalry, the Greek general quickly hailed the skirmish as an opportunity, 'Thank heaven they did not come upon us in any great force, but were only a handful of men; so that the injury they did us was not large, as it might have been; and at least it has served to show us what we need.' Lose small in a minor skirmish and adapt, using that experience as the basis to change, avoid large-scale defeat and achieve victory instead.

Gain the space and time to recover

Whereas a victorious general should act swiftly and re-engage an already defeated enemy before they can reorganize and adapt, to recover from a defeat a general and his vanquished army usually need to put some space between themselves and the forces who defeated them. The purpose is both to allow their own soldiers time to recover and rebuild their confidence, and to prevent the enemy from gaining momentum and turning one victory into a string of successes. The later Byzantine military chronicles, drawing heavily on the earlier Greek and Roman writings, provide clear advice to commanders on how to recover from a military defeat. Their guidance largely was to break contact with the victorious enemy, put physical space between them, and introduce delays either through distance or drawn-out negotiations.

To recover from defeat on the battlefield usually requires time for a general to rebuild their forces, restore their troops' confidence and morale, and slow or stop the momentum of a victorious enemy. It was precisely this challenge which faced General Fabius when dealing with a seemingly invincible Hannibal, destroying Roman commanders and armies at will. Fabius' delaying strategy frustrated Hannibal by denying him a continuing run of successful battles. The delays created other problems for the Carthaginian too, as he faced the problems of attempting to sustain, feed and motivate an army heavily reliant on mercenaries and Gauls in a hostile foreign country. Fabius also denied Hannibal freedom of movement, as he was shadowed by Roman troops who refused to engage in battle on the Carthaginian's terms. The delaying tactics allowed for Rome to rebuild her armies and for the soldiers to develop confidence in engaging the Carthaginians on a smaller scale, while diminishing Hannibal's mystique.

Immediately following their defeat at the battle of Leuctra (371 BC), the beaten Spartans were keen to quickly seek a new battle with the Thebans, to attempt to reverse their humiliating loss. However, Jason of Pherae convinced them otherwise, highlighting the difference between themselves as a defeated army and the victorious Thebans. Jason's advice was for the Spartans to take the time to recover, to rebuild their strength, and only then to make a fresh attack on the Thebans' unconquered and now experienced army. To rush back into battle following such a significant loss and against the very same soldiers who had just so convincingly defeated them would have been foolish.

Or launch a rapid counterattack

However, though riskier, the immediate counterattack option is available to a general who has been defeated. In this case, instead of taking the time and space to regroup and recover, launching a counterattack straight away, to catch a victorious and complacent enemy off their guard, can work. As

Onasander argues in his guidance to generals, a measure of good fortune can do more harm than misfortune, in that a recently successful army might reduce their vigilance and become careless and contemptuous towards their defeated opponent – an opportunity for a general to exploit.

Soon after the unexpected naval victory over the Carthaginians at Mylae (260 BC) in the First Punic War, the Romans enjoyed a run of successes, lifting the siege of Segesta (in Sicily) and then capturing the Sicilian city of Macella from the Carthaginians. Following that series of wins, the Roman forces and their allies appeared to entirely forget that they were still at war. The Carthaginian general Hamilcar got word that the Romans and their allies had argued over the awarding of prizes for the victories and had set up camp separately from each other. Thanks to this intelligence, Hamilcar took his entire army and launched a surprise attack on the Roman allies in their camp, slaughtering some 4,000 soldiers. A few battles might have been won but the war was not, and the Roman allies paid dearly for their mistake.

Post-battle celebrations are frequently alluded to as times when victorious armies can be taken by surprise. The Romans and their allies entirely forgot about the Carthaginian threat and, in their celebrations, focused on themselves and who should receive what honours and awards. Their internal squabbles allowed the Carthaginians to counter a loss at sea with a victory on land. On many occasions in these accounts, battlefield victories were quickly overturned and the situations reversed even in the course of one day, situations in which 'the conquerors were obliged to resign their victory to the conquered.'

A well-executed counterattack can catch a recently victorious army unprepared, both mentally and physically. The ability to rapidly reverse a defeat is demonstrated in Roman general Lucius Marcius' efforts against the Carthaginians in Spain, around 211 BC, following the destruction of Roman armies in the battle of Upper Baetis. Livy provides an account of what the Roman forces under Marcius achieved in the course of just a few days, arguing, 'When it seemed that the Roman armies were annihilated, and Spain lost, one man recovered this desperate state of affairs.'

Marcius had been serving as a soldier under Gnaeus Cornelius Scipio when the Roman general was killed. Livy describes Marcius as 'possessing a mind and genius far superior to the condition in which he had been born.'

Following the defeat of the Roman forces at the hands of the combined Carthaginian armies in Spain, Marcius gathered up the surviving Romans, drafted some more from nearby garrisons, fortified a camp and united his troops with another surviving Roman army under General Tonteius. The soldiers unanimously elected Marcius as general of this united army and immediately prepared for war. The Carthaginian general Hasdrubal Gisco soon marched on the Roman camp with the expectation of easily finishing off what he assumed would be the few, demoralized remnants of the surviving Roman force in Spain. Instead, thanks to Marcius' organizational skills, preparedness and leadership, Hasdrubal's forces had to face a large, motivated and well-commanded army.

As the Carthaginians approached the fortified camp, in an overconfident and disorganized manner, the Romans charged out to meet them, angry and seeking revenge. The Carthaginians were shocked. Their expectation of easy victory was shattered and instead they faced a coordinated and violent attack by determined troops in significant numbers. Hasdrubal's forces fled the field, and the eager Romans had to be physically restrained from pursuing them – Marcius had bigger plans. The Carthaginians, once they were sure that the Romans were no longer in pursuit, returned to their camp still shaken by the day's events. But Marcius now ascertained that the Carthaginians had failed to adequately post guards around their encampment. Determining that it would be easier to attack Hasdrubal's camp than continue to successfully defend their own, Marcius ordered a night attack on the enemy camp. In a scene reminiscent of Scipio Africanus' later efforts in North Africa, Marcius' forces surrounded the Carthaginian base and set fire to the tents. In the ensuing chaos and confusion, the Romans were able to slaughter the unprepared and often-unarmed Carthaginian soldiers.

The Roman cavalry ensured that any enemy soldiers who did escape were killed, to prevent them warning the neighbouring Carthaginian camp some miles away. Not that it would have mattered much, says Livy, because having destroyed the first camp by night, Marcius moved straight on to the next, which was equally poorly guarded and entirely unprepared for attack. The result was a swift double victory for the Romans: 'Thus, in a night and a day, two camps of the enemy were carried, under the conduct of Lucius Marcius.'

The losses to the Carthaginians over the course of the two days were reportedly in the tens of thousands. The consequence was that a peace settled over Spain, now both sides had experienced significant defeats and neither was willing to risk any further major battle. The ability of a general to turn a defeated force into a victorious one by determined leadership, swift reorganization, and retaking the initiative on the battlefield, highlights one approach for overcoming defeat. But such a tactic usually also relies on a complacent enemy, already made overconfident and careless by their own success. The example provides insight into both overcoming a defeat and the importance of maintaining vigilance following a victory.

Refusal to accept defeat: A fighting mindset

Even in situations such as surprise attacks, there is something to be said for a general's personal conduct and the unwillingness to accept defeat. One approach for a general facing defeat is simply to refuse to give up. This gets us to the mindset of a general who rejects a pessimistic outcome even when the situation initially appears irretrievable. In early warfare there are many accounts of such indomitable leadership, demonstrating how through personal valour, and a fighting attitude, a general could rally soldiers who might otherwise have given up the fight as lost. In the case of Roman general Cerialis, in Germany, the story is of a commander refusing to give up hope despite being taken by surprise and in the face of a real possibility of defeat and the wholesale slaughter of his army. The enemy had approached the Roman camp from different directions and caught the Romans completely unawares:

> So sudden was their onslaught that Cerialis, who had not spent the night in camp, was still in bed when he heard almost simultaneously that the fighting had begun and that the day was lost. He cursed the messengers for their cowardice until he saw the whole extent of the disaster with his own eyes. The camp had been forced, the cavalry routed, and the bridge over the Moselle, leading to the outskirts of the town, which lay between him and his army, was held by the enemy. But confusion had no terrors for Cerialis. Seizing hold on fugitives, flinging himself without any armour into the thick

> of the [fight], he succeeded by his inspired imprudence and the assistance of the braver men in retaking the bridge.

Cerialis rapidly took control, refused to panic and reversed the direction of the battle, taking the fight to the attacking enemy. Regardless of his motivation – perhaps not wanting a reputation for losing his military camp through a lack of commitment (having allegedly spent the night outside the camp with a local lover) – Cerialis desperately fought back and ultimately claimed victory. Certainly, he might have been killed in his recklessness and the story would have been different. But he chose to fight, rallied his soldiers, and won the battle.

This account highlights a *fighting* mindset, one that refuses to accept defeat and pushes forward to victory. Roman forces were often defeated in battle, but for centuries they proved themselves able to recover from their losses and, time and again, turn the tables and inflict defeat on those tribes and nations who had triumphed over them. The Romans would dig deeper, be hungrier, and fight back with renewed strength and determination. They had the will to win. Polybius describes this when reflecting on the Romans' disastrous loss at the battle of Cannae (216 BC), noting that their defeat in this conflict was far from the final outcome of the Second Punic War:

> For though the Romans were now incontestably beaten and their military reputation shattered, yet by the peculiar virtues of their constitution and by wise counsel they not only recovered their supremacy in Italy and afterwards defeated the Carthaginians, but in a few years made themselves masters of the whole world.

There is a common factor in these accounts, revealing the formidable nature of an enemy who refuses to accept a battlefield defeat as the final outcome in a war.

Chapter 9

Why Is Speed of Action So Important?

Speed on the march, energy in attacks, cold steel.

General Alexander Suvorov

It may seem unusual to dedicate an entire chapter to speed in warfare. However, the frequent instances within the early texts where speedy action was identified as the primary factor in a battlefield victory warrant this attention. Good generals understand both why speed matters, and how to use it in overwhelming and defeating their enemies, as is apparent in descriptions of the battlefield successes of Alexander, Hannibal, and Caesar (to name just a few).

Speed denies the enemy time

Speed of movement and rapid action bring numerous advantages for a general and impose a number of problems on the enemy. Rufus' judgement on Alexander the Great was that of all the talents displayed by the young Macedonian general, it was Alexander's speed of action that was his greatest military skill. Alexander knew what he was doing in choosing to act swiftly, understanding the impact that it would have on his opponents.

Receiving reports that the Mallians and Oxydracians were the most warlike and numerous forces in the direction he was leading his Macedonian army (modern-day Pakistan), and hearing that they were preparing to fight him, Alexander moved quickly to the attack. As Arrian wrote, Alexander travelled rapidly, 'with the express design of attacking them before they had arranged their plans, and while there was still lack of preparation and a state of confusion among them.' Whether it was large scale movement of forces or smaller scale ambushes, the principle was the same – to act swiftly before the enemy understood clearly what was happening or could effectively counter it. A general who moves fast denies the enemy time: time to prepare, to comprehend, and time to react or adapt. And time, once lost, can never be recovered.

To move quickly is about more than just getting somewhere fast. Speed of action requires determination, a plan and forethought, a clear purpose and a strong resolution. A general who acts swiftly usually recognizes there are significant costs and risks as well as benefits and rewards and, having weighed these up, determines to commit their forces. An army which appears unexpectedly, in size and with determination, will immediately sow doubt in the minds of the enemy opposing them. In taking rapid action a general is displaying confidence in their own forces, an assurance and confidence which will likely unnerve a more cautious and usually stationary adversary: a confident army facing an uncertain and hesitant one is at a clear psychological advantage. The effect that speed of movement can make on an enemy is well-illustrated in the account of Caesar's swift march to engage a German force during his Gaul campaign:

> he arrived at the camp of the enemy before the Germans could perceive what was going on; who being suddenly alarmed by all the circumstances, both by the speediness of our arrival and the absence of their own officers, as time was afforded neither for concerting measures nor for seizing their arms, are perplexed as to whether it would be better to lead out their forces against the enemy, or to defend their camp, or seek their safety by flight.

Caesar's rapidity denied the Germans time to weigh up their options. The resulting uncertainty and fear became clear to the Romans, and they took advantage of the Germans' evident loss of confidence to launch their attack. The result was an unsurprising victory to Caesar and his Roman army over an unprepared enemy in a state of confusion and terror. This was not a one-off strategy for the Roman commander. One of the most famous statements attributed to Julius Caesar, 'Veni, vidi, vici' ('I came, I saw, I conquered') was displayed on a sign during the victory procession celebrating his defeat of King Pharnaces II and the Pontic forces at the battle of Zela (47 BC). The statement reflected the speed of his action and rapid defeat of his enemy. As a general, Caesar consistently used speed to good effect in his campaigns against all enemies, barbarians and Romans alike.

Speed overcomes limitations

In commencing his march on Rome and beginning the civil war, Caesar used rapid movement of military forces to catch his enemies off-guard; what his forces lacked in size they made up for with their speed. Appian captures this in his account of Caesar marching into Italy under arms to take control of Rome in 49 BC. Assuming that Caesar would be slow in coming, the Senate ordered Pompey to raise an army of 130,000 men. However, despite having marched to Italy with just 5,000 soldiers, Caesar took good advantage of the terror he caused with bold, swift actions.

Rather than wait for the rest of his army to arrive from Gaul, Caesar immediately took the initiative. He deployed his available soldiers to take control of key locations, catching his enemy off guard. He had already committed himself to war when he crossed the Rubicon river with his armed troops, an act which has become synonymous with his own comment, 'The die is cast.' The decision was taken and he unwaveringly backed himself with his swift deployment of soldiers. Caesar's actions and evident determination unnerved his opponent Pompey, who fled Rome and left Italy. Consequently, in just sixty days Caesar had gained control of all Italy without bloodshed. The actual fighting in the civil war that took place between Caesar and Pompey was to occur outside the borders of Italy.

Pompey fled to Greece and he did not expect Caesar to pursue him until winter was over, due to the bad weather and lack of safe anchorages for the fleet Caeser would need to transport his army. He therefore ordered his admirals to keep watch at sea and dispersed his army into winter quarters. But Pompey had once again failed to understand his opponent, or learn the lesson from Caesar's previous rapid march into Italy. Instead of waiting, Caesar took immediate action:

> [He] hastened to Brundusium about the winter solstice, intending to strike terror into his enemies by taking them by surprise. Although he found neither provisions, nor apparatus, nor his whole army collected at Brundusium, he, nevertheless, called those who were present to an assembly and addressed them as follows: 'Fellow soldiers – you who are joined with me in the greatest of undertakings – neither the winter weather, nor the delay of our comrades,

> nor the want of suitable preparation shall check my onset. I consider rapidity of movement the best substitute for all these things.'

Here is an insight into Caesar's thinking and strategy; speed would overcome what was lacking. Swift action would be enough to make up for his smaller forces, the difficult conditions and his lack of supplies. Was this reckless? Yes but, more importantly, did it work? The answer ultimately is who won, which must be the ultimate measure of a general's success. And, yes, Caesar did ultimately defeat Pompey soon after.

Speed helps both to conquer and to avoid defeat

Hannibal's sixteen-day march through the Alps and into Italy with his army is all the more incredible considering that he also had to battle local tribes during the advance. Catching the Romans by surprise was a consistent aspect of Hannibal's actions. His use of speed was a regular feature of his successes, as well as an effective strategy for getting himself out of trouble. When he found his forces surrounded by Fabius' army and his own in a precarious position he moved fast to deny the Romans time to take advantage of their good fortune. Quickly developing and putting into action an unexpected stratagem, Hannibal confounded the Roman army that very night, creating chaos and uncertainty with a herd of oxen, fire and noise in the darkness that confused the Romans, dumbfounded Fabius, and secured his army's safe escape. The plan was successful as much because of the confusion it created as the speed with which it was delivered. Speed is about denying time to the enemy as well as grasping opportunities yourself.

Secure allies, scare the enemy, win without fighting

Speed of action has an impact on both the enemy and allies, as the timing of the arrival of an armed force can impact on critical decisions. In these ancient accounts it is apparent that the resolution inherent in such rapid action not only unnerved enemies, but strengthened the commitment and support of otherwise wavering or hesitant allies. When the Romans were facing revolt in Gaul, rapid action by Caesar and his army removed the threat without further conflict and saw alliances restored. Caesar 'arrived there unexpectedly and sooner than anyone anticipated' resulting in the Remi sending ambassadors 'to tell him that they surrendered themselves and all their possessions to the protection and disposal of the Roman people.'

Any force can be caught out by the rapid movement of their enemies. Parthian king Artabanus recognized a growing threat to his kingdom and took speedy action to counter his enemies and shore up the support of his allies. He marched immediately to counter Tiridates, a rival to his throne, arriving with a sizeable army in the vicinity of Seleucia (modern day Iraq), where Tiridates was located. Tiridates was unnerved to hear of Artabanus' unlooked-for arrival at the head of an army, not far away and ready to engage in battle. Panicking, Tiridates fled back to Syria, his own forces abandoning him along the way and some even going over to Artabanus' side. Through sheer speed and determination Artabanus had secured a victory without a fight and expanded the number of those allied to him.

Following the battle of Leuctra (371 BC), Jason of Pherae rapidly marched his forces to liaise between the victorious Thebans and the defeated Spartans, keen to enhance his own power and that of his state of Thessaly. Getting there was a problem given hostilities between himself and his neighbours, the Phocians, but rather than avoid their territory he managed a secure passage by sheer speed of movement. Jason had his naval fleet manned, giving the impression that he would send his forces by sea, but instead gathered his mercenaries and cavalry and marched them straight through Phocis – to the absolute astonishment of his enemies. Xenophon says the first many Phocians knew of Jason and his forces being in their territory was when they witnessed him with their own eyes, marching past their cities. The audacity and speed with which he moved negated any advantage that the Phocians should have had. The Phocians could not have asked for a better opportunity to strike, yet Jason's sudden appearance caught them entirely unprepared, so that they could not even organize their own forces let alone coordinate an attack, though it was within their own borders. By seizing the initiative without delay, Jason avoided conflict altogether and was able to safely take his army through enemy territory in time of war.

Chapter 10

How Do You Avoid Hubris and Over-Confidence?

When you are in any contest, you should work as if there were – to the very last minute – a chance to lose it. This is battle, this is politics, this is anything.

General Dwight Eisenhower

A successful general faces the problem of ensuring that victories do not go to their head and that they remained grounded in the reality of war. Even during a successful campaign, any general can find themselves unexpectedly defeated on the battlefield. Victors can become the conquered and the previously defeated reverse their fortunes to become conquerors themselves. Success can often encourage over-confidence in a general's perspective of their abilities, setting the scene for a deadly date with reality.

Recognize the human tendency towards over-confidence

A great risk for any general is initially to overestimate their own armed force's capabilities and minimize those of their enemy. This is particularly common after experiencing early successes. In the opening stages of the Peloponnesian War, the Athenians' initial victories over the Spartans led to an unrealistic evaluation of their own military capabilities:

> So thoroughly had the present prosperity persuaded the citizens that nothing could withstand them, and that they could achieve what was possible and impracticable alike, with means ample or inadequate it mattered not. The secret of this was their general extraordinary success, which made them confuse their strength with their hopes.

In reality, the Athenians faced a formidable foe in the Spartans and their allies, who would eventually defeat them and tear down the walls of their city. Athens' run of initial success did not continue, over-confidence and hubris led to poor decision-making and, ultimately, to the loss of the war. The problem, as Caesar argued when reflecting on warfare, was that 'in most cases men willingly believe what they wish'. There is a human preference of and tendency towards the positive; cheerful information is much more welcome than negative reports, particularly when it applies to ourselves or our performance, and such a preference is evident in the early accounts of warfare. Thucydides depicts this tendency to over-optimism during an incident with Athenian allies in the early stages of the Peloponnesian War, noting that their initial judgement had been based more on their wishes than any sound reasoning, reflecting the tendency in human nature for people to carelessly hope for what they most desire to happen but employing the full force of critical reasoning to reject what they do not want.

In practice, a general risks minimizing any problems with a preferred plan or action, while adopting a more robust and critical argument against options they do not favour. In warfare, such unquestioning acceptance of the 'best case scenario' can lead to disaster.

Avoid minimizing the enemy

Without reckoning on the fact that the enemy is equally willing to fight and kill in order to survive or conquer, generals and armies can find themselves defeated by armed forces that they underestimated or, in their own over-optimistic view, considered to be all but beaten. The requirement to recognize this reality is reflected in the modern saying, 'the enemy gets a vote.' In his campaign against Crete, Roman general Marcus Antonius (father of Mark Antony) led an initial attack on the island which resulted in utter destruction of the Roman forces. The failure was a direct result of the Roman general's overconfidence and corresponding unrealistic planning:

> Marcus Antonius made the first attack upon the island with such expectation of victory and confidence that he carried more fetters [chains for prisoners] than arms on board his ships. And so he paid the penalty of his rashness; for the enemy cut off most of his ships and hung the bodies of their prisoners from the sails and tackle; and then spreading their sails the Cretans returned in triumph to their harbours.

Such overwhelming and unwarranted optimism, minimizing the strength of the enemy, resulted in total defeat. But Antonius is far from alone in showing such hubris before battle. Describing the scene before the battle of Pharsalus (48 BC) where Caesar would defeat Pompey, Appian captures the mindset amongst Pompey and his army:

> going to the battle in an unreasoning, a reckless, and contemptuous way as though it were already won. Many of them adorned their tents with laurel branches, the insignia of victory, and their slaves prepared a magnificent banquet for them. Some, too, of them began already to contend with each other for Caesar's office of Pontifex Maximus.

Hubris is a completely self-imposed handicap. Such disregard of the enemy is based entirely on a general's mindset and thinking and is, therefore, entirely avoidable. Unwarranted assumptions of superiority can prove costly but are within the power of a general to control. This overconfidence can be understood as a form of self-delusion and self-deception – the enemy might have some effect by their own efforts at deception, but the ultimate responsibility is, of course, down to oneself. A general can, therefore, avoid such a mistake by maintaining a cautious and questioning approach to both their own capabilities and those of their enemies. In providing advice to their Spartan allies, the Corinthians made plain how such unwarranted feelings of superiority over one's enemies reflect poor thinking, often with devastating consequences.

The Corinthians argued that there are three great mistakes that can be made, a lack of common sense, a lack of courage, and a lack of vigilance. They noted that none of these could be overcome by feelings of superiority of one's own strength or contempt towards an enemy, which had proven so disastrous in history and reflected not strength but foolishness. The Corinthians highlighted this well, overconfidence was simply idiocy. Such 'arrogance through ignorance', rather than reasoned, sober, and informed judgements, is a way of thinking which often leads to disaster.

During the First Punic War, the Roman naval fleet under the leadership of Gaius Duilius, sailed out to attack the Carthaginians in what we know as the battle of Mylae (260 BC). The Carthaginians had great repute and experience as a naval power and, on seeing the Roman fleet, they immediately steered their ships towards them and readied themselves to attack, entirely confident of an easy victory. According to Polybius, the Carthaginians carelessly disregarded their formation because of their contempt for their opponent's inexperience, behaving as if the battle was already won. Such overconfidence and lack of discipline came at a huge cost. The Carthaginians did notice an unusual piece of equipment on the Roman ships as they approached them, but disregarded this and sailed on. It was a fatal error.

Hoisted high in the bows of the Roman ships was a new boarding device called a 'raven' (*corvus*) that the Romans had designed and installed on their vessels Its name came from a beak-like iron hook that could be fastened to an enemy ship. As the undisciplined Carthaginians sailed close to them, the Romans lowered these devices, and the Carthaginians found their vessels held fast to the Roman ships. The ravens allowed the Roman troops to swarm aboard the enemy ships, turning the naval engagement into something more like a land battle, with hand-to-hand fighting on the ships' decks. The leading 30 Carthaginians ships were lost with their entire crews, including their flag ship. The rest of the Carthaginian fleet turned and fled, with an eventual loss of 50 of their original 130 ships.

The defeat went beyond the loss of ships and sailors and its effects were psychological on both sides. The Carthaginians' contempt for their enemy's naval inexperience and their consequent lack of caution not only resulted in defeat but, as Polybius highlights, saw the Romans gain confidence that they could control the sea and renewed their determination to prosecute the war with Carthage. As for the Carthaginians, they now knew that they faced a tough fight and were no longer in control of the seas. For the Romans it was a massive morale boost; they had adapted ships with new equipment and matching tactics. The Romans had shown that they could not only contest the Carthaginians on the seas but defeat them.

Seek out honest counsel and guidance

The counter to such self-deception is to maintain a link with reality, in which endeavour genuine, honest counsel and guidance appear to be crucial. When Spartan king Archidamus saw his son fighting recklessly against the Athenians, his advice to him was grounded in reality, 'Either attack in greater strength or be less courageous'. Such plain speaking was a feature of many Spartan kings.

Years later, Archidamus' counsel to his Spartan commanders before the outbreak of the Peloponnesian War echoed his namesake's earlier guidance. Archidamus emphasized the importance of clear thinking and warned them against underestimating their Athenian adversaries. The Spartan king provided the type of counsel which later, after his death, the Corinthians would offer the Spartans. Archidamus' early guidance and caution would become prescient. In considering the challenges of any conflict, the Spartan leader argued that they needed to acknowledge there was likely little difference between their own thinking and that of their enemies, and that their enemies' plans were likely to be considered and thoughtful – thus they should place their hope in their own preparations and planning instead of simply hoping their enemies would make mistakes.

This cautious and realistic approach is the antithesis of hubris. The Athenians themselves also had a cautious leader in Admiral Pericles, whose sage counsel was forgotten soon after the commencement of the conflict and after his death. Pericles consciously tried to keep the Athenians grounded: he would remind them of the threats against them when they became over-confident, but when they became despondent without justification then he would bring them back to a spirit of confidence. He argued the Athenians would be victorious if they could remain focused and act cautiously, maintain their navy, and avoid trying to expand their empire. Pericles' main concern about the outcome of the war was not the actions of the Spartans but the likelihood of the Athenians making mistakes. Pericles proved prescient. The Athenians' decision to launch their forces on a campaign in Sicily, and the resulting military disaster, ultimately laid the foundations of Athens' defeat in the war. The loss of both Archidamus and Pericles early in the conflict proved challenging for Sparta and Athens respectively.

Warfare is inherently confusing, and the progress of battles and campaigns always contains an element of uncertainty before and during the clash of arms. Consequently, there is a constant risk of a general simply accepting what they *want* to believe. To counter this, other sources of information, potentially contrary to what the general is thinking or wanting, are required. The problem is often one of rank (the proverbial difficulty of 'speaking truth to power') together with the perceived (or actual) preference and reward for positive news. Therefore, a general needs to overcome this default position by actively encouraging alternative and critical perspectives. How to achieve this? Vegetius provides practical guidance:

> It is the duty and interest of the general frequently to assemble the most prudent and experienced officers of the different corps of the army and consult with them on the state of both his own forces and the enemy's forces. All [overconfidence], as most pernicious in its consequences, must be banished from the deliberation.

To obtain alternative perspectives a general has to actively seek out and encourage honest feedback and guidance and create the conditions in which such free and frank advice will be offered. Even then, there remains the real risk of subordinates simply telling a general what they think the leader wants to hear, instead of what is considered less palatable news, albeit closer to reality. Roman general Germanicus had an interesting approach to ensure that what his commanders were telling him to his face was indeed the unvarnished truth. Gaining intelligence that the German leader Arminius was preparing an attack, Germanicus wanted to know whether or not his soldiers were mentally prepared for battle and if they had confidence in his leadership. He knew that directly asking for his commanders' thoughts risked them simply giving him a false impression of the situation:

> Tribunes and centurions, he knew, oftener reported what was welcome than what was true; freedmen had slavish spirits, friends a love of flattery. If an assembly were called, there too the lead of a few was followed by the shout of the many. He must probe their inmost thoughts, when they were uttering their hopes and fears at the military mess, among themselves, and unwatched.

Germanicus was determined to obtain the honest perspectives of his soldiers so one night he disguised himself, left his tent in secret, and walked around the military camp incognito. The approach proved successful and he was able to overhear his soldiers' discussions during their meals and around the camp. Based on what was said in these private and unguarded conversations, the general was satisfied that he had his soldiers' full support and that they were confident about the battle to come. Thus Germanicus was able to implement his battle plans with assurance.

Germanicus' observation that there was an element of flattery in the advice of his friends is echoed throughout the literature, with a consistent theme of the risk that flatterers present to a general. The reporting of overly positive news, unrealistically glowing reports, and fawning praise of a general's performance and judgement are a real danger for any commander. The result of such insincerity by subordinates denies the commander an understanding of the reality of a situation and instead promotes that very over-confidence, self-deception and hubris which often proves deadly on the battlefield.

Actively counter flattery

At the commencement of Alexander's Persian campaign, the Macedonian king experienced a number of delays, first due to illness, then the need to hold lengthy ceremonies, and finally by a side operation against hill tribes. Because of all the delays, Persian king Darius was persuaded by his advisers that Alexander was no longer a threat and that there would be no Macedonian invasion of Persia. Arrian explains that Darius had formed up his army in a favourable location to fight the Macedonian forces, one with the necessary space to make best use of his vast army and counter Alexander's smaller forces. Just one of Darius' counsellors did argue that Alexander was still a threat, saying that 'Alexander would certainly come to any place where he heard Darius might be; and he exhorted him by all means to stay where he was.' However, Darius came to the decision which was 'most agreeable to his own wishes... being influenced by those who gave him the advice which they thought would be pleasant to him', and persuaded himself that Alexander would no longer advance into Persia because of his fear of fighting Darius.

As a result, the Persian king moved his forces, giving up his strategically favourable position for a location in which he could gain little advantage with the size of his military or his cavalry, and one which 'surrendered to Alexander and his troops an easy victory.' As Arrian observes, for Darius the worse advice prevailed – because it told him exactly what he wanted to hear. As history shows us, Alexander did seek out Darius and his Persian army, engaging and defeating them at the battle of Issus (333 BC), thereby establishing the foundations for his final defeat of Darius at the Gaugamela some two years later.

Warnings about the dangers of flattery appear consistently in early writings. Agrippa provided sobering guidance to the Emperor Augustus (Octavian) that flatterers could be expected to bring about a person's destruction rather than save them. Given human nature, it was difficult for a general to overcome the human desire for praise, but it could be achieved. Roman general Gaius Marius went so far as to label the over-confident as traitorous – 'traitors to their country' is what he called those soldiers overly keen to rush carelessly into battle.

Similarly, when General Demaratus had been rudely spoken to by a fellow Spartan, Orontes, the insult was pointed out to him by a bystander. Rather than expressing anger towards Orontes, Demaratus replied to the man who had commented, saying, 'He hasn't done me any wrong; for it is those who speak to gain favour who do harm, not those who openly speak with hatred.' Recognizing the greater risks presented by flattery and overly positive advisers is crucial for any general in avoiding such disastrous guidance and maintaining a link with reality.

Chapter 11

How is Warfare Fundamentally Human and Why Does Psychology Matter?

No system of tactics can lead to victory when the morale of an army is bad...
General Antoine-Henri Jomini

Once the mass of the defending infantry become possessed of low morale, the battle is as good as lost.
General Douglas Haig

Machines don't fight wars. Terrain doesn't fight wars. Humans fight wars. You must get into the mind of the humans. That's where the battles are won.
Colonel John Boyd

Generals need to understand themselves, the people they lead into battle and the people they fight against. Ultimately, comprehension of human nature and psychology is crucial to a general as it forms the basis of fighting. By understanding how soldiers behave under stress on the battlefield, how emotions shape actions, and how opponents will likely think and behave, a general is best placed to anticipate, plan and act from an informed perspective. Recognizing this fundamentally important aspect of warfare, the ancient authors emphasize the necessity of understanding the human element in the preparation, conduct and aftermath of battle.

Human emotions matter

Human emotions remain central to warfare and a general who wants to win cannot ignore them. Fears and hopes, confidence and morale, confusion and clarity all co-exist within the human mind. The willingness to fight and the confidence about achieving victory are essential human characteristics of the personnel who make up the armed forces that generals lead. To think 'war' a general must also think 'humans'.

In reflecting on the nature of conflict, Sallust argues that there has previously been lengthy debate about what was more important in warfare – the mind or the body? The debate centred on whether mental or physical strength mattered most. After considering King Cyrus of Persia, and the Athenians and Spartans, Sallust concludes that the question has been well and truly answered, and that 'mental power has the greatest effect in military operations.' The general's mind is where decisions and judgements are made, insights gained, impressions solidified, and appropriate tactics for the situation identified. What happens in the mind of a general and in the minds of their soldiers matters most.

The description of warfare as 'months of boredom punctuated by moments of sheer terror' is an apt description of the nature of conflict, both ancient and modern. Days, weeks, months and even years go by in which major battles may be few and far between. In these early histories, even when armies drew up opposite each other for battle there was no guarantee that an actual clash of arms would occur, and the same armies would often return to camp to fight another day, or sometimes not at all. Such periods of delay and uncertainty are still a feature of warfare and are difficult for any military commander to manage. This was something that the early writers recognized. Polybius notes that there is nothing more difficult for soldiers than waiting out a prolonged suspense, but as soon as a decision to enter conflict is made then these same soldiers are able to endure even the worst of conditions. The extended waiting, boredom and uncertainty of war cannot help but have an impact. So, a good general will use that aspect of the human condition to their advantage.

Creating uncertainty and drawing out events to unnerve or frustrate the adversary plays on such human emotions. Soon after Cyrus was defeated and the Greek mercenary army became trapped in Persia, General Clearchus was approached by a Persian envoy requesting a decision on what the Greeks intended to do. Would they establish a truce? Would they choose to fight? What would it be? But Clearchus deliberately remained vague, withholding his intended course of action from the Persians and delaying any decision. He explained to his commanders that he wanted to keep his enemies in a state of uncertainty for as long as he could. All warfare has elements of ambiguity, the type which creates stressors on commanders, soldiers and civilians alike. Actively increasing this uncertainty, knowing the anxiety it causes an enemy, can be helpful to a general and his soldiers.

Reality bites

Emotions, mindsets and cognitive biases display a consistency across human history, particularly when it comes to warfare. Prior to conflict, people usually think about their own strength, abilities and future far more positively than they should. This occurs far too often to be attributed to an individual mistake but is a regular feature of human thinking. In what is referred to as the Mytilenian Debate, Thucydides captures this point with the argument that even the most consequential decisions are usually made mostly on hope, both individuals and groups usually overestimating their own abilities and power. Further, once such decisions are made and a course of action decided upon, it becomes almost impossible to change people's minds, regardless of how obvious and grave the threat or risk they face. However, once they are at war, both communities and individuals find they are dealing not in hopes but in facts, their own power countered by an equally determined enemy, and reality comes back at them with a vengeance.

War quickly focuses people's minds on the reality of their circumstances, and sometimes this 'wake-up call' can be the motivation a community, city or nation needs to rapidly mobilize all their resources against a clear and present danger. When Hannibal crossed the Alps, marched his army into Rome's backyard, and gained a series of victories in Italy in short order, the Roman population was propelled into immediate and drastic action. The direct threat of annihilation and the reality of Hannibal's then-undefeated army marching through Italy itself resulted in the Romans gearing up for war. Remembering how the city had previously been sacked by the Gauls (387 BC), they were very conscious that such an event could well happen again. The psychological shock resulted in fast, decisive action and the raising of armies which would put a stop to Hannibal's rampant campaign and eventually defeat him.

An initial victory or defeat significantly impacts future battles

One of the most significant impacts on mindset is an army's initial victory. To defeat an enemy boosts morale and confidence, and creates in both commander and soldiers a positive expectation concerning future engagements. The psychological impact of victory is one reason that generals and their armies are able to repeat successful outcomes, particularly against the same opponents. Further, the ability to build a string of battlefield successes on the initial win brings a tremendous psychological advantage – each new victory makes the army even more difficult to defeat.

For a defeated force, naturally, the opposite is true. Early defeats discourage and demoralize the surviving generals and soldiers. Rallying his forces before the naval battle of Actium (31 BC), Octavian highlighted the advantages they held over an enemy they had defeated in previous smaller engagements on land. He argued, 'it is a natural characteristic of human nature everywhere, that whenever a man fails in his first contests he becomes disheartened with respect to what is to come.' This point is also made by Tacitus who says, 'conquered troops, however bold their language, never show the same courage.'

Speaking to his commanders before the battle of Issus (333 BC), when the Macedonians had already fought successfully against the Persians at Granicus (334 BC), Alexander emphasized their advantage. His soldiers should take courage from the previous dangers they had overcome and remember the upcoming struggle would be between a victorious army and an enemy they had already once defeated in battle. The previous century, Athenian admiral Phormio had made a similar observation noting 'beaten men do not face a danger twice with the same determination.'

Livy captures the psychological impact of prior defeats on confidence and morale in recounting how the victorious Roman legions approached the previously defeated Masaesylian forces: 'The Masaesylians not only dared not await [the Romans] first charge, but could not bear even the sight of the standards and arms; so powerful was either the recollection of their former defeats, or their present fears.' Success breeds success and failure is difficult to overcome, and these points can be exploited by a good general.

However, while a victorious army starts in a better psychological position, a good general can also turn a defeated force around. A once-defeated army can be led to victory given the right leader. Spartan general Xanthippus was chosen by the Carthaginians to lead their army, following a series of battlefield disasters against Rome in the First Punic War. Under Xanthippus, the Carthaginians went on to defeat the Roman general Regulus and his army at Bagradas river in 255 BC. Polybius reflects on this accomplishment, observing how a wise commander could take a previously losing army and make it victorious again. Polybius argues the truth of Euripides' observation that 'one wise counsel conquers many hands.' The Spartan general had restored the fortunes of Carthage, renewed the confidence and fighting spirit of its soldiers and defeated an enemy who had appeared invincible.

There are other elements in victory and defeat and their impact on generals and soldiers. *How* an armed force succeeds or fails matters greatly. An armed force which goes into battle anticipating victory only to find itself defeated can become thoroughly demoralized, given its previous overconfidence and expectations. In contrast, an armed force expecting to lose a battle only to come out victorious is affected very differently. A victory against a seemingly stronger opposition creates an impression on both sides, the winners rapidly gaining confidence and the defeated forces beginning to question and doubt themselves.

Plutarch argues that the Gauls' sacking of Rome in 387 BC was a direct result of a series of unexpected Roman military failures. The poor performance of Roman generals and their armies, and their subsequent battlefield defeats, had emboldened the Gauls. Instead of the Romans appearing formidable opponents, the Gauls realized they could be beaten. As a result of the Gauls' new confidence, they marched their forces to Rome and sacked the city. A year or two earlier, such an event would have seemed entirely incredible to both the Romans and the Gauls.

Defeating an enemy at their strongest point

Another way for a general to use psychology is by attacking and defeating the enemy at their strongest point. That point could be the soldiery, weapons, defensive structures, or any element in which the enemy placed their utmost confidence. The psychological shock to a force witnessing the destruction of the military capability on which they feel most assured is profound. The strategy of attacking an enemy's strongest point is certainly a risky one, but when successful will achieve a thoroughly disproportionate impact – shattering the enemy's self-confidence and making them easier to defeat in future battles. The success of such a tactic also ensures that the question of which force is the stronger has been unequivocally answered. Alexander the Great would deliberately select strong points in which he knew the enemy placed their confidence as priorities to overcome. This can be seen in his determination during the sieges of the cities of Tyre and Gaza. Arrian makes clear Alexander's reasoning, 'the more impracticable it seemed to be, the more resolutely Alexander determined that it must be captured,' because of the impact it would have on his enemy. The strategy is found in numerous early accounts of warfare to achieve a similar effect.

Following a power struggle between pro- and anti-Roman forces in the Cimmerian Bosporus (modern day Black Sea area), in AD 49 the Romans and their allied Adrosi forces attacked the fortified city of Uspe. The rapid defeat of what had been perceived by locals as an impenetrable fortress, and the slaughter of 10,000 of its inhabitants, dealt a devastating psychological shock to the surviving population. Tacitus explains, 'The destruction of Uspe struck terror into the rest of the people, who thought safety impossible when they saw how armies and ramparts, heights and difficult positions, rivers and cities, alike yielded to their foe.'

The tactic was not new and had been repeatedly made use of by Roman generals. During the Second Illyrian War (220–219 BC), the Roman consul Lucius Aemilius Paulus travelled with his army to Illryia (Balkans region) to take on Rome's former ally, Demetrius of Pharos. On arriving in Illyria, Aemilius recognized that the enemy placed enormous confidence in the strength of their fortified city of Dimale. The locals believed their fortress city to be impregnable, so Aemilius determined that it would be his first target to attack and conquer in order to strike terror into the population. The strategy proved effective. The Romans showed themselves to be the stronger force by taking Dimale in just seven days. The loss of their supposedly unassailable fortification shattered the confidence of the local people and the opposition collapsed. If the Romans could overcome their strongest defensive position so quickly the Illyrians believed there was nothing more they could do to resist them, just as the Roman consul had intended.

Overcoming an adversary's particular fighting strength or a military capability in which they are most assured and invested can similarly result in a disproportionate impact on their confidence and sense of security. When preparing Syracusan naval forces for the sea battle to come, Spartan general Gylippus made the following points about the Athenians' belief in their naval prowess:

> When men are once checked in what they consider their special excellence, their whole opinion of themselves suffers more than if they had not at first believed in their superiority, the unexpected shock to their pride causing them to give way more than their real strength warrants; and this is probably now the case with the Athenians.

The Syracusan naval forces under overall command of General Gylippus subsequently defeated the Athenians in that battle and Gylippus proved correct in his judgement, both of the Athenians' over-confidence in their maritime superiority and the shattering impact that a loss at sea would have on their psyche. Indeed, the defeat also revealed to all the other Greek states that the Athenian navy was not invincible .

Ability to overcome the worst setbacks

There are other aspects that shape human perceptions on both sides of a conflict. The ability of a general to overcome losses or disasters which an enemy believed would prove fatal can have a profound psychological impact, convincing their opponents that a force is simply unconquerable and instilling in them a sense of hopelessness. Around 16 AD, during General Germanicus' campaign in Germany, the Roman leader was transporting soldiers in a fleet of ships across the Amisia river. A fierce storm hit them, resulting in widespread destruction and loss of life amongst the soldiers. The wreckage of the ships and the myriad bodies of soldiers and horses washed up on shore, in full view of the German tribes.

At the sight of such devastation, the Germans saw an opportunity for victory over the remaining Roman forces. However, Germanicus was determined to counter the threat and avoid any perception of weakness despite his losses. He despatched a force of some 30,000 soldiers led by

Caius Silius against one German tribe (the Chatti), while with an even larger force he attacked another of the German tribes (the Marsi). These attacks were at a scale and strength so entirely unexpected by the Germans that it led to complete despair among them. Captured German prisoners revealed the extent of the tribes' total demoralization – that they had witnessed the destruction of the Roman fleet, riverbanks strewn with dead soldiers and horses, yet still the Romans had launched attacks with the same courage, fighting spirit and seemingly greater numbers of soldiers. The impression of an unconquerable force, one that could recover from any disaster and still fight on, proved devastating to Rome's adversaries.

Bold action

Overt confidence and bold action by a general and their armed forces can also prove unnerving for an opponent, as we can see in multiple instances. To counter Spartan general Cleomenes' campaign in the region, the Achaeans raised a force of 20,000 soldiers and 1,000 cavalrymen under King Aratus. With his own force of less than 5,000 soldiers, the Spartan general did not hesitate but met the Achaean army and prepared for battle. In the face of such a confident opponent, ready to engage despite being heavily outnumbered, Aratus became fearful and withdrew his force, to the anger of his own Achaean soldiers and the mocking of the Spartans who wanted to fight. This ability to get inside the minds of their adversaries is something that good generals will exploit.

Julius Caesar, though cautious, would also act boldly to discourage and demoralize the enemy. When preparing for combat against German general Ariovistus, Caesar confidently marched his forces right up to the German camp. Ariovistus had thought that the Romans would be too intimidated by his great force to risk an attack, yet here was Caesar and his army now camped opposite him. To compound his concerns, Ariovistus noticed that his own soldiers had been similarly unnerved by the Romans' sudden appearance and clear confidence. Caesar had psychologically defeated both General Ariovistus and the German troops before any combat had commenced.

In the same way, before fighting began at the battle of Issus (333 BC), Alexander the Great mentally rattled Darius and his vast Persian army, by deliberately having his own Macedonian forces engage in a protracted and measured march on to the battlefield, to further shake the confidence of an already fearful king:

> Having thus marshalled his men, [Alexander] caused them to rest for some time, and then led them forward, as he thought the enemy's approach was very slow. For Darius was no longer leading the foreigners against him, as he had arranged them at first, but he remained in his position, upon the bank of the river, which was in many parts steep and precipitous; and in certain places, where it seemed more easy to ascend, he extended a stockade along it. By this it was at once evident to Alexander's men that Darius had become cowed in spirit.

The calculated actions of Alexander indicate an inherent confidence, in contrast to Darius' static forces hiding behind defences despite their obvious numerical superiority – some 600,000 Persians against a Macedonian force of around 47,000. Alexander's control and willingness to fight against such odds only compounded Darius' fears. Of course, such bold action may backfire if a general finds that they are facing an enemy ready and willing to engage.

During the First Punic War, Rome's Admiral Pulcher launched a fleet in an effort to surprise the Carthaginian maritime force at Drepana and trap them in the harbour. Pulcher did manage to catch them and their Admiral Adherbal by surprise, but the Carthaginians' response shocked Pulcher and demonstrated how fragile a general's own confidence can be. The Roman admiral had assumed that the Carthaginians would be so intimidated by his unexpected appearance that they would stay in the harbour and refuse to engage in a naval battle. On the contrary, on seeing the Romans arrive the Carthaginians immediately readied their fleet to attack. Pulcher himself was shocked by his enemy's eagerness for battle and immediately recalled those of his ships that had sailed towards the harbour, ordering them back out to sea. Taking advantage of the Romans' confusion and the chaos of their attempts to withdraw, the Carthaginian admiral quickly regained the initiative and attacked. In the naval battle that followed, Pulcher's fleet was soundly defeated by Adherbal and his Carthaginian ships. After the engagement, the victorious Admiral Adherbal was praised and celebrated in Carthage, while Admiral Pulcher found himself relieved of command and on trial in Rome, only narrowly avoiding the death penalty.

Unexpected action unnerves

Unexpectedness can be unnerving, an unfamiliar or unlikely action giving a general a psychological advantage over the enemy commanders and soldiers who have been surprised by it. However, a general hoping to turn such initial alarm into battlefield success needs to press home their advantage and take the fight to the enemy while they are still uncertain, fearful and disorganized. The battle of Marathon (490 BC) proved a turning point in Greek history not only as a battlefield victory but in terms of the Greeks' self-confidence.

At Marathon, some 40 kilometres north of Athens, a heavily outnumbered Greek force consisting largely of Athenians with some Plataean allies (around 10,000 and 1,000 soldiers respectively) faced off against a vast Persian army of perhaps 200,000. The Athenian line spread out to cover the entire Persian front, General Miltiades gave the order to attack, and the Athenian troops began racing towards the enemy, less than a mile away. Watching the Greeks advance, the Persians prepared to meet them, thinking it suicidal for such a small force to take them on. Contrary to the Persians' expectations, however, not only did the Greeks attack but neither the Athenians nor the Plataeans stopped running – they rushed head on at the Persian lines. Herodotus states that it was the first time he knew of in history where an army had charged the enemy at a run.

The psychological impact of the unexpected tactic on the Persians was enormous. The Greeks had not only attacked the far larger force but in a way that was entirely unforeseen – smashing into the Persian ranks at speed, with great violence and confidence. The impact on the numerically superior Persians was evident in the result of the battle, a significant Greek victory with the surviving Persians fleeing the field. The effect on the Greeks was similarly profound. Herodotus argued that these Athenian soldiers were the first to face down the Persians without fear, whereas before the victory at Marathon just hearing the name 'Persian' had produced terror in them. Athens' victory showed all of the Greek states that even with smaller numbers the mighty Persian army could be defeated.

Physical action

In early accounts of battles between a moving force and a static one, there appears to have been a psychological advantage for the side taking action as against the one standing and awaiting the attack. There can be little doubt that the Athenians running towards their enemies helped morale; their blood was up, adrenalin flowing, running at speed and entirely committed. In contrast, the Persians were static, waiting, ceding the initiative to the Greeks. Caesar himself recognized the importance of having soldiers keep active rather than standing still, as a means of encouraging the fighting spirit and morale of soldiers.

At the battle of Pharsalus (48 BC) where Caesar finally overcame Pompey, there was a stark difference in approach between the two Roman generals. In the battle, Pompey would order his infantry not to rush forward or throw their javelins, but to keep their position and await the attack of Caesar's soldiers and only then use their spears to engage in hand-to-hand combat. In contrast Caesar was critical of such an approach, arguing that the impact of weapons is more powerful and the spirits of soldiers heightened when they are able to run at the enemy. Those who must stand and wait quickly become demoralized and make easy targets for their enemies. Caesar understood how soldiers thought and felt, and the effect on them of activity or inactivity on the battlefield. It is no surprise that at Pharsalus Caesar had his men actively launch their spears into Pompey's static ranks of soldiers, ultimately proving successful.

Even when not engaged in battle, Julius Caesar disliked his soldiers being idle and would deliberately find ways to keep them active and engaged. In this way, the men remained energetic, focused and ready. Suetonius highlights Caesar's style of leading his army and his clear understanding of how to keep those he led focused and ready to fight:

> He valued his soldiers neither for their personal character nor for their fortune, but solely for their prowess, and he treated them with equal strictness and indulgence; for he did not curb them everywhere and at all times, but only in the presence of the enemy. Then he required the strictest discipline, not announcing the time of a march or a battle, but keeping them ready and alert to be led on a sudden at any moment wheresoever he might wish. He

> often called them out even when there was no occasion for it, especially on rainy days and holidays. And warning them every now and then that they must keep close watch on him, he would steal away suddenly by day or night and make a longer march than usual, to tire out those who were tardy in following. When they were in a panic through reports about the enemy's numbers, he used to rouse their courage not by denying or discounting the rumours, but by falsely exaggerating the true danger. For instance, when the anticipation of Juba's coming filled them with terror, he called the soldiers together and said: 'Let me tell you that within the next few days the king will be here with ten legions, thirty thousand horsemen, a hundred thousand light-armed troops, and three hundred elephants. Therefore some of you may as well cease to ask further questions or make surmises and may rather believe me, since I know all about it. Otherwise, I shall surely have them shipped on some worn out craft and carried off to whatever lands the wind may blow them.'

In other words, stop panicking and focus your energy on the fight to come. Caesar built the army he wanted by understanding his soldiers' fears and directing their focus to the actual job at hand. A good general understands that fear is normal and tries to counter it within their own forces while maximizing it in their opponents, knowing that fear can be debilitating regardless of whether the fears are based on reality or not.

Human fear, panic and blame

Polyaenus identifies the power of groundless human terrors clearly in his *Stratagems of War*, noting that 'all vain and imaginary fears are termed *panics*.' When a small force of Alexander's army took control of the Rock of Sogdiana, a local stronghold, his opponents panicked at the unexpectedness of the event, they were so shocked at the sight of a small number of Macedonian soldiers, that they assumed they were instead facing a much larger, well-armed force, and so immediately surrendered.

In the face of an unexpected shock, and devoid of other intelligence, Alexander's opponents envisaged a far greater force opposing them and simply gave up. This is not unusual in war. In the absence of information and against a background of fear and uncertainty, people tend towards pessimism.

Discussing the siege of Tyre by Alexander, Curtius Rufus reflects on the impact that uncertainty and panic can have. He notes that the besieged Tyrians were inclined to believe any information despite it coming from unreliable sources; based on their fears they would readily accept the very worst news. There is an argument that people tend to overestimate success in good times and the reverse, overplay their losses or impending disaster, when they are fearful. This appears to be a consistent observation in classic accounts of warfare and subsequently reinforced through the ages.

A general also needs to recognize that soldiers themselves can increase the fear and uncertainty of a situation and promote panic among their own ranks. Tacitus offers the example of a small military force led by Roman commander Alfenus Varus, who marched against a Roman opponent's fort in AD 69, during Rome's civil war. Some of the opponent's men were killed and some escaped, but the majority of the soldiers in the fort simply surrendered to Varus' small force. To minimize the disgrace of losing the fort, those soldiers who escaped then exaggerated the strength and fighting abilities of Varus' force, creating panic within their own army. An embarrassing loss was thus compounded by baseless information, leading to increased fear amongst the ranks, entirely unwarranted by the actual threat itself.

Another consistent human behaviour in war is that when things go wrong, people readily turn to blaming each other. Though ultimately successful, when Alexander's soldiers faced a setback during their siege of Tyre, Rufus notes that what followed was what usually happens in disasters – everybody began blaming each other. Hundreds of years later during yet another of Rome's many civil wars, Appian painted a picture of panic in the city: 'Having heard that an army was advancing with hostile intentions, there was nothing that they did not fear. The Senate was struck with consternation since they had no military force in readiness. As is usual in cases of panic they blamed each other.' Another observation on human behaviour under great stress is made by Tacitus, commenting on a similar debacle, 'The result was what always happens in a hopeless disaster: everybody gave orders and nobody obeyed them.' Human behaviour certainly appears consistent in reaction to the many difficulties which emerge in war.

The impact of appearances

Of the human senses, sight is arguably the most significant and certainly matters in conflict. What the eyes tell us significantly influences human emotions, including affecting morale, fear and confidence. Tacitus in his account of Germany describes a tribe which was not only physically imposing but would deliberately,

> make the most of their natural ferocity by the help of art and opportunity. Their shields are black, their bodies dyed. They choose dark nights for battle, and, by the dread and gloomy aspect of their death-like host, strike terror into the foe, who can never confront their strange and almost infernal appearance.

This tribe dressed to strike fear into their opponents, and it worked. As Tacitus concludes, 'For in all battles it is the eye which is first vanquished.' Physical appearances do have an effect on both a general's own forces and the enemy. Onasander provides clear advice that during any conferences with the enemy, a general should select the strongest, tallest, fittest and best-armed soldiers to accompany him. In this way the enemy, and specifically the opposing general, would conclude that the entire force opposing them was of such a high standard and strength because people are impacted more by what they have seen than by what they hear.

When Greek mercenaries were escaping Persia, General Clearchus marched his Greek army past the city of Opis, in front of a Persian general and his army – the *manner* in which Clearchus' army advanced clearly impacted perceptions on both sides. The Greeks marched two abreast, Clearchus consistently halting and re-starting the front ranks of the army, which created a rippling flow effect through the columns of soldiers as they slowly paraded past the onlooking Persians. The strategy proved effective even with the Greeks themselves, thinking that their army was enormous, and left the Persians absolutely astonished at what they saw.

Summing up the tendency for people to exaggerate based on what they hear, what they imagine, and what they expect, Syracusan general Hermocrates preparing his colleagues to counter the Athenians observed:

> We should also be reported, I am certain, as more numerous than we really are, and men's minds are affected by what they hear, and besides the first to attack, or to show that they mean to defend themselves against an attack, inspire greater fear because men see that they are ready for the emergency.

Hermocrates ties his solid appreciation of human nature into his strategy, as a good general should. What soldiers hear and see impacts how they feel and, ultimately, how they fight.

In AD 69, Batavian chief Gaius Julius Civilis had fomented an uprising in Germany, resulting in the destruction of local Roman forces. Soon after, Civilis faced off against another Roman force. According to Tacitus, 'Civilis set the standards of the defeated cohorts round him in a ring to keep their fresh honours before the eyes of his men, and to terrify the enemy by reminding them of their disaster.' The use of an army's battle standards to motivate soldiers, as well as the value of capturing enemy standards, is a reminder that warfare is fought by humans and emotions matter. A military standard is, in reality, merely an inanimate object (metal, wood, material). However, it is invested with so much significance that soldiers risk their very lives to protect or regain a unit's military standard. This was recognized by the Romans, who would at times use this emotional attachment to motivate their soldiers to fight harder, by throwing their own unit's military standard into the enemy ranks:

> neither party could make the least impression on the other, until Quintus Victorius... and Caius Atilius ...had taken a course often tried in desperate conflicts; snatching the standards from the officers who carried them, and throwing them among the enemy. In the struggle to recover the standards, the men of the second legion first made their way out of the gate.

Such a tactic was also employed by Julius Caesar, demonstrating the emotional element of warfare and how such emotions impact on the motivation, willingness and effort soldiers will exercise in battle. The fear of losing a standard could move soldiers to give that extra effort that might well carry the day. Of course, there were losses could have the opposite effect and entirely demoralize an army.

The general on the battlefield

Despite being just one individual, the position of the general on these ancient battlefields had a disproportionate importance for the army. Soldiers understood that in battle a general was usually facing risk to life and limb just as they were. For the general, being physically present and part of the battle gave them an opportunity to directly influence the fight and even rally their soldiers by directly involving themselves in combat. Alexander the Great and Julius Caesar were two such commanders, well-known for throwing themselves into the fray, leading and inspiring through personal example, and having an effect on the outcome of battles by their example and on-the-spot directions. These fighting generals could motivate their men at first hand, but that advantage came with the potentially devastating downside that their injury or death could entirely destroy their soldiers' hope and confidence. The loss of the most senior military commander had such a psychological effect on the whole army that this single event alone could determine the outcome of the battle.

General Mago, Hannibal's brother, had followed Hannibal and Hasdrubal's lead into Italy. Mago arrived in northern Italy by sea in 205 BC. He successfully established himself with allied Gauls in the region and in 203 BC the Roman forces marched against him, at Insubria. The Roman legions found the fight against the Carthaginians fierce and difficult, but the critical moment came when General Mago was seriously wounded. Livy reflects on the impact that losing a general on the battlefield can have, particularly when the general is in the thick of the fighting, 'As long as Mago stood in front, the troops stepped back slowly, preserving their ranks and not relaxing their ardour in fighting; but when they saw him falling, from a wound in his thigh …and carried off the field almost lifeless, in an instant they all betook themselves to flight.' When Mago was seen to be injured and carried from the field the fight was over; the Carthaginian army gave up hope and fled. This was not of course unique to the Carthaginians. The death or serious wounding of a general on the battlefield would often result in the outcome being predetermined due to his soldiers' loss of heart.

Early psychological operations

While psychological operations are a recognized aspect of modern warfare such activities are far from new. The Romans understood the impact of parading defeated and captured kings, generals and nobles back in Rome, during triumphs to boost their own citizens' confidence. Such displays were also used to remind their enemies of the military might of Rome, reinforcing the perception of an all-conquering empire and minimizing the chance of future conflict or uprisings. Word did spread of these triumphs, and it became well known that captured senior military commanders could find themselves utterly humiliated by being paraded as a trophy in Rome before possibly being put to death. Further, outside of the triumphant processions in the capital, the Romans were well aware of the power of psychological operations in the homelands of their adversaries.

Following the destruction of Crassus and his Roman army by the Parthian general Surena, and knowing that the defeat would embolden their enemies, General Mark Antony's Roman army returned to Syria. Antony allocated forces to General Publius Ventidius who went on to vanquish the Parthians at Mount Gindarus in 38 BC. Defeating an enemy force of some 20,000 soldiers, including King Pacorus, the Romans then sought to minimize future resistance. They beheaded the Parthian king and took their gory trophy on a tour around the province, displaying it in all the Syrian cities that had revolted against Rome. This psychological form of aggression successfully ensured the Romans regained control with no more fighting. Such grisly displays were not uncommon and were designed to dishearten an enemy by demonstrating the victor's invincibility, very often proving highly effective at suppressing further resistance.

Another such case is when Spartan general Clearchus learned that his Thracian enemies had moved their supplies into the mountains and planned to simply wait out his siege. He summoned the Thracian envoys to come before him and as they looked on he had one of his prisoners executed, the body cut into pieces and distributed to the Spartan tents, as if for a meal. On seeing this, convinced that Clearchus would do anything to win, including resorting to cannibalism, the Thracians surrendered to the Spartans. Efforts to manipulate human emotions are a consistent element of warfare ancient and modern.

Generals are human too

Given the uncertainties, complexities, fears and risks involved in war, it is perhaps no surprise that we find historical accounts of the doubts, second-guessing, despondency and even the total psychological breakdown of generals in war. Many, of course, appear to have been able to adapt to circumstances in front of them and found ways to achieve victory; defeat did not need to be final, and doubts and personal moments of despondency could be overcome. When Julius Caesar was defeated by Pompey at the battle of Dyrrachium (48 BC), he is recorded as experiencing some hours of doubt and despair, believing that his own poor generalship had led to the defeat. But having reflected on his failure, Caesar adjusted his plans, rallied his soldiers, and ultimately prevailed over Pompey at Pharsalus in 48 BC. Of course not all generals could have done this, and some were simply overwhelmed by their circumstances and the chaos and confusion of battle.

During a Roman military campaign in Greece in 195 BC, General Flamininus came up against King Nabis, who was in command of the then-walled city of Sparta. Flamininus surrounded the city, then deliberately kept the inhabitants in a state of constant alarm for three days, 'sometimes harassing them with assaults, sometimes enclosing several places with works, so as to leave no passage open for flight.' Nabis tried to give orders and instructions to counter the Roman army, but 'was so stunned by the horror and confusion that prevailed all around, as to become incapable either of giving proper directions, or of hearing what was said, and to lose, not only his judgment, but almost his reason.' After the three days, Nabis realized he could not cope with the situation and sent an envoy to the Romans to seek peace.

The cognitive failure of leaders in battle, even those who had been successful commanders before, accords with our own sporting proverb that, 'You are only as good as your last game' or in this case 'A general is only as good as their last battle.' In Roman history perhaps the most famous case of mental collapse in a general was what happened to Pompey. Despite his numerous successes and reputation as a great leader, in his final battle against Julius Caesar at Pharsalus in 48 BC, Pompey simply ceased to function. Plutarch describes Pompey's reaction on witnessing his cavalry being beaten and fleeing the battlefield. Seeing this, Pompey seemed to lose his senses, simply leaving the field without a word and returning to his tent, where he sat down and waited for the battle to be over. When Caesar's forces started attacking the camp defences, Pompey appeared to regain some sense of the situation, but only enough to discard his general's uniform, change into inconspicuous clothing, and run away himself. Such a complete breakdown on the battlefield, even in a senior leader, was actually not unusual.

Chapter 12

Why Does Managing Politicians, Peers and Soldiers Matter?

I asked the general where the enemy was. He replied that he did not know. He said the fact was, that he was so embarrassed with orders from Washington moving him first to the right and then to the left that he had lost all trace of the enemy.

General Ulysses S. Grant

It is sometimes tougher to fight my superiors than the French.

General Heinz Guderian

I don't know what effect these men will have upon the enemy, but, by God, they terrify me.

Duke of Wellington

In addition to fighting an enemy, a general usually faces the real and pressing challenges of dealing with political leaders, of competition from their peers, and all the machinations of leading and managing the soldiers under their command. All these complexities also represent threats, not only to their position as generals and their egos as military commanders but, at times, to their very lives.

Politicians

Most Greek and Roman generals were accountable to politicians or other leaders, making this a critical aspect for these senior military commanders to manage. Generals usually operated under a level of authority, a leader, group or institution (e.g. the Roman Senate) from whom they received their position, authority and directions and to whom they were accountable. This guidance and accountability would influence and limit the actions generals could take, where they could go, what they could do, and the resources available to them.

One example of this is apparent in the actions of an Athenian fleet, prior to the conflict with Sparta, when the Athenians were providing support to their Corcyrean allies in a naval engagement against the Corinthians. While the Athenians would sail in close support of the Corcyreans when the Corinthians threatened to overwhelm them, the Athenian naval commanders initially would not participate in the battle because of orders from Athens to avoid such engagements. Only once the battle was in full swing and part of the Corcycrean fleet looked as if it would be defeated did the Athenian fleet finally engage in the fight. Until the situation for their allies became desperate, their instructions from political superiors acted as a brake on how far the Athenians could support their allies.

A crucial aspect of civilian control over the military is that the political class usually holds the power to hire and fire generals. Being promoted to the position of general represents a significant achievement, just as being removed from command signals disgrace. In the ancient world, promotion to the most senior rank could open the door to glory, success and wealth, whereas being sacked from it would bring loss of status, exile or even death. Thucydides himself was an Athenian admiral during the Peloponnesian War who was deemed to have failed in not coming to the aid of a besieged Athenian force in time, so was removed from command and exiled from Athens. Indirectly, this proved a benefit to future generations as Thucydides used his time to research and write one of the most outstanding accounts of warfare in history. However, for most generals, losing their command meant the end of their military career and the end of their chance for glory. For a few, there might be an opportunity to return when time had passed, or if the state became desperate enough. However, the chances were that they would never again attain the same high rank.

Even more galling, a general who was removed might well find a peer and competitor appointed to replace them. Roman general Paetus had been feeding false information and accounts back to Rome on the progress of his campaign in Armenia, minimizing his own failings and hiding the disastrous terms on which he had been forced to treat for peace with Parthian general Vologeses. When it was known that Paetus' forces had actually fled Armenia, Emperor

Nero 'consulted with the chief men of the State whether they should accept a dangerous war or a disgraceful peace. There was no hesitation about war.' But it was not General Paetus who would be leading the Roman army. Instead, Rome appointed General Corbulo, 'who had known our soldiers and the enemy for so many years, was appointed to conduct it, that there might be no more blunders through any other officer's incapacity; for people were utterly disgusted with Paetus.' In this case, Paetus' replacement was justified. However, there were generals who had to avoid being removed from command even when they were pursuing a winning strategy.

As previously mentioned, in the face of Hannibal's invasion of Italy General Fabius would save the Roman Republic by wearing down Hannibal through delay, avoiding unfavourable engagements, and allowing Rome time to rebuild its diminished armies. However, Fabius initially faced hostility from a Roman Senate keen to engage Hannibal immediately, despite lacking the strength or skill at that time. As Livy notes, General Fabius 'kept away from the popular assemblies, in which he did not command a favourable hearing, and even in the Senate he was not heard with favourable ears, when his eloquence was employed in praising the enemy, and attributing the disasters of the last two years to the temerity and unskilfulness of the generals.'

Fabius' words in the Senate were unwelcome, albeit accurate, but he did have the wisdom to avoid such hearings and audiences while continuing to pursue his strategy. In the longer term, and in the face of brutal and devastating failures by his peers against the Carthaginians, Fabius was able not only to convince the Roman Senate, populace and citizenry of the wisdom of his approach, but would be recognized and honoured as the saviour of the Roman Republic, proving his ability to successfully manage the politicians as well as the enemy.

To assist in winning the confidence of their political overseers, and achieve recognition and honours, a general not only had to win battles, but also have their victories formally recognized and publicly celebrated. Florus' account of the Gaetulian War (AD 3–6) between Rome and the Gaetuli (North Africans), demonstrates how perceptions of victories matter and why it did not necessarily help a general to be humble about their achievements:

> Augustus put down the Musulami and Gaetulians who dwell near the Syrtes, through the agency of Cossus, who thus gained the name of Gaetulicus, a title more extensive than his actual victory warranted. He entrusted the subjugation of the Marmarides and Garamantes to Quirinius, who likewise might have returned with the title of Marmaricus, had he not been too modest in estimating his victory.

Julius Caesar had no such problems with modesty, using his own written accounts of his campaigns against the Gauls to publicize his victories to the Roman populace. Undoubtably, he had to first win on the battlefield, but subsequently publicizing his conquests helped to solidify his popularity and gain recognition. A noteworthy feature of Roman culture was the 'triumph', a formal procession through the streets of the capital. These victory parades were an important public recognition of a general's battlefield victories, bringing glory, honour, recognition, and public adulation for the battle or campaign success. However, these parades were not a given, even after a successful military campaign.

A general had to seek formal approval from the political authorities (usually the Senate and later the Emperor) for permission to celebrate a triumph through the capital. Such approvals were not guaranteed and not all generals' requests for a triumphal entry into the city were approved. This could be for a variety of reasons, from the relatively small scale of a victory to petty rivalries, politics, or even concerns over the potential increase in popularity of a general. Consequently, there were always challenges for generals in managing their political relationships, even after victories on the battlefield. And challenges in the form of political interference could come long before a campaign had even begun, so generals had to be adept at managing expectations and any concerns of their political masters, both to get a campaign approved and to secure their own position as its leader.

Like the ancients, today's generals need to manage the relationships with their political masters to secure their support, keep them onside or even sway their opinions in favour of the commander. The ability to entirely change political leaders' minds is perhaps best demonstrated by Scipio Africanus in the lead-up to launching his army into Africa against the Carthaginians. Following accusations of Scipio's having failed to prepare his forces properly for the campaign, and calls to have him removed from the command, a political delegation was dispatched from Rome to Sicily to review his efforts. In a brilliant display of how a general can handle their political overseers, Scipio succeeded in impressing the visiting officials with perhaps the first ever large-scale military wargame:

> While they were on their way to Syracuse, Scipio prepared to clear himself, not by words but facts. He ordered all his troops to assemble there, and the fleet to be got in readiness, as though a battle had to be fought that day with the Carthaginians, by sea and land. On the day of their arrival he entertained them hospitably, and on the next day presented to their view his land and naval forces, not only drawn up in order, but the former performing evolutions, while the fleet in the harbour itself also exhibited a mock naval fight. The praetor and the deputies were then conducted round to view the armouries, the granaries, and other preparations for the war. And so great was the admiration excited in them of each particular, and of the whole together, that they firmly believed that under the conduct of that general, and with that army, the Carthaginians would be vanquished, or by none other.

Scipio's superb preparation and presentation saw the reviewing dignitaries 'return in the highest spirits, as though they were about to carry to Rome tidings of a victory, and not of a grand preparation for war.' With the politicians taken care of, Scipio was secure in his position and could refocus his efforts on the African campaign ahead.

Peers

Generals not only have to reassure politicians but are continually dealing with their peers, fellow generals (or those wanting to be appointed to the role) and the jealousies, undermining and backstabbing which can occur between commanders supposedly on the same side. Striving for opportunities, recognition and awards costs generals time, effort, and sometimes, particularly in the case of civil wars, their own lives and those of their soldiers. Even short of open hostilities or actual physical combat, competition among the top echelons can be fierce.

Generals are not immune to human emotions, their own or those evident around them. Overinflated egos, desire for recognition, promotion, and glory can be recognized in many great leaders. Alexander, Hannibal, Scipio Africanus and Julius Caesar were all known for their ambition and determination to succeed, and certainly ego was a very real factor in understanding any of them. Livy makes an observation on the human condition, recognizing the constant competition between men over 'land, money, and honours'. Amongst these great generals, the quest for honour and glory was significant and could be all consuming. Such ambitions could even extend beyond their immediate success – many of them longed for their achievements to be seen to have truly surpassed their peers, both living and dead. Consequently, despite the fate of armies, cities, even nations and empires being in their hands, petty jealousies, selfish ambitions and undermining of their peers were often a characteristic of these military commanders.

Crassus' defeat by the Parthians, a disaster described as putting the entire Roman Republic at risk, appears to have been a result of jealousy of his peer Julius Caesar and a desire to achieve his own warfighting success to match, if not outdo, Caesar's campaign in Gaul. In the case of Crassus' ambitions, the desperate attempt for personal glory cost him his own life, the life of his son, and some 20,000 Roman soldiers, killed or sold into slavery. Rather than the praise and recognition that he desired, history instead associates Crassus' name with stupidity, disaster, and humiliating defeat. For Rome, the costs of such vanity were also reflected in the numerous civil wars experienced during the nation's history. Florus reflects on the egos and the ambitions of generals when describing Julius Caesar and his rival Pompey:

> Caesar's power now inspired the envy of Pompeius, while Pompeius' eminence was offensive to Caesar; Pompeius could not brook an equal or Caesar a superior. Oh, the wickedness of it! They strove for the first place, as though the fortunes of a great empire could not find room for both of them.

Though successful, Caesar's own fate, murdered by peers in the Senate, was arguably the foreseeable outcome of the general's seemingly unending ambition and quest for power.

It is human nature for people to want to maximize credit and minimize blame attached to themselves in any situation. In warfare this is no less the case, and generals can be expected to maximise their credit for successful battles and campaigns as well as minimize any blame for battlefield losses. Tacitus' sage observation rings true across the ages – namely that in war everyone claims credit for a victory, but defeat is blamed on one person alone. This can be seen in the behaviour of Greek commanders following the naval victory over the Persians at the battle of Salamis (480 BC).

Following the division of spoils from the battle, the Greek admirals sailed to the temple of Poseidon, to award a prize for valour to the most deserving leader. Each commander was given two votes to cast, one for whom they judged the bravest and one for the second bravest. As every commander considered themselves the most courageous, they each put their own name first, while the majority gave their second vote to Themistocles. The result was that no admiral received more than one vote, but Themistocles was the clear winner of the vote for second. As a result of these leaders' high opinions of themselves and mutual jealousies, no decision was reached and the Greek commanders sailed away without an award being issued. As some justice, Herodotus notes that it was Themistocles' name that became famous and he was recognized as the most capable military leader in Greece at the time. Further, in recognition of his success, Themistocles was honoured by Sparta with numerous awards and, on departing the city, was given an escort of 300 Spartan horsemen who accompanied him all the way to the border, an honour previously unheard of. Not bad for an Athenian admiral!

For the Greeks in this instance, at least the problem of egos and competition became evident only once victory had been achieved. Other historical accounts capture the consequences of animosity and personal ambition measured in lives lost and battlefield disasters. During Hannibal's initial entry into Italy, Publius Cornelius Scipio (father of Scipio Africanus) and General Longus commanded two separate Roman armies opposing Hannibal's forces. As was the Roman practice for some time, command of co-located armies alternated each day between their respective generals. When Publius Scipio became ill, General Longus saw his opportunity for individual glory, to secure victory by his own hand before Scipio recovered. As Polybius argues, because the desire to engage Hannibal was based on Longus' ambitions, his judgement and subsequent actions would naturally be flawed.

Hannibal had gained intelligence on the two generals opposing him. He had been told that Publius Scipio was a mature and cautious leader, whereas

Longus was inexperienced and impetuous. This made Hannibal determined to provoke General Longus into battle. While Publius Scipio was ill and Longus held command of both armies, which were not co-located but separated by some distance between the two camps, Hannibal succeeded in goading the glory-seeking Longus into a fight. Longus launched his forces, piecemeal fashion and against Scipio's advice, in what would become the battle of Trebia river (218 BC). In the fight, Longus' forces suffered a serious defeat, handing Hannibal his first major victory on Italian soil. This is far from an isolated example, particularly in Roman history, with leaders' desire for individual success over their peers often resulting in actions which would have been comedic if they had not proved so tragic for soldiers, armies and nations.

Severe animosity between generals supposedly on the same side is not uncommon. Livy's account of the war between Rome and the Veientines in Italy demonstrates the commanders' open hatred for each other and the consequences. The author's description of Lucius Virginius and Manius Sergius showed how bitter rivalry between the military leaders resulted in the deaths of their own soldiers and battlefield defeat:

> For both the Roman commanders had more quarrels among themselves, than spirit against the enemy... [Virginius], when word was brought that most of the forts were attacked, the fortifications scaled, and that the enemy were pouring in on both sides, kept his men under arms, saying that if there was need of assistance, his colleague would send to him. His arrogance was equalled by the obstinacy of [Sergius]; who, that he might not appear to have sought any aid from an adversary, preferred being defeated by an enemy to conquering through a fellow-citizen. His men were for a long time cut down between both: at length, abandoning their works, a very small number made their way to the principal camp; the greater number, with Sergius himself, made their way to Rome. Where, when he threw the entire blame on his colleague, it was resolved that Virginius should be sent for from the camp, and that lieutenant generals should take the command in the meantime. The affair was then discussed in the Senate, and the dispute was carried on between the colleagues with (mutual) recriminations. But few took up the interests of the republic, (the greater number) favoured the one or the other, according as private regard or interest prejudiced each.

Petty rivalries and jealousies could lead to sound military advice being disregarded, risking even an empire itself. When Alexander crossed into Asia, senior Persian commanders met to consider options. With Darius not yet with his army and the Persians not having fully gathered their forces, they were facing the numerical superiority of the Macedonians. Persian commander Memnon recommended against an engagement but proposed immediately to destroy all crops, vegetation, and even towns in Alexander's path. The plan was a logical one – to deny the Macedonian leader the means to feed and supply his army and force his retreat without a fight. But the recommendation was entirely disregarded. Fellow commanders were suspicious of Memnon and attributed his plan to an attempt to secure his own position. Thus, on this occasion it appears that no action was taken to hinder the advance of the Macedonian army and Alexander was able to continue his march into Asia and lay the foundations for later victories over Darius and the Persian army.

Such petty jealousies extend to even the most successful of generals. Roman writer Cornelius Nepos, analysing the lives of prominent commanders, argues that Hannibal 'surpassed other commanders in ability …and, had not his efforts been paralysed by the envy of his countrymen at home, he would appear to have been capable of getting the mastery over the Romans. But the jealous opposition of many prevailed against the ability of one.'

Fabius versus Scipio: Italy or Africa

During the Second Punic War, when the Romans had started to get the better of Hannibal in Italy, Roman leaders began to debate over the best strategy to defeat Carthage. The question boiled down to whether Rome should continue focusing on destroying the Carthaginians in Italy or take the fight into Africa, to attack Carthage itself. These conflicting approaches reveal the intense personal rivalry between two great Roman generals, Fabius and Scipio. Fabius, so successful at blunting Hannibal's forces in Italy, argued, 'Let there be peace in Italy before war in Africa.' Scipio, who wanted to lead the overseas campaign, argued for taking the fight to Carthage, 'Let the Roman camp overhang the gates of Carthage rather than that we should again behold the rampart of the enemy from our walls.'

Ultimately, the Senate decided they would send forces into Africa with Scipio in command, but the argument between Fabius and Scipio had created a bitter atmosphere. During the discussions, Scipio openly admitted to comparing himself with Fabius, not only seeking to emulate the same glory and honours that Fabius had attained, but to exceed them. Even after his eventual success in Africa that led directly to Carthage's surrender and the end of the Second Punic War, Scipio was still verbally sparring with Fabius, comparing and contrasting their honours and awards. What is apparent is just how much attention even highly successful generals can still pay to each other's recognition and legacies. According to Polyaenus:

> Fabius having been honoured with the surname of Maximus, and Scipio only with that of Magnus, Scipio, with some degree of pique at the superior distinction of Fabius, asked him how it was; that he, who had only saved the Roman armies, should be surnamed Maximus, while himself, who in close action had engaged Hannibal, and beat him, should have no higher distinction than that of Magnus. Why, replied Fabius, if I had not preserved the men; you would have no soldiers, with whom to have fought and conquered him.

And this obsessive competitiveness could go even further, beyond generals comparing themselves to living contemporaries. As Scipio argues, 'I am confident, that it is usual with all the most exalted minds, to compare themselves, not only with the illustrious men of the present, but of every age.' The constant comparison with their peers, living and dead, reflected the driving ambition, ego and outlook of many great generals.

In a telling engagement, Livy recounts a meeting that reportedly occurred between Scipio and Hannibal years after the end of the Second Punic War. Scipio was in Ephesus and met with Hannibal (then exiled from Carthage). The discussion, not surprisingly, turned to generalship and generals. This conversation between two of the greatest commanders of the ancient world is worth including at length. Scipio began with a question to Hannibal as to whom the Carthaginian thought was the greatest general ever to have lived. Hannibal replied:

> 'Alexander, king of Macedonia; because, with a small band, he defeated armies whose numbers were beyond reckoning; and because he had overrun

> the remotest regions, the merely visiting of which was a thing above human aspiration.' Scipio then asked, 'to whom he gave the second place?' and he replied, 'To Pyrrhus; for he first taught the method of encamping; and besides, no one ever showed more exquisite judgment, in choosing his ground, and disposing his posts; while he also possessed the art of conciliating mankind to himself to such a degree, that the nations of Italy wished him, though a foreign prince, to hold the sovereignty among them, rather than the Roman people, who had so long possessed the dominion of that part of the world.' On his proceeding to ask, 'whom he esteemed the third?' Hannibal replied, 'Myself, beyond doubt.' On this Scipio laughed, and added, 'What would you have said if you had conquered me?'
>
> 'Then,' replied the other, 'I would have placed Hannibal, not only before Alexander and Pyrrhus, but before all other commanders.' This answer, turned with Punic dexterity, and conveying an unexpected kind of flattery, was highly grateful to Scipio, as it set him apart from the crowd of commanders, as one of incomparable eminence.

Scipio Africanus would have been pleased.

On being a leader of soldiers

The final aspect of this discussion is on the challenges that generals face in managing and leading their own soldiers. A general not only has to lead but also to convince their soldiers to fight, or refrain from fighting, in the face of fear, fatigue, stress, over-confidence, desire for plunder, homesickness, boredom, terror and all the vagaries of human emotions experienced over the course of a military campaign. Many generals (e.g. Alexander, Roman and Carthaginian generals) had the power and authority to put to death their soldiers for any number of reasons. Such great authority and options available to generals are well-known, an example being the Roman practice of decimation (killing every tenth soldier in a military unit following particularly disastrous and poor conduct of an army in battle), highlighting just how much power ancient military leaders had over the men under their command. Nevertheless, even with such options available, managing soldiers is often a challenge and a general is faced with the difficulty of dealing with this collective of humans upon whom their success (even their own life) depends, throughout the most stressful of situations.

Many of these generals were able to inspire their soldiers, achieve loyalty and obedience through shared hardships, to gain victories, and the subsequent spoils of war for the soldiers. However, early writers also capture the risk to generals who could not motivate their soldiers through personal example or victories on the battlefield. Sometime around 482–480 BC, a Roman army was raised to fight the Aequi under a General Fabius (not the later defender of Rome). This Fabius seemed to display strengths in the planning and conduct of war, but was detested by his soldiers.

On the day of battle against the Aequi forces, Fabius routed the enemy by means of his cavalry, but when ordering his infantry to pursue the fleeing enemy they refused. Incredibly, against orders, the infantry conducted an about face and returned to camp, venting angrily at the cavalry and yelling their disdain for their general. Fabius had no solutions and appeared to lack the basic ability to manage his own soldiers. Whatever the circumstances of the soldiers' contempt of their general (it is not quite clear to us), Fabius was evidently unable to change their attitude. Instead, according to Livy, Fabius 'returned to Rome, not having so much increased his military glory as irritated and exasperated the hatred of his soldiers towards him.'

The early literature is replete with warnings of the risks to commanders of soldiers being idle, whether in camp or on campaign. Preventing men from doing nothing might mean exposing them to danger, but was considered far better than letting them become bored, soft and lazy. As Onasander argues, a general's soldiers must be kept occupied to ensure they are always ready and willing to fight. Julius Caesar also took measures to ensure his army was active: 'Caesar, wishing to keep his soldiers from being spoiled by idleness, the great enemy of discipline, was making frequent expeditions in Illyricum and Dalmatia and thus hardening his army by endurance of danger and experience in warfare.' Mutinies among the ranks were a recognized danger and did occur. Bored soldiers on distant campaigns, or posted far from Rome, could present a direct threat to generals themselves. Soldiers frustrated with camp life, perhaps struggling to secure supplies and food, with time on their hands and weapons readily available, represented a real risk for commanders. Consequently, there have always been clear reasons for generals to ensure their soldiers remain engaged, active and subject to discipline.

At times, a general needs to convince their soldiers of the need to fight harder, to endure longer and to push through setbacks and difficulties. At other times, he may need to restrain such desire for action. Fabius' advice to one of his junior commanders, Lucius Paulus, highlighted the challenge and the potential outcomes of giving in to his soldiers' untimely desire to engage with Hannibal early in his Italian campaign. He told Lucius Paulus, 'For your own soldiers will desire the same thing as those of the enemy.' Fabius had experienced such challenges with his own troops in the face of Hannibal's successful slaughter of Roman armies. The difficulty was restraining his soldiers' enthusiasm for battle before they were ready and before they had the measure of the military genius of the African general. But it was no easy task:

> Fabius, keeping his attention fixed no less upon his own troops than on the enemy, first shows that his resolution was unconquered by the former. Though he well knew that his procrastination was disapproved, not only in his own camp, but by this time even at Rome …

Despite the enormous pressures Fabius faced, he was able to manage both the politicians and his own soldiers who were frustrated by supposed inaction and simply wanted to fight. The general understood what was at stake and by giving his soldiers time to build their skills and familiarity with a brilliant adversary, victory eventually came, albeit not in the timeframe that his soldiers (or the politicians) originally desired.

Not all generals prove so successful in restraining their men. During the Roman civil war (AD 69), at a particularly violent moment when multiple Roman leaders were contending for control of the Empire, desperate for men and armies to fight for them, some generals proved unable to control their own soldiers' desire for plunder or slaughter. Tacitus highlights how one general, Primus Antonius:

> courted the goodwill of his troops and used every word and every action to pave his way to power. He allowed his men to appoint centurions themselves in place of those who had fallen, and thus gave them a taste for insubordination; for their choice fell on the most turbulent spirits. The generals no longer commanded the men, but were dragged at the heels of their caprices.

Better generals understand that they are ultimately reliant on their soldiers as a fighting force and, when necessary, will proactively make decisions to avoid losing control. They can recognize when soldiers have reached their limits and take decisions accordingly. During the Roman campaign against Bato, in AD 6–9 (modern-day Balkans), Tiberius eventually 'saw that the soldiers were not for enduring further delay and were anxious to end the war in some way even if it involved danger; therefore, fearing that if they remained in one place together they might revolt, he divided them into three parts.' By splitting his force, Tiberius dealt with his soldiers' frustrations, sent them off into action against various opposing forces, and ultimately proved successful in the campaign. There comes a time when soldiers simply cannot handle any more delays and need to fight even if the circumstances are not as desired. At such moments, further delay risks the military commander losing their force altogether and actually ensuring a disaster.

When managing his army's escape from Persia, Xenophon faced numerous difficulties in maintaining the soldiers' morale in the face of their many fears and frustrations. On reaching the Black Sea, efforts at securing ships to transport the entire army were underway, but there were no guarantees and plenty of risks. Xenophon sought to take precautions in the event that enough vessels could not be procured, but his soldiers refused to even listen to other options. The general recognized the gravity of the situation and his solders' fraught emotions, so avoided putting the question to the vote, knowing they would react badly. Instead, Xenophon waited until, as anticipated, the Greeks found themselves unable to secure enough ships to transport their whole force. Once the soldiers saw the limited number of ships and understood the truth of the situation, they resolved themselves to keep going on foot to escape Persian-controlled territory. Xenophon had successfully managed his soldiers' emotional state and was able to continue the escape with an army now ready to deal with the reality of their circumstances.

Even Alexander the Great reached the limits of what his own soldiers would endure. It was not an enemy who brought an end to Alexander's campaign, but his own men. Alexander marched his army towards the Hyphasis river, determined to continue his war so long as any hostile force remained to be fought. On hearing stories of the warlike people beyond the Hyphasis, Alexander was excited to test himself and his army against new challenges and enemies. However, on seeing their general's seemingly insatiable desire for yet more conquests in the face of so many dangers, his Macedonian army became demoralized. Meetings were held in the camp at which even the most ardent soldiers complained of their situation, with others vowing that they would not go any further, even if it was Alexander leading the way.

Soon after, Alexander himself realized that he would be unable to convince his soldiers to advance any further into the unknown on a campaign which appeared to have no end. Recognizing they had reached their limit, Alexander turned his army around and commanded them to begin their return home. Alexander knew what all good generals understand; that a general is nothing without his armed force.

Chapter 13

What Makes a Poor General?

It was a serious performance to demand, and it was fraught with many risks. … But the only alternative was to do nothing and attempt nothing. That would have been the worst of bad generalship, and it was an occasion when risks must be taken.

General John Monash

A competent leader can get efficient service from poor troops, while on the contrary an incapable leader can demoralize the best of troops.

General John J. Pershing

Before considering what makes a good general, it is also worth deliberately reflecting upon what makes a poor one. As much as history gives an insight into good and great generals, it also provides witness to leaders on the other side of conflicts, those who are unsatisfactory and incompetent.

Overwhelmed by circumstances

Thucydides' account of the Peloponnesian War finished with events in 411 BC, the assumption being that he died before completing his work. The conflict went on until Athens surrendered in 404 BC, with Xenophon's account taking up where Thucydides' stopped, and covering the final seven years. The war proved to be no easy victory for the Spartans and their allies and there was much to tell on both sides before the end. In 410 BC, a Spartan fleet led by Admiral Mindarus had been defeated by the Athenian forces and left stranded far from home. The surviving Spartan vice-admiral, Hippocrates, dispatched a message back to Sparta which was captured by the enemy and sent to Athens. The few short words in the message present an image of a poor military commander. It read: 'Ships gone; Mindarus dead; the men starving; at our wits' end what to do.' Still, thousands of years later, we are seeing an admiral completely overwhelmed by circumstances, a leader entirely out of his depth. No plan, no solutions, no clue.

The issue is not so much about defeat; even good generals can be defeated. But the manner of the loss and the conduct of the commander before, during, and after it gives much insight into poor generals and poor generalship. Ancient writers are often highly critical of those who have proved inept in the role, using them as examples of the type of behaviour, thinking and actions to be avoided. These historic accounts show how an otherwise formidable fighting force could be undone by the general's flawed decision making and that incompetent leaders could destroy their own forces through their mediocre and uninspiring performance.

In 256 BC during the First Punic War, the Carthaginians found themselves on the receiving end of heavy losses at the hands of the Romans, once at sea (Cape Ecnomus), and once on land (battle of Adys). These battles were disastrous for the Carthaginians, and Polybius makes it abundantly clear where the blame lay – it was a direct result of the incompetence of their commanders. The failures were not due to the soldiers and sailors, but were entirely down to the Carthaginian generals and admirals.

Lack of accountability

Poor generalship often leads to defeat. It can also have a deleterious effect on the soldiers. At his trial over the loss of his army in Italy, Roman general Fulvius Flaccus was openly derided to his face when called before the Senate to explain how it was that his army had been destroyed by Hannibal at the first battle of Herdonia (212 BC) and how he, the senior commander, had managed to make it safely back to Rome. Livy records Senator Blaesus' scathing criticism of Fulvius:

> 'Many generals,' he reiterated, 'had by indiscretion and ignorance brought their armies into most perilous situations, but none, save Gnaeus Fulvius, had corrupted his legions by every species of excess before he betrayed them to the enemy; it might therefore with truth be said, that they were lost before they saw the enemy, and that they were defeated, not by Hannibal, but by their own general.'

Senator Blaesus was not finished and went on to highlight how Fulvius' conduct after the battle had brought even further disgrace to the general. The senator pointed out that other Roman generals who had led their armies to annihilation on the battlefield had 'preferred falling in the battle to abandoning their armies when in the power of the enemy. But Gnaeus Fulvius was almost the only man who returned to Rome to report the annihilation of his army.' Instead of accepting responsibility for the defeat, Fulvius disgracefully 'shifted the blame from himself to his soldiers' – *it wasn't me, it was them*. Here is another aspect of poor generalship; trying to avoid accountability and refusing to accept responsibility. Thousands of years after the event it is clear to see in Fulvius a general more interested in his own survival and a corresponding total disregard for the men he was appointed to lead and look after.

Military ignorance

There are clear examples of generals who were appointed to the position due to political connections, wealth or family status, who understood nothing of warfare. During the Roman civil war (AD 68), Vitellius successfully defeated a rival on the battlefield and had been proclaimed Emperor. Despite this initial success, Vitellius would last just eight months in the role before being defeated by another rival, Vespasian. Tacitus' critique of Vitellius is brutal but offers valuable details about what made him such a woeful general. Of General (then Emperor) Vitellius, Tacitus writes:

> He was ignorant of soldiering, incapable of forethought: knew nothing of drill or scouting, or how far operations should be pressed forward or protracted. He always had to ask some one else. At every fresh piece of news his expression and gait betrayed his alarm. And then he would get drunk. At last he found camp life too tedious, and on learning of a mutiny in the fleet at Misenum he returned to Rome. Every fresh blow terrified him, but of the real crisis he seemed insensible. For it was open to him to cross the Apennines and with his full strength unimpaired to attack the enemy while they were worn out with cold and hunger. But by breaking up his forces he sent his keenest soldiers, stubbornly loyal to the last, to be killed or taken prisoner. The more experienced of his centurions disapproved of

> this policy and would have told him the truth, if they had been consulted. But the emperor's intimates refused them admittance. He had, indeed, formed a habit of regarding wholesome advice as unpleasant, and refusing to listen to any that was not agreeable, and in the long run fatal.

Tacitus gives us an image of a general so hopeless as a military commander as to be deadly to his own soldiers and himself: an ignorance of military command and warfare, an inability to identify a winning strategy, a leader bored by life in the camp, a drunk, unable to mask his fear, wasting his best soldiers and refusing to accept sound advice. While many of Vitellius' soldiers remained loyal even to their deaths, not all soldiers respond to poor generals with such obedience or accommodation.

Hope-based judgement

For some military commanders, the result of their poor leadership is embarrassment and shame, rather than death for themselves or their army. Soldiers have proved willing to abandon leaders who show themselves inept in basing plans and actions solely on hope. Plutarch writes of the Spartan commander Sphodrias, courageous in battle but lacking sound judgement. Desiring personal glory, Sphodrias determined on his own initiative to surprise the Athenians and seize the port of Piraeus, to deprive the city of access to the sea. The plan was to conduct a night attack and take the Athenians unprepared. But in the execution of the plan Sphodrias failed, and badly. Instead of moving his forces into position at night he was instead caught on the open plain outside the town when daylight arrived. As the Athenian town came to life, his soldiers abandoned him, seeing all too clearly the futility of the attempted 'surprise' attack. Deserted by his men, Sphodrias entirely lost his nerve and withdrew to Thespiae.

Poor decision making

It is worth making a further distinction. Sometimes poor generalship can come from previously successful generals making wrong decisions. At times even successful commanders simply make mistakes or errors of judgement, a point worth emphasizing as previously good generals may take rash actions or fail to *continue* making sound military decisions.

Quintus Metellus Scipio (father-in-law of Pompey) achieved an initial victory against Julius Caesar's forces when Caesar was attacking Scipio's camp in North Africa. However, he and his allies failed to carry through their success, allowing Caesar to regroup. Appian makes clear it was the poor generalship of Caesar's opponents – who should have simply worn him down with delays, allowing him to exhaust his supplies, given that he was in hostile territory – that led to their defeat. Instead, they chose to go into battle against an almost full-strength opposing force under Caesar's command at the Thapsus (46 BC). The final result was defeat for Scipio and victory for Caesar. Scipio's poor decision gives an example of how victors can rapidly become the vanquished. Despite the modern-day bravado of slogans like 'failure is not an option', in warfare failure is always a possibility, regardless of previous success. To ignore this reality and fail to take it into account is poor generalship.

Scipio Africanus was from a military family, the son and nephew respectively of two successful military generals in their own right. His father and uncle had both fought the Carthaginians in Spain during the early part of the Second Punic War. Despite previous victories, poor decision-making by Scipio's father, Publius Cornelius Scipio, had led to the battlefield death of himself and Scipio's uncle, Gnaeus Cornelius Scipio, as well as the devastation of the two Roman armies that they led. General Publius Scipio had made hurried decisions under the pressure of circumstances and his determination to attack a Carthaginian ally, the Iberian military leader Indibilis. Thus, 'Scipio, though a wary and provident general, overpowered by difficulties, adopted the rash measure of going to meet Indibilis by night, with the intention of fighting him wherever he should meet him.' In attempting to force an engagement with Indibilis before the Spanish leader's Carthaginian allies could support him, the Roman abandoned his usual considered and sound approach to generalship, instead taking unnecessary and ultimately disastrous risks.

Publius Scipio initially succeeded in surprising Indibilis and his army but could not deliver a decisive blow, and the Iberian chief's forces were able to hang on until reinforced by Hasdrubal Gisco and Mago's Carthaginian armies.

The combining of the Iberian and Carthaginian armies into one massive force turned the battle against the Romans and Publius and much of his army were slaughtered. Hasdrubal and Mago then joined with Hasdrubal Barca's army, operating against Gnaeus Cornelius Scipio. Gnaeus and his Roman army found themselves pursued by three Carthaginian armies and were eventually destroyed despite the Roman general's efforts to evade the enemy. These dual engagements were known as the battle of the Upper Baetis (211 BC) and resulted in the death of two renowned Roman generals and much of their armies. The Roman commander's rushed decision-making and eagerness led to unfavourable battles against three great Carthaginian generals.

Making life easy for the enemy

Another aspect of poor generalship is allowing the enemy to maintain freedom of movement, unimpeded and unchallenged. Instead of putting them in a difficult position, or presenting them with dilemmas and only bad options, poor generals allow an enemy to determine the pace and nature of engagements themselves. Recall Vegetius' observation that 'what is beneficial to you is detrimental to your enemy and what is of service to him always hurts you.' Poor generals fail to act on such sound guidance.

When the Sabines began attacking and besieging Roman territories early in the nation's history, two Roman armies were formed and deployed to counter the threat. One, led by General Nautius, immediately took the fight to the Sabines, devastating their territories during a series of nightly attacks, successfully using small forces to create mayhem for the enemy in their own lands. The second Roman army was led by General Minucius who, in clear contrast:

> had neither the same success nor the same energy of mind in conducting his business; for after he had pitched his camp at no great distance from the enemy, without having experienced any considerable loss, he kept himself through fear within the camp. When the enemy perceived this, their boldness increased, as sometimes happens from others' fears; and having attacked his camp by night, when open force did not succeed well, they on the following day drew lines of circumvallation around it.

Even then Minucius' response was not to fight, nor even to pressure the Sabine forces still working to form a protective ring around his camp, but instead to send five horsemen through a gap in the enemy lines to inform Rome that his army was besieged. As Livy notes, on the news reaching Rome, 'Nothing could have happened so unexpected, nor so unlooked-for.' The army sent to counter the enemy had instead been surrounded by them.

General Varus – the Eagles have fallen

The destruction of an entire Roman army, almost down to every soldier, in the German forest of Teutoburg in AD 9 is recognized as one of the greatest military disasters Rome ever suffered. Numerous Roman authors reflect on the failings of General Varus Quintilius, upon whose shoulders the disaster firmly rested. Paterculus (himself a Roman army officer and author) notes that Varus 'lost his life and his magnificent army more through lack of judgement in the commander than of valour in his soldiers.' Other commentators agreed and provide a rich description of the failings of this general prior to and during the battle. Consequently, Varus' generalship performance in Germany and with his Roman legions is worth analysing, drawing upon the multiple accounts of the disaster by Paterculus, Suetonius, Florus, and Cassius Dio. Varus demonstrates multiple failures of leadership and offers an example of how such individual failings could be compounded, resulting in annihilation on the battlefield. Both his decisions and actions give a comprehensive answer to the question, 'What makes a poor general?'

Argued by Paterculus to have been 'a man of character and of good intentions', Varus nevertheless oversaw the destruction of three legions, three divisions of cavalry and six cohorts, perhaps some 15,000 soldiers in all. Varus had enriched himself as governor of Syria and when placed in charge of the Roman army in Germany as consul he appears to have had a similar intention to increase his personal wealth. But Germany was not Syria. Varus' first mistake was his lack of understanding of the German peoples he governed. As Florus observed, 'the Germans had been defeated rather than subdued,' they were a governed but not a *conquered* people. Yet Varus made judgements and decisions as if he could keep them under control solely by his position and proclamations.

On the same lines, Paterculus makes the observation that Varus 'entered the heart of Germany as though he was going among a people enjoying the blessings of peace' and, instead of a summer campaign to ensure that locals did not rise up, spent his time issuing and overseeing laws and legal procedures. The Roman general was making rapid changes to German society, issuing orders as if they were mere slaves and extracting money from them. Initially at least, the Germans appeared to abide by Varus' judgements and approach, but this was merely a pretence. They brought him fictitious lawsuits, setting up disputes amongst each other, and praising Roman justice. Their apparent compliance brought Varus 'to such a complete degree of negligence, that he came to look upon himself as a city praetor administering justice in the forum, and not a general in command of an army in the heart of Germany.'

Varus' lack of understanding of the Germans was matched by his lack of appreciation of his and his army's position and circumstances – he was a foreign leader of a foreign force, ruling over a warlike people, far from the security of Rome and surrounded by angry, capable and numerous adversaries. It was in these circumstances that the Germans began taking up their weapons again, in secret, under the leadership of Arminius. A plan was developed to lure Varus and his army into territory well-known to the German tribes, and unfamiliar to the Romans. Varus was actually informed of the plot by one of the German chiefs, but was so confident of peace that he disregarded the warning. Indeed, possibly because he frequently met and dined with two of the principal leaders of the planned revolt, Arminius and Segimerus, Varus refused to believe the warnings to be on his guard. Instead, the Roman general rebuked those giving him such advice, saying they were slandering men he considered his friends. At the same time, German communities had been requesting soldiers be sent to outlying villages, supposedly to assist with keeping law and order but in reality to disperse and divide the Roman forces into smaller and more vulnerable units. Varus complied with these requests and instead of keeping his legions together allowed groups of soldiers to be distributed around the German territories.

Word was now deliberately spread of an uprising far away from the Rhine and the Roman stronghold, intended to ensure that Varus would take his legions out into unfamiliar and hostile territory, which he did. He gathered his forces and began marching through what he believed to be regions friendly to Rome. German chieftains excused themselves from his presence, pretending they were going to rally their troops to come to his aid. Instead, they took charge of their readied forces, put to death the isolated bands of Roman soldiers they had previously asked for, and then headed towards Varus and his army, who were now attempting to make their way through the Teutoburg Forest.

The terrain had been well selected for the battle, with mountains and thick forests and marshes. The Roman legions struggled to make their way through the forest with their soldiers, wagons, a number of women, children and servants, as well as beasts of burden. Rather than a cohesive fighting force, Varus' army was advancing through the forests in a spread-out line and scattered groups. Violent rain and winds further separated the already dispersed forces. The ground became slippery, roots and logs slowed them down, with falling branches coming down in the storm adding to the chaos. The Romans were unprepared for the conditions, unfamiliar with the territory, and grappling just to manoeuvre their widely dispersed army. At the same time, having moved up through the dense thickets unseen, along paths they were familiar with, the Germans had silently surrounded the disorganized Roman forces. It was then that the Germans struck.

In the initial attack the Germans launched volleys from a distance, but then, with the Romans unable to offer any self-defence, the attackers closed in. Varus' legions had not been proceeding in military order 'but going along helter-skelter among the wagons and the unarmed, and so, not being able to form readily in a body, and being fewer at every point than their assailants, they suffered greatly and offered no resistance at all.' Varus does not appear to have reconnoitred the area, compounding his lack of knowledge of the terrain and conditions, and, crucially, he had no idea of the location (even the existence) of the enemy. The Roman general had, entirely unbeknown to him, placed his army in the middle of a battlefield that the Germans had selected for him. And he remained unaware until the moment of attack, by which time the fate of the Roman general and his army had already been determined.

The Germans had chosen a logical place to attack, deliberately designed to minimize the Romans' ability to mass and coordinate their military strength, and where they held the advantage. The Germans brought the battle to their enemy at the very worst location and time for Varus and his army, thanks to their leader's clever planning, forethought and military genius. Arminius and the combined German forces achieved the ambush brilliantly, assisted in large part by Varus' very poor generalship. But the initial attack was just the beginning of the disaster. Over a four-day period, the Romans were continually harassed and attacked; their numbers ever diminishing as they tried to advance through the forest. They struggled to form up their lines to engage the Germans, hampered by the dense forest and narrow spaces. In their efforts to attack the enemy, the Roman infantry and cavalry found themselves constantly colliding with the trees and with each other. The Romans' tactics were ill-suited to the situation they found themselves in, and they proved unable to adapt. A comparison between their equipment and that of the Germans is informative. The continued bad weather hampered the Roman soldiers with their heavy armaments, the violent winds and heavy downpours 'would not allow them to go forward or even to stand securely, and actually deprived them of the use of their weapons. They could not manage successfully their arrows or their javelins or, indeed, their [wood and leather] shields (which were soaked through).' In contrast, the Germans were adapted to the conditions, enjoying much more freedom of movement, 'being for the most part lightly equipped and with power to approach and retire freely, [they] suffered less from the effects of the storm.' Then came the final blow.

As news of the German successes spread and it became clear just how incapable the Romans were at fighting back, German tribes who had been wavering in their support now poured into the fight. The rapidly diminishing number of Roman troops were overwhelmed by the growing numbers of the enemy. Recognizing the unfolding disaster, Varus and other senior officers, already wounded from the fighting and fearing capture, took their own lives. Given the situation Varus had led his army into, Paterculus scornfully remarks, 'The general had more courage to die than to fight.' His final act proved disastrous for the morale of those Romans who had survived to that point. When news of Varus' death by his own hand became known to the remaining soldiers, most appear to have simply given up. Realizing the hopelessness of the situation in their general's decision, the soldiers entirely lost their fighting spirit:

> When this news was spread, none of the rest, even if he had strength still left, defended himself longer. Some imitated their leader; others, throwing aside their arms, allowed who pleased to slay them. To flee was impossible, however one might wish it. Every man and horse, therefore, was cut down without resistance…

This was, however, not quite the end for the few survivors. The carnage that followed was horrendous. As Paterculus notes, the Germans – whom the Romans 'had always slaughtered like cattle, whose life or death had depended solely upon the wrath or the pity of the Romans' – were in no mood to show any pity for the defeated soldiers. According to Florus, 'Never was there slaughter more cruel than took place there in the marshes and woods.' Florus writes that some of the surviving leaders had their eyes removed, others their hands cut off, while they sewed up the mouth of one and shouted insults at him. Varus' body, which had been buried by his soldiers, was dug up and desecrated, his head cut off and sent back to Rome. Tacitus describes the scene when, some six years after the battle, Roman general Germanicus and his army arrived at the site. What they found was the stuff of nightmares: soldiers' heads nailed to trees, bones heaped up into piles, and indications of the human sacrifice of survivors.

In terms of the psychological aspect of the victory, the Germans captured two of the three legions' eagles, military standards which held enormous significance for the Roman military and society. At the time he was writing, Florus confirmed that the Germans still possessed the eagles; an enduring mark of shame for Rome. Varus' defeat and the annihilation of his legions had been an absolute disaster for the Romans and their belief in their military superiority. 'The result of this disaster', writes Florus, 'was that the empire, which had not stopped on the shores of the Ocean, was checked on the banks of the Rhine.'

On hearing news of the destruction of the Roman army, Emperor Augustus (Octavian) is said to have shouted furiously, 'Varus, give me back my legions!' Augustus was terrified that the Germans and Gauls would march into Italy and against Rome itself. Because of this fear, Germans and Gauls living in Rome were all sent away, even those who were members of the Pretorian Guard (protecting Augustus himself). Quickly attempting to raise an army to counter a possible invasion, Rome forcibly conscripted one in every five men under the age of 35, and one in every ten over that age. Only after some time, when it became clear that the German forces were not advancing to the Rhine, did Augustus' alarm recede.

In the immediate aftermath, mutual fears kept the opposing forces on either side of the Rhine. But the military disaster and General Varus' failings remained at the forefront of Roman thoughts. Varus' inadequate generalship had been exposed by a clever, well-led and motivated enemy under Arminius, and the Roman's poor decision-making had led to an entire army being slaughtered. And not just any army. The Roman force in Germany was described as one 'unexcelled in bravery, the first of Roman armies in discipline, in energy, and in experience in the field.' General Varus had presided over the annihilation of Rome's premier fighting force, and he had only himself to blame.

Chapter 14

What Makes a Good General?

I used to say of Napoleon that his presence on the field made the difference of forty thousand men.

Duke of Wellington

The directing mind [of the general] must be at the very head of the army – must be seen there, and the effect of his mind and personal energy must be felt by every officer and man present with it, to secure the best results.

General William T. Sherman

The entirety of this book has been focused on the fundamental role of the general in warfare. The enduring questions of war examined in these chapters are ultimately the responsibility of generals to address. Where generals' planning, decisions and actions result in solid answers to these questions before, during and after battle, it is fair to conclude that they have exhibited good generalship. The judgements generals make and the actions they take are consequential; they can mean victory or defeat, life or death. The brutalities, complexities and human emotions that feature in war make the general's position a crucial one in the conduct of a war and the outcome on the battlefield. Returning to the quote at the start of this book:

> Iphicrates used to [compare] an army marshalled for action to the human body. The phalanx he called the breast, the light-armed troops the hands, the cavalry the feet, and the general the head. If any of the inferior parts were wanting, the army he said was defective; but if it wanted a general it wanted everything.

In both ancient and modern times, finding a general to lead an armed force is usually not difficult; there are in most cases numerous people eager and willing to take up the senior position. Finding a *good* general, however, can be difficult and might mean the difference between victory or defeat, survival or destruction. Therefore, it is worth deliberately addressing the question 'What makes a good general?'

A master of generalship

An initial response to what makes a good general will reflect a combination of various individual characteristics, decisions and actions. Just as Varus' weaknesses, poor thinking, poor tactics, and lack of situational understanding, were all combined and compounded to a disastrous end, a good general will bring together wide knowledge, considered decisions and timely actions in order to maximize their chances of success. Fortunately, early authors provide detailed analysis of these factors when examining the lives of generals recognized for their greatness, measured by their successes on the battlefield. Livy and Plutarch each offer a study of the Greek general Philopoemen, acclaimed by both Greeks and Romans for his excellent generalship. What comes through in Livy's description is a thinking commander, constantly evaluating, planning and selecting appropriate actions, a lifetime invested in understanding warfare:

> Philopoemen was possessed of an admirable degree of skill and experience, in conducting a march, and choosing his station; having made these points his principal study, not only in times of war, but likewise during peace. Whenever he was making a journey to any place and came to a defile where the passage was difficult, it was his practice, first, to examine the nature of the ground on every side. When journeying alone, he meditated within himself; if he had company, he asked them, 'If an enemy should appear in that place, what course ought he to adopt, if they should attack him in front; what, if on this flank, or on that; what, if on the rear; for he might happen to meet them while his men were formed with a regular front, or when they were in the loose order of march, fit only for the road.' He would proceed to examine, either in his own mind, or by asking questions, 'What ground he himself would choose; what number of soldiers, or what kind of arms (which was a very material point) he ought to employ; where he should deposit the baggage, where the soldiers' necessaries, where the unarmed multitude; with what number and what kind of troops he should guard them, and whether it would be better to prosecute his march as intended, or to return back by

> the way he came; what spot, also, he should choose for his camp; how large a space he should enclose within the lines; where he could be conveniently supplied with water; where a sufficiency of forage and wood could be had; which would be his safest road on decamping next day, and in what form the army should march?' In such studies and inquiries, he had, from his early years, so frequently exercised his thoughts, that, on anything of the kind occurring, no expedient that could be devised was new to him.

Here was a general proactively thinking on all matters of warfare, engaging his mind constantly, questioning others, and testing his own thinking. And this was thinking towards a practical end – the conduct of war. Plutarch observes that Philopoemen's successes throughout his numerous battles are evidence of a skilful general, not just one favoured by fortune. He defeated the most warlike of the Greeks, the Cretans and the Spartans by strategy and bravery, and he developed new tactics and trained up his soldiers to achieve his victories – Philopoemen's 'leadership made good soldiers'. Philopoemen is the very model of a master ancient general.

Takes control

The willingness of a general to take control of their soldiery and shape them into an effective fighting force, rather than simply accepting whatever standard of personnel they are given, speaks volumes. To restate Florus' observation, 'It is a true proverb which says that a general has the army he deserves.' Generals such as Philopoemen proactively developed the soldiers they had into the type of armies that they wanted, armies formidable to their enemies.

Athenian general Iphicrates similarly innovated and improved his armies, their tactics and their weapons, to create the most effective fighting force possible with the resources available to him. As Cornelius Nepos argues, Iphicrates 'was much engaged in the field; he often had the command of armies; he never miscarried in an undertaking by his own fault; he was always eminent for invention, and such was his excellence in it, that he not only introduced much that was new into the military art, but made many improvements in what existed before.' We read how Iphicrates got the army he wanted by taking control and by getting the individual soldiers to operate as a cohesive fighting force, capable and confident in the use of their new weapons and new tactics through training and discipline. A good general takes the responsibility to build their armed forces into the most formidable band of warriors, able to succeed on any battlefield that they face.

Have an eye to everything

Such readiness, training and preparation only occurs through deliberate and dedicated effort and care at all levels. A good general pays close attention to every aspect of preparing for war, just as much as the conduct of the fighting when conflict has begun. A general and their armed forces are ready because of the deliberate investment of time and effort, without short cuts or half measures. Cornelius Nepos offers the maxim that 'nothing should be despised in war' – if it matters, then the general should be across it, before, during and after the fight. As Xenophon shows, it is not enough for a general to give orders, they need to ensure that the orders have been followed. In preparation for launching an attack, Xenophon issued orders to the army's different elements – to the heavy infantry, light infantry and peltasts – on weapons readiness and resupplies. He then sent out trusted aides to ensure that his orders had actually been followed. This is the action of a general with a sound understanding of human nature, who knew that these things needed to be checked, and knew whom to trust to ensure that they had been successfully carried out.

Alexander the Great gives an example of a general who paid close attention to his soldiers. In his preparations for conquering the island city of Tyre, Alexander was always on the scene, encouraging his soldiers and ensuring the standard of work he desired. Arrian describes a commander who was present, observant, willing to act, and who openly recognized and rewarded hard-working individual soldiers. Good generals get the behaviour they want by publicly rewarding effective performance and punishing poor performance. Such rewards and punishments establish the standards to be achieved, ensuring that both officers and troops clearly understand the required behaviour on and off the battlefield.

During the siege of an enemy Thracian fort, Roman general Sabinus ensured that during the nighttime pause in the fighting his soldiers did not lose nerve or focus. He understood the impact of the conditions, the efforts of the enemy and the uncertainty of his own soldiers. As night closed in and a storm approached, the Thracian soldiers were attempting to unnerve the Romans with loud shouts and yelling followed by periods of absolute silence. Sabinus went through his army's lines, encouraging the soldiers not to be fooled by the enemy's efforts and to avoid giving their besieged enemy any opportunities. He made it clear that each man was to stay focused and ready and should not waste their javelins by throwing them at noises in the dark when they were unable to see the enemy. Sabinus checked everything with his own eyes, was physically present, and addressed his soldiers directly. He calmed the soldiers, ensured that they did not waste weapons, emphasized their required jobs, and took all necessary steps to guarantee that they maintained pressure on their trapped adversary.

Reflecting on General Catiline's efforts when he was facing a tough fight and his final battle, Sallust provides insight into the importance of the general's focus, awareness and conduct during battle, 'Catiline, during this time, was exerting himself with his light troops in the front, sustaining such as were pressed, substituting fresh men for the wounded, attending to every exigency, charging in person, wounding many an enemy, and performing at once the duties of a valiant soldier and a skilful general.' Sallust describes Catiline as having 'an eye to everything' during the fighting. Theough he was killed in the battle, his personal conduct was singled out for specific praise and allows further insight into good generalship.

To truly have 'an eye to everything' a general needed to place themselves in the right position to understand what was happening and have the ability to influence it. Roman military officer and author Marcellinus provides advice for military commanders on the leader being both visible and taking action:

> And if it should be necessary to engage with the enemy in battle, ...take thy place steadily among the standard-bearers themselves, as a prudent encourager of daring at the proper opportunity; exciting the warriors by leading them on with caution, supporting any troops which may be thrown into disorder

> by reserves, gently reproving those who hang back, and being present as a trustworthy witness of the actions of all, whether brave or timid.

Scipio, before his successes in Africa, was already displaying such leadership qualities, being cautious but physically present, able to make quick decisions and speak directly to his soldiers. During the siege of New Carthage in Spain:

> Scipio took part in the battle, but [considered] his safety as far as possible; for he had with him three men carrying large shields, who holding these close covered the surface exposed to the wall and thus afforded him protection. So that passing along the side of his line on higher ground he contributed greatly to the success of the day; for he could both see what was going on and being seen by all his men he inspired the combatants with great spirit. The consequence was that nothing was omitted which was necessary in the engagement, but the moment that circumstances suggested any step to him he set to work at once to do what was necessary.

A good general is physically present, with almost literally 'an eye to everything', making the right decisions at the right time in order to achieve victory.

Leading by example

Good military commanders inspire their soldiers to fight, to keep pressing the enemy, to lift their efforts and performance. Orders alone are usually not enough. As has been shown, an untrusted general could be entirely ignored by his soldiers. But good generals win trust and confidence by their actions and presence, motivating their men with the will to fight and maintain their formation and focus even in the face of setbacks, exhaustion, the fear of death and the horrors of the battlefield. A general who would fight and conquer, or die fighting alongside them, was a general whom the soldiers would follow. Threats such as decimation could only go so far; instilling fear has its limits, particularly in the face of other fears such as those presented by a formidable enemy. Instead, a general visible on the battlefield and in the fight was a general that soldiers respected and wanted to fight for.

The personal examples given by great leaders like Alexander and Caesar were a powerful motivation and inspiration to their soldiers. These generals were able to rally their armies and instil the will to fight because they took to the battlefield alongside their men. Sharing the dangers with the soldiers was a risk, but more important was the impact it had on the troops and the ability to rapidly influence the battle through on-the-spot decisions and actions.

The importance for a general of being seen in the fight and leading by example clearly mattered. Florus credits the gladiator Spartacus, who led a famous slave revolt in Italy, with fighting as a military commander should during his final battle when he was at last defeated by Roman forces (71 BC). He notes that, 'Spartacus himself fell, as became a general, fighting most bravely in the front rank.' Despite the fear and hatred that Spartacus had generated amongst the Roman populace, Florus recognized the personal bravery and example of this gladiator-turned-general.

At the battle of Pharsalus against Pompey (48 BC), Caesar is described as running frantically amongst his soldiers, pleading with them to make a further effort to take Pompey's fortifications. Caesar knew that the entire campaign could be finished that day and rallied his soldiers by being amongst them, fighting with them and urging them on. And it worked. Caesar's army finished the campaign against Pompey that very day. Plutarch makes it clear that this was no one-off for Caesar, citing earlier battles, he observes:

> And if Caesar himself and Asinius Pollio had not come out of the camp to help the men, and checked the pursuit, the war would have been at an end. In another battle, also, the enemy had the advantage in the encounter, on which occasion it is said that Cæsar, seizing by the neck the man who bore the eagle and was running away, turned him round, and said, 'There is the enemy!'

Caesar was willing to be in the thick of the fight when needed and demonstrate to his soldiers that they would all fight or die as one. As Suetonius notes, if a battle was in doubt, Julius Caesar would send away the horses, his own first, to make it clear that he and his soldiers would have to stand their ground and fight – fleeing was not an option. For a general to be in the midst of the fighting was dangerous, and that was precisely the point. Leadership by example is a crucial aspect of good generalship.

Alexander the Great's willingness to fight and lead by example in battle is also legendary. His readiness to share the dangers and hardships of fighting and campaigning across the most difficult terrains and conditions helped him to build an army of soldiers who respected him and followed him into lands unknown. Such personal courage and leadership was also critical beyond the battlefield. Rufus gives a picture of Alexander's efforts in the small things that helped him win the approval and respect of his soldiers. Alexander exercised alongside his men, his clothing and appearance was similar to theirs, and he displayed the same energy they did. Once, when the army was in the desert and very short of water, a party sent to find a source had located little more than a trickle which they poured into a helmet and brought to Alexander. Rather than drink it, in full view of all Alexander tipped the water into the sands – he would share his soldiers' thirst. According to Arrian, the effect of this gesture was equivalent to the general having given every soldier a drink. Arrian says, 'This deed beyond all others I commend as evidence of Alexander's power of endurance and self-control, as well as of his skill in managing an army.'

Alexander was not alone in his willingness to share the circumstances of his soldiers and lead by example. Of Roman general Marcus Valerius, Livy notes, 'Never was a general on a more familiar footing with his soldiers, by his performing all the duties among the lowest of the soldiers without reluctance.' A leader willing and able to carry out the tasks of the ordinary soldiers, to do the work that they expected others to do, clearly has an impact on the people they lead. And such behaviour is noticed by all junior to the general. Xenophon highlights the fact that soldiers look to their commanders to set the example to follow and why these leaders' behaviour and actions were so disproportionally important:

> The soldiers outside have their eyes fixed upon you; if they think that you are faint-hearted, they will turn cowards; but if you show them that you are making your own preparations to attack the enemy, and setting an example to the rest – follow you, be assured, they will: imitate you they will.

Soldiers watch their general closely and make their judgements accordingly. A good general earns the respect of their subordinates by their personal example, both on and off the battlefield.

Thinking like a general

Personal example and physical conduct matter but so does the distinction between a general and a soldier. Yes, a general needs to lead by example but their *thinking* must be different and a good soldier does not automatically make a good general. The case of Marcus Centenius provides an example of what happens when these differences were ignored. Centenius was distinguished amongst the centurions for his physical size and courage, and Publius Cornellius Sulla convinced the Roman Senate to make him a general. Sulla argued that given Centenius' experience as a soldier fighting against Hannibal's forces, he was acquainted with the enemy and could outwit Hannibal in the field. The argument 'was not promised more foolishly than it was believed; as if the qualifications of a soldier and a general were the same.'

The Senate agreed and with an army of some 8,000 men Centenius marched through Italy towards Hannibal, nearly doubling his initial force through volunteers joining the newly appointed general. Livy notes the predictable outcome of the battle between a general and his experienced army and a centurion with an inexperienced force – Hannibal chalked up another battlefield victory and the Romans another defeat. Centenius did not know enough to realize his impending doom, and that of his army.

The contrast between the role of a soldier and that of a general is captured by Tacitus in the words of Roman general Marcus Antonius Primus. Primus' soldiers were eager to attack the city of Cremona without a plan or adequate preparation. In response, Antonius gave his soldiers a well-reasoned explanation on why rushing into an attack on the city was a bad idea. In doing so, he provided a detailed insight into how a general and a soldier think differently and the crucial role the general plays:

> He assured them that he had no wish to rob them of the glory and the reward they so well deserved. 'But,' he said, 'an army and a general have different functions. It is right that soldiers should be greedy for battle, but the general often does more good not by [rashness] but by foresight, deliberation and delay. I have done all I could to aid your victory with my sword: now I will serve you by the general's proper arts of calculation and strategy.

Tacitus walks us through a general's thinking, as Antonius talks to his soldiers about his understanding of the situation and what it meant. The discussion is worth including at length as it provides a rare insight into an ancient general's mindset, expressed in his own words as he engages with those under his command:

> 'The risks that face us are obvious. It is night; we know nothing of the lie of the city; the enemy are behind the walls; everything favours an ambush. Even if the gates were open, we cannot safely enter except by day and after due reconnoitring. Are you going to begin storming the town when you cannot possibly see where the ground is level and how high the walls are? How do you know whether to assault it with engines and showers of missiles, or with [protective shields] and shelters?' Then he turned to individuals, asking one after another whether they had brought hatchets and pick-axes and other implements for storming a town. When they answered no, 'Well,' he said, 'could any troops possibly break through walls or undermine them with nothing but swords and javelins? Suppose it proves necessary to construct a mound and to shelter ourselves with mantlets and fascines, are we going to stand idle like a lot of helpless idiots, gaping at the height of the enemy's towers and ramparts? Why not rather wait one night till our siege-train arrives and then carry the victory by force?'

This interesting account provides a great insight into how a good general thinks. The calculation, the strategy, the willingness to deal in considered facts rather than unfounded hopes all increase the chances of success and minimize the risk of failure. From the *Mytilenian Debate* described by Thucydides, we are told that wisdom and good decisions are more formidable to an enemy than unconsidered brute force. A thinking general presents a difficult challenge for any adversary. Livy emphasizes this point when reflecting on the early successes of Rome, noting 'that the Roman commonwealth was more powerful by reason of its generals than its army.'

Acting cautiously

The importance of caution on the part of military commanders was a consistent theme of ancient discussions on good generalship. Emperor

Augustus detested haste and recklessness in his generals, instead he argued for cautious commanders rather than bold ones, that what is done well is done quickly enough, and to 'be active but not rash' (*festina lente*). Further, Augustus said that a war or battle should not be undertaken unless the benefits outweighed the risks, likening those who sought small gains at great risk to those who went fishing with a golden hook – nothing they caught could ever compensate for its loss. In the years after Varus' defeat by the German tribes, Roman general Tiberius successfully campaigned in Germany, giving an example of a considered and cautious commander. Velleius Paterculus offers the following praise of Tiberius' generalship:

> Nothing in the course of this great war, nothing in the campaigns in Germany, came under my observation that was greater, or that aroused my admiration more, than these traits of its general; no chance of winning a victory ever seemed to him timely, which he would have to purchase by the sacrifice of his soldiers; the safest course was always regarded by him as the best; he consulted his conscience first and then his reputation, and, finally, the plans of the commander were never governed by the opinion of the army, but rather the army by the wisdom of its leader.

Here was a cautious general who proved successful because of his analysis and considered actions.

This caution and watchfulness is applicable to enforcing camp discipline, fortifying positions, reconnoitring the surroundings, understanding both one's own soldiers and those of the enemy. It is not timidity but carefulness, avoiding over-confidence and minimizing assumptions – aiming to keep a general's own armed forces secure and bring the greatest calamities on the enemy. An armed force can be destroyed by a poor general, but in the hands of a general who considers his options it takes on a disproportionate strength. Additionally, a general who is willing to learn and adapt can prove formidable to enemies. The willingness to change one's mind in light of mistakes – one's own, or better still, the mistakes of others – is another indication of a good general.

Returning to the example of Tiberius' efforts in Germany not long after Varus' slaughter, we find evidence of a general willing to learn and adapt to avoid repeating the mistakes of a fellow general. Suetonius provides a description of this shrewd leader, who took the time to learn from Varus' mistakes and change his own behaviours and actions as a result, becoming far more deliberate and cautious than he had previously been. Finding that Varus had acted carelessly and neglected basic precautions against being surprised, Tiberius deliberately sought counsel and discussions with his commanders before taking major actions. He checked every detail, actively avoided opportunities for his enemy to surprise or ambush him and took time to clarify any ambiguity in his directions to his officers. General Tiberius changed his own behaviour in response to the failures of a peer. His willingness to reflect and adapt in this way ensured his own campaign was successful, avoiding the disasters of Varus and presenting his German enemies with a far more difficult opponent – one whom they proved unable to defeat.

Taking bold action

A general will always face risks whenever they engage in battles, which can unfold in unanticipated ways. What caution and preparation does is to set as many conditions as possible to maximize the chances of success. However, caution alone is not enough. Just as the expression goes that 'The safest place for a ship is in harbour, but that is not what a ship is for', so too a general's purpose is to fight and win in war. While caution is one aspect of establishing the foundation for victory so too is daring, and there is often a balance to be achieved between the two.

When considering Julius Caesar, Suetonius argues that it is difficult to say whether it was his caution or his daring that was most apparent in his conduct of war. His caution was evident in his constant use of scouts and reconnaissance to ensure that he never led his army into an ambush. Further, to cross over to Britain he waited until he had collected key intelligence on harbours and necessary navigation and landing requirements for a fleet. In contrast Suetonius points out how, when Caesar was away from his camp in Germany and it came under siege, he disguised himself as a Gaul and made his way through enemy territory to take command, or how he launched his fleet in winter, risking the weather and the enemy blockades to arrive in Dyrrachium to take on Pompey. Sometimes Caesar would go into battle only after careful planning, at other times he would seize an opportunity to immediately launch an assault, while he would also use surprise going into battle at the end of a long march or sometimes during violent storms, attacking when his enemies (and even his own soldiers) least expected it.

Daring is important to take an enemy by surprise, to instil confidence in a general's own army and fear in the opponent. As Pompey notes in a letter to the Roman Senate, 'Actions speak louder than words.' Seemingly risky decisions, even on the spur of the moment, were often built on a good general's previous success and a knowledge of the capabilities of his own soldiers and those of the enemy, as well as an understanding of human nature and the human condition in warfare. Caution alone was not enough, a general needed to take action and win on the battlefield, to not simply avoid defeat but to achieve victory. As Peloponnesian naval commander Teutiaplus observed, the successful general is the one who guards against risks on their own side, recognizes when the enemy is at greatest disadvantage, and uses this as the moment to attack. A good general takes the fight to their enemy.

Demonstrating military genius

Truly great generals do demonstrate military genius. Such commanders are able to see what others do not and take advantage of the uncertainty of human conflict, displaying excellence and exceptional acumen in the conduct of warfare. Polybius credits Hannibal with such genius, arguing that the Carthaginian general had a mind for warfare and strategy, being a commander who tended towards unexpected options for both attack and defence. The Greek writer goes further, arguing that in the early part of the Second Punic War, Roman losses were not due to any inferiority of weapons or tactics, but to Hannibal's military genius. Polybius points out that once a general with the genius to match Hannibal came onto the scene, then it was only a short time until Rome defeated Carthage. That comparable military genius was Scipio Africanus who, even early on, had shown himself to be a masterful general:

> The fact was, he had decided not to do any of the things he had publicly announced, but to invest suddenly the town in Spain to which they had given

> the name of Carthage. ... He was now but twenty-seven years of age, and yet he in the first place took in hand a situation pronounced by most people as desperate owing to the serious nature of the recent reverses, and secondly in dealing with it he put aside the measures obvious to anyone and planned out and decided on a course which neither his enemies nor his friends expected. There was nothing in all this that was not due to most close calculation.

The refusal to accept a situation that everyone else has determined to be hopeless and the capacity to develop an unexpected plan of attack indicate a good general. It might be argued that measuring a general's quality by means of successful battles and victories is a form of 'victor's fallacy', but it is entirely fair to judge leaders precisely on their results on the battlefield. The military genius of these truly great generals is evident in their ability to consistently achieve victories across multiple battles, against numerous enemies, in different locations and in varying situations and circumstances.

Being relentless

Personal drive, ambition, military genius, and a will to win all appear common to truly great generals. In comparing Caesar and Alexander, Appian describes them as 'men of the greatest ambition, both were most skilled in the art of war, most rapid in executing their decisions, most reckless in danger, least sparing of themselves, and relying as much on audacity and luck as on military skill.' Appian's point about daring over strategy might be debatable, given previous analysis of these generals and their planning and preparedness, but there is something undeniable about the willingness of these truly great commanders to act boldly and take the fight to the enemy. What is also undeniable is that generals such as Alexander, Hannibal, Scipio and Caesar actively liked to fight, they loved the thrill of battle. As Arrian notes of Alexander, he had an uncontrollable passion for battle and glory. There was also a relentlessness, a personal ambition which drove these generals to overcome whatever obstacle was put in their way. When facing Alexander in his initial push into the eastern Persian empire, the Persian general Bessus,

> was laying waste the country at the foot of Mount Caucasus, in order to prevent Alexander from marching any further, both by the desolation of

> the land between the enemy and himself and by the lack of provisions. But none the less did Alexander keep up the march, though with difficulty, both on account of the deep snow and from the want of necessaries; but yet he persevered…

Alexander pushed through, refusing to be stopped by his enemy, the harsh elements or lack of supplies. The Macedonian general was unstoppable.

It is with Alexander that we reach a good finishing point in answering the question, 'What makes a good general?' In reflecting on this great military commander's ability to overcome any and all challenges, Arrian observes that 'no military enterprise which Alexander undertook was ever unsuccessful.' Regardless of the enemy, terrain, weather, circumstances, or other possible challenges, Alexander overcame them all to prove victorious on the battlefield and he provides the definitive insight.

Ultimately, a good general finds a way to win.

References

Details of the sources of accounts and quotes are provided in this Reference section. Unless otherwise indicated, all quotations in the book are drawn from the following public domain texts: Ammianus Marcellinus, *The History of Ammianus Marcellinus.* Translated by C. D. Yonge (1911), London: G. Bell & Sons Ltd; Appian, *The Roman History.* Translated by Horace White (1912). In four volumes (Vols 1–4). Loeb Classical Library, London: William Heinemann Ltd; Aristotle, *The Athenian Constitution.* Translated by Sir Frederic G. Kenyon (1914), London: G. Bell; Aristotle, *Politics: A Treatise on Government.* Translated by William Ellis (1912), London: J. M. Dent & Sons Ltd; Arrian, *The Anabasis of Alexander.* Translated by E. H. Chinnock (1884), London: Hodder & Stoughton; Caesar, *'De Bello Gallico' and Other Commentaries.* Translated by W. A. McDevitte with an introduction by Thomas De Quincey (1915), Everyman's Library (702); Cassius Dio, *Dio's Rome.* Translated by Herbert Baldwin Foster (1905). (Vols 1–6) New York: Pafraets Book Company; Cornelius Nepos, [*Lives of Eminent Commanders*] in *Justin, Cornelius Nepos and Eutropius.* Translated by Rev. John Selby Watson, MA (1856), London: Henry G. Bohn; Florus, *Epitome of Roman History.* Translated by E. S. Forster (1929), Loeb Classical Library, London: William Heinemann Ltd; Herodotus, *The History of Herodotus*, Translated into English by G. C. Macaulay (1890), In two volumes (Vol. 1) London: MacMillan and Co; Livy, *The History of Rome.* Translated by Daniel Spillan and Cyrus Edmonds and William A. M'Devitte (1850, 1853, 1858, 1860). In four volumes (Vols 1–4). London: Henry G. Bohn; Plato, *Dialogues of Plato (Laws).* Translated by Benjamin Jowett (1892). In five volumes (Vol. 5). New York: Charles Scribner's Sons; Plutarch, *Plutarch's Lives.* Translated by Aubrey Stewart and John Long (1894, 1899, 1892). In four volumes (Vols 1–4). London: George Bell & Sons; Polyaenus, *Stratagems of War.* 2nd edn. Translated by R. Shepherd (1796); Polybius, *The Histories of Polybius.* Translated by W. R. Paton (1922–1927). In six volumes (Vols 1–6). Loeb Classical Library, London: William Heinemann Ltd; Sallust, *Conspiracy of Catiline and the Jugurthine War.* Translated by J. S. Watson (1896). Philadelphia: David McKay; Suetonius, *The Lives of the Twelve Caesars.* Translated by Alexander Thomson, revised and corrected by T. Forester (1909), London: George Bell & Sons; Tacitus, *The Annals.* Translated by Alfred John Church and William Jackson Brodribb (1876), Cambridge, MA: Hackett Publishing Company, Inc.; Tacitus, *The Histories.* Translated by W. H. Fyfe (1912), Oxford: Clarendon Press; Tacitus, *The Agricola and Germany of Tacitus.* Translated by Alfred John Church and William Jackson Brodribb (1868), London: MacMillan and Co.; Thucydides, *The History of the Peloponnesian War.* Translated by Richard Crawley (1903), London: J. M. Dent & Sons; Vegetius Renatus (Flavius), *The Military Institutions of the Romans.* Translated by Lieutenant John Clarke (1767); Velleius Paterculus, *Compendium of Roman History.* Translated by F. W. Shipley (1924), Loeb Classical Library 152, London: William Heinemann Ltd; Xenophon, *The Works of Xenophon.* Translated by H. G. Dakyns (1890, 1892). In four volumes (Vols 1–2), London: MacMillan and Co.

Introduction

The quote 'Iphicrates used to [compare]…it wanted everything' is from Polyaenus, *Stratagems of War*, 3.9.22.

The quote 'Cato the Elder...of lasting utility' is from Vegetius, *Military Institutions of the Romans*, 2.3.

The quote 'misconduct in the common affairs... enemy in the face' is from Vegetius, *The Military Institutions of the Romans*, 1.13.

The quote 'No state can either be happy... terror of our arms' is from Vegetius, *The Military Institutions of the Romans*, 1.13.

Carl von Clausewitz' distinction between the character of war and the nature of war is based on Carl von Clausewitz, *On War* and discussions of the human elements of warfare, particularly in Book 1, and acknowledgements of the changing character of how 'modern' wars are fought, for example refer to Book 3, Chapter 17.

The reference to Keegan's argument on the human in battle is based on John Keegan, *The Face of Battle,* Barrie & Jenkins Ltd, London, 1988, p. 263.

The reference to Liddell Hart's statement on human nature is based on B. H. Liddell Hart, *Thoughts on War*, Faber & Faber, London, 1944, p. 219.

Polybius' argument on the two ways to learn and the necessity of historical knowledge is from Polybius, *The Histories*, 1.35.

The paragraph discussion on the selection of Athenian generals, their authority and accountability, and the selection of Spartan generals, their authority once outside Sparta's borders and their accountability is drawn from Antony Andrewes, *Greek Society*, Penguin Books Ltd, Harmondsworth, 1967, pp. 174–5, 203 (Athenian generals); pp. 175, 191–2 (Spartan generals). The discussion on the selection of Roman generals is based on numerous accounts across the ancient literature, including Livy and Plutarch. The aristocratic and noble underpinnings of both Spartan and Athenian societies and the consistent trend of generals coming from families of nobility is discussed at length by M. T. W. Arnheim, *Aristocracy in Greek Society*, Thames and Hudson, 1977, for example p. 102, Ch. 5, and p. 186. Arnheim notes that the Spartans replaced a traditional aristocracy with an aristocracy of military 'best men' (p. 102). Athenian generalship being largely limited to the nobility is also highlighted by Antony Andrewes, *Greek Society*, Penguin Books Ltd, Harmondsworth, 1967, p. 242. A reading of the lives of Roman generals similarly highlights that they were selected from the aristocratic, wealthy and powerful families. For example, see Livy and Plutarch's numerous accounts.

The discussion on military skill rather than virtue as the basis for selecting a general, and the associated quote, is from Aristotle, *Politics*, 5.1309b.

The quote 'as the generals...were exhausted' is from Aristotle, *The Athenian Constitution*, 26.

For the ages of Alexander, Pompey, Hannibal, and Scipio Africanus, refer to: Plutarch, *Alexander*, 9; Plutarch, *Pompey*, 6.3; Polybius, *The Histories*, 3.13 (Hannibal's age of 26 is widely accepted based on the timing of his birth and timing of the death General Hasdrubal in 221 BC. This resulted in Hannibal being elected by the Carthaginian army in Spain to take over from Hasdrubal and lead them); and Polybius, *The Histories*, 10.6 for Scipio Africanus.

For insights into the triumph, refer to: Plutarch, *Romulus*, 16, *Poplicola*, 9, *Camillus*, 7, *Pompey*, 14 & 45, Plutarch, *Caesar*, 27 & 60; Josephus, *The Jewish Wars*, 5.3–7; Livy, 10.7 & 46, 26.13 & 21; Tacitus, *The* Annals, 2.41; Cassius Dio, *Dio's Rome*, 40.41; as well as Robert Payne, *The Roman Triumph*, Pan Books Ltd, London, 1962.

The account of four triumphs awarded in 71 BC is based on Robert Payne, *The Roman Triumph*, Pan Books Ltd, London, 1962, p.111.

The account and quoted words of Roman citizens singing about Germanicus come from Suetonius, *The Twelve Caesars,* Gaius Caligula. 6.

The story of Julius Caesar distributing wealth to his soldiers is based on Plutarch, *Caesar*, 17.

The reference to Eisenhower's statement on morale is based on Dwight D. Eisenhower, *Crusade in Europe*, Doubleday, New York. 1948, p. 210.

The quote 'generals cannot... obtained it' is from Polyaenus, *Stratagems of War*, 5. Preface.

Chapter 1: How Do You Understand Yourself?

The quote 'A general is not easily overcome... enemy's forces' is from Vegetius, *The Military Institutions of the Romans*, 3.26.

The quote 'Thus a vigilant... both in numbers and strength' from Vegetius, *The Military Institutions of the Romans*, 3.9.

The quote 'If you know your enemy... in every battle' is from Sun Tzu, *The Art of War*, 3.18.

The statement about a commander needing to learn by experience of being commanded and the associated quote is from Aristotle, *Politics*, 3.1277b.

The discussion of Pompey's efforts at convincing his father's soldiers not to abandon General Strabo, the hatred of Strabo, and affection of the populace and soldiers for Pompey is based on Plutarch, *Pompey*, 1 & 3.

The account of Julius Caesar weeping after reading of Alexander's battlefield successes and comparing them to his own then-modest achievements is drawn from Plutarch, *Caesar*, 11.

The discussion and quotes from Plato suggesting a general who does not know victory cannot be said to have understanding comes from Plato, *Laws*, 12.

The quote 'It is a true proverb which says that a general has the army he deserves' is from Florus, *Epitome of Roman History*, 1.34.

The account of Metellus taking command of the Roman army in Africa and related quotes are from Sallust, *The War with Jugurtha*, 44 & 45.

The account of Alexander telling his officers that the Persians had more people in their ranks but the Macedonians would have more people who would fight is from Curtius Rufus, *The History of Alexander*, 4.14.5.

Discussion on General Agesilaus with reference to Sparta's walls is from Plutarch, *Plutarch's Moralia*, Agesilaus 29.

Discussion on Thermopylae, Leonidas and Xerxes and the lack of men who would fight in his army is based on Herodotus, *The Histories*, 7.201–210. The estimate of 5,000-plus soldiers is based on Herodotus' figures, which are unclear and at times appear contradictory – refer to Herodotus, *The Histories*, 7.201–202 for initial Greek numbers and 7.228 and 8.25 which indicates 4,000 Peloponnesians killed in the battle.

The quote 'Upon a complaint ... more soldiers' is from Polyaenus, *Stratagems of War*, 2.1.7.

The quote 'The ancients, taught by experience, preferred discipline to numbers' is from Vegetius, *The Military Institutions of the Romans*, 3.1.

Alexander's quote 'to preserve discipline...' and associated discussion is from Arrian, *The Anabasis of Alexander*, 3.9.

The quote 'At Corinth... the most skilful captain' is from Cornelius Nepos, *Lives of Eminent Commanders*, Iphicrates, 2.

The quote 'The courage of a soldier... dragged to slaughter' is from Vegetius, *The Military Institutions of the Romans*, 1.1.

The quote 'if that discipline is neglected, there is no longer any difference between the soldier and the peasant' is from Vegetius, *The Military Institutions of the Romans*, 2.23.

The comparison of the Macedonian phalanx to the Roman formations and soldiers is based on Polybius, *The Histories*, 18.31–32. The explanation of the Roman legion and various elements is drawn from Polybius, *The Histories*, 6.19–42.

The quote 'At last Alexander's men... only darts' is from Arrian, *The Anabasis of Alexander*, 1.15.

The account of the Roman spears against the Gauls' shields is based on Julius Caesar, *The Gallic War*, 1.25.

Statement on the superiority of Roman weaponry and the inferiority of German swords is based on Polybius, *The Histories*, 2.33.

Discussion of Crassus' defeat at the hands of the Parthians is based on Plutarch, *Crassus*, 22–31.

Scipio's quote 'Go, therefore...lives away' is from Polybius, *The Histories*, 15.10.

Discussion on Demaratus' advice to Xerxes is from Herodotus, *The Histories*, 7.101–103.

The remarks about Spartans asking not about the enemy's numbers but their location is from Plutarch, *Plutarch's Moralia*, Agis 3.

The quote 'it is indispensably necessary…' is from Vegetius, *The Military Institutions of the Romans*, 3.10.

The observation that victory usually goes to the side who refuse to break ranks, whose confidence and will to fight remained unbroken, and who fight until the other side break ranks and flee the field of battle is based on John Keegan's discussion of Ardant du Picq's analyses of historical (including ancient) battles. Refer to John Keegan, *The Face of Battle*, Barrie & Jenkins Ltd, London, 1988, p.60.

The quote 'Length of service or age alone … in his profession' is from Vegetius, *The Military Institutions of the Romans*, 2.23.

The description of the soldiers sent to Corbulo in Syria is based on Tacitus, *The Annals*, 13.35.

The discussion on Caesar seeking to engage Pompey given he was leading veterans is from Frontinus, *The Stratagems*, 1.3.2.

The account of Hannibal's army learning from their Spanish campaigns is based on Polybius, *The Histories*, 3.35.

'For the enemy's forces… lay in victory' is from Polybius, *The Histories*, 3.89.

The concern of Hannibal about his army, after emerging from winter quarters at Capua, and the associated quote is from Livy, *History of Rome*, 23.45.6.

The quote 'For soldiers [unused] to fighting for a length of time must be considered in the same light as recruits' is from Vegetius, *The Military Institutions of the Romans*, 3.9.

The account of Longus attacking Hannibal when his army was unready is based on Polybius, *The Histories*, 3.72.

The figures of 47,000 for the Macedonian army and 1,000,000 infantry and 40,000 cavalry of the Persians come from Arrian, *The Anabasis of Alexander*, 3.12, 3.8 & 3.13. The related quote 'The success… cowed their spirits' is from Arrian, *The Anabasis of Alexander*, 3.11.

The quote 'Two armies…equal match' is from Vegetius, *The Military Institution of the Romans*, 3.1.

Pericles' reflection on the difficulty that the Spartans would face in developing a naval capability and associated discussion is based on Thucydides, *The Peloponnesian War*, 1.142.

The account of the Battle of Pylos is based on Thucydides, *The Peloponnesian War*, 4.1–41, with and discussion of the Spartans recognising their error of judgement based on 4.18

Chapter 2: How Do You Understand the Enemy?

The quote 'It is essential… brave or cowardly' is from Vegetius, *The Military Institutions of the Romans*, 3.9.

Polybius and Livy are the two main ancient authors who give accounts of Hannibal.

This discussion on Hannibal's intelligence on Flaminius, ambush of Flaminius' army at Lake Trasimene, and importance of understanding the opposing commander is based on Polybius, *The Histories*, 3.80–3.85 with the quote 'There is no denying…' from 3.81.

The account of Fabius is based on Florus, *Epitome of Roman History*, 1.22.

The quote 'Whether the victory… conquer him afterwards' is from Livy, *History of Rome*, 23.16.

The quote 'for our shortness… men of Gaul' is from Julius Caesar, *The Gallic War*, 2.30.

'Caesar at first … men would dare' and account is from Julius Caesar, *The Gallic War*, 2.8.

Account of the Belgae approach for attacking fortifications is based on Julius Caesar, *The Gallic War*, 2.6.

The account of Caesar trying to draw Ariovistus into battle, discovering the reason for the delay, associated quote 'that among the Germans…' and the subsequent battle and aftermath is described at Julius Caesar, *The Gallic War*, 1.48–53.

The quote 'The Romans… would be sufficient' is from Livy, *History of Rome*, 10.28.

The account of the Spartan engagement with Hydarnes and associated quote is based on Herodotus, *The Histories*, 7.135.

The account of Xerxes being unable to comprehend the Greeks' preparation to fight against such odds, and his waiting four days and then attacking on the fifth, is based on Herodotus, *The Histories*, 7.210.

The account of Xerxes' commander's response to hearing of the Olympic awards and associated quote is from Herodotus, *The Histories*, 8.26.

Discussion of Crassus' defeat at the hands of the Parthians is based on Plutarch, *Crassus*, 22–31.

The account of Alcibiades and the associated quotes are based on Thucydides, *The Peloponnesian War*, 6.91.

Nicias' discussion on the Athenians needing to understand the Spartans is based on Thucydides, *The Peloponnesian War*, 6.1.

Flamininus' quote, 'The kingdom of Macedonia had been hitherto supported by its reputation, not by real strength; and that even that reputation had, at length, vanished' is from Livy, *History of Rome*, 33.8.5.

The quote 'The Romans had been apprised… however poor' comes from Livy, *History of Rome*, 9.40.

The quote 'One would suppose… greater part at the Trasimenus' is from Livy, *History of Rome*, 22.46.4.

The account of the Romans obtaining a Carthaginian ship, using it as a model for building their own fleet, and training sailors even before the ships were built is from Polybius, *The Histories*, 1.20–21.

The quote 'The Thebans pay… able to do before' is from Plutarch, *Lycurgus*, 13.

Account of the depth of Spartan and Theban phalanxes and losses are based on Xenophon, *Hellenica*, 6.4–15.

The discussion on the civil war and associated quote 'never before had…among the vanquished' is from Appian, *The Civil Wars*, 4.137.

The account of Alexander's success over the Telmissians is based on Arrian, *The Anabasis of Alexander*, 1.27.

Chapter 3: How Do You Prepare and Plan?

The discussion on Vegetius' advice and associated quotes are from Vegetius, *The Military Institutions of the Romans*, 3. Preface.

The quote 'These evolutions… on actual service' is from Vegetius, *The Military Institutions of the Romans*, 1.26.

The quote 'for them alone… preparation for war' is from Plutarch, *Lycurgus*, 21.

The account of the Athenians building the 200 warships and their availability when Xerxes attacked Greece is based on Herodotus, *The Histories*, 7.144.

The account of Marcus Aemilius' and Servius Fulvius' naval disaster is based on Polybius, *The Histories*, 1.36–1.37.

The reference to the Byzantine Emperor's guidance is based on Maurice, *Strategikon*, 8.2.19.

Account of Artabanus' advice to Xerxes is based on Herodotus, *The Histories*, 7.49.

The statement on a general or the lowest ranking soldier being of no value without food or supplies is based on Xenophon, *Anabasis*, 1.3.

Starving an enemy rather than force of arms is recognized in Frontinus, *The Stratagems*, 4.7.1.

Guaranteeing that an army had everything secured within camp is based on Vegetius, *The Military Institutions of the Romans*, 2.11.

The quote 'Threatened with this gathering storm… a few days' is from Tacitus, *The Histories*, 4.22.

The quote 'When provisions once begin to fail… too late' is from Vegetius, *The Military Institutions of the Romans*, 3.3.

Plutarch's point on money being the sinews of war is from Plutarch, *Cleomenes*, 27.

Pericles' statement on Sparta's lack of funds and delays in procuring it, and the quote 'but the opportunities of war wait for no man' are from Thucydides, *History of the Peloponnesian War*, 1.142.

The quote 'appointed Gaius Lutatius...anticipated battle' is from Polybius, *The Histories*, 1.59.

Pericles' discussion on what Athens needed to do to prevail in the war and the later ignoring of his advice and subsequent consequences is based on Thucydides, *The Peloponnesian War*, 2.65.

Artabanus' advice to Xerxes on evaluating risks and acting boldly is based on Herodotus, *The Histories*, 7.49.

Themistocles' guidance on cautious planning is based on Herodotus, *The Histories*, 8.60.

The account of plans being successful if they were well-considered is from Polybius, *The Histories*, 9.12.

Nicias' advice that success is not from wishes but sound judgements is based on Thucydides, *The Peloponnesian War*, 6.13.

The account of people considering things after the event rather than before is based on Curtius Rufus, *The History of Alexander*, 8.2.1.

The Corinthians' guidance to the Spartans on planning and associated quote is from Thucydides, *The Peloponnesian War*, 1.120.

Hannibal's statement, 'Rarely does that man... fluctuating nature of war', and account of the prebattle meeting between Hannibal and Scipio Africanus is from Livy, *History of Rome*, 30.30.11–20.

The account of the Aetolians' disaster and associated quote are from Polybius, *The Histories*, 2.3–4.

The account of the engagement of Drusus' army and the German tribe is based on Cassius Dio, *Dio's Rome*, 54.33.

The account of the debate over a naval engagement against the Persians is based on Arrian's *The Campaigns of Alexander*, 1.18 and the account of the debate prior to the battle of Granicus is based on *The Campaigns of Alexander*, 1.13.

Account of Cornelius Scipio's cavalry engagement with Hannibal, associated quote, and appearance in Italy to meet Hannibal as the Carthaginian emerged from the Alps is from Livy, *History of Rome*, 21.29 and 21.39.

The quote 'It is the nature of war... for your advantage' comes from Vegetius, *The Military Institutions of the Romans*, 3.26.

Lycurgus' reference to doing more harm to the adversary is from Plutarch, *Plutarch's Moralia*, Lycurgus, 24.

Archidamus' quote 'This decision...to your opponents' is from Thucydides, *The Peloponnesian War*, 1.85

The reflection on Sparta's failure to take their advantage and on their helpfulness to their Athenian enemies, with associated quote, are from Thucydides, *The Peloponnesian War*, 8.96.

The quote 'Those designs are best... moment of execution' is from Vegetius, *The Military Institutions of the Romans*, 3.26.

The quote 'communicate the designs... no one but yourself' is from Vegetius, *The Military Institutions of the Romans*, 3.26.

The quote '[Himilco] with the Carthaginian fleet ... of his invasion' is from Polyaenus, *Stratagems of War*, 5.10.2.

Chapter 4: How Do You Select a Battlefield?

Leonidas' rationale for the selection of Thermopylae as the battlefield is based on Herodotus, *The Histories*, 7.177.

The account of Boudicca and the battle between the Britons and Suetonius' army and associated quote is drawn from Tacitus, *The Annals*, 14.31–37. The argument that it was customary for Britons to be led by women in war is from Tacitus, *The Annals*, 14.35.

The account of Popillius' battle with the Gauls and the quote '...being a fierce people... slain with the sword' are from Livy, *History of Rome*, 7.23. Quote is from the Loeb edition (1919).

The description of the battle of Adys is based on Polybius, *The Histories*, 1.30.

For the discussion of the maxim 'Allow the enemy an escape route', Frontinus is an example of one of many ancient authors who highlight the importance of allowing the enemy a path of escape to avoid the risks of fighting desperate men. Refer to Frontinus, *The Stratagems*, 2.6.

The account of Aemilius and his Roman force's battle with the Aequi and Volsci is drawn from Livy, *History of Rome*, 2.42.

The quote 'At the Aegospotami... an easy victory' is from Polyaenus, *Stratagems of War*, 1.45.2.

The account of Celer's surprise of Catiline's forces and the quote is from Sallust, *The War with Catiline*, 57, with the discussion of the lead up to and result of the battle at Pistoria from 57–60.

The quote 'But on a march... without loss' is from Vegetius, *The Military Institutions of the Romans*, 3.6.

The account of the Battle of Ilipa is based on Livy, *History of Rome*, 28.14–28.15 and the quote 'as the day... engaged the enemy' is from Livy, *History of Rome*, 28.15.2–4.

The account of the Battle of Adrianople is from Ammianus Marcellinus, *The History of Ammianus Marcellinus*, 31.12–31.13. The quote 'scorched the Romans... as he could' comes from Marcellinus, 31.13.

The account of Fabius and associated quote, 'The first hope... reduced by delay', is from Florus, *Epitome of Roman History*, 1.22.

The discussion of Alexander's siege of Tyre is based on Curtius Rufus, *The History of Alexander*, 4.2. The reference to his warning is based on Curtius Rufus, *The History of Alexander*, 4.2.5

Chapter 5: How Do You Employ *Stratagems* Against the Enemy?

The accounts of the Greeks' use of the horse to deceive the Trojans are in Homer's *Odessey*, 8.12 and Virgil's *Aeneid*, 2.

The quote 'while superior conduct . . . least danger' is from Polyaenus, *Stratagems of War*, 1.Preface.

The quote 'Good officers... exposing their own forces' quote is from Vegetius, *The Military Institutions of the Romans*, 3.9.

The description of Frontinus' wide range of stratagems is based on Frontinus, *The Stratagems*, 1.

Caesar's observation to his soldiers on surprise in war is from Appian, *The Civil Wars*, 2.53.

In the section 'Scipio Africanus and the greatest battle that never was', the account of Scipio's planning, reconnaissance and attack on the Carthaginian camp is based on Polybius, *The Histories*, 14.2–14.5.

The quotes 'thunderbolt' and 'Carthaginian craft devised a new stratagem' are from Florus, *Epitome of Roman History*, 1.22.

The account of the Battle of Lake Trasimene is contained in Livy, *History of Rome*, 22.3–22.7. The quote 'A shout being raised on all sides...' is from 22.4.7. The quotes 'from the noise and tumult...' and 'more use of ears...' are at 22.5.3. The quote 'We have been defeated...' is from 22.7.8.

The account of Nero's deception of Hasdrubal and Hannibal and the Battle of Metaurus is from Livy, *History of Rome*, 27.43–51. Nero's quote is from Livy, *History of Rome*, 27.45.1.

Polybius lists Roman deaths at Cannae as 70,000 (*The Histories*, 3.117), with 5,700 of Hannibal's forces lost, while Livy puts the Roman deaths at more than 50,000 (*History of Rome*, 25.6.13) and 8,000 on the Carthaginian side (*History of Rome*, 22.52.6).

The account of Spartan king Cleomenes' stratagem against the Argives is based on Polyaenus, *Stratagems of War*, 1.14.1.

The description of Alexander's deception of Porus is based on Arrian, *The Anabasis of Alexander*, 5.11.

The account of Scipio's stratagem against Hasdrubal Gisco is based on Frontinus, *The Stratagems*, 2.3.4.

The account of Postumius' deception of the Carthaginians is from Frontinus, *The Stratagems*, 2.1.4.
The description of Viriathus' stratagem against the Segobrigenses is based on Frontinus, *The Stratagems*, 3.11.4.
The quote 'Novelty and surprise…no effect' is from Vegetius, *The Military Institutions of the Romans*, 3.26.
The reference to attacks from unexpected directions is based on Frontinus, *The Stratagems*, 3.9.
The quote 'Most of them… to defend themselves…' quote is from Arrian, *The Anabasis of Alexander*, 6.6.
The account of the surprise attack on the Spartans at Pylos is based on Thucydides, *The Peloponnesian War*, 4.36.
The account of Xenophon in Persia and quote 'The cavalry…a larger one' is from Xenophon, *Anabasis*, 6.3.
The account of Antigonus' deception and quote 'should abruptly introduce … were at hand' are from Polyaenus, *Stratagems of War*, 4.6.19.
The account of Caesar's deception with cavalry and associated quote, 'Caesar formed a design… they immediately fled', is from Polyaenus, *Stratagems of War*, 8.23.12.
The account of Admiral Diotimus' deception against the Spartan fleet is from Polyaenus, *Stratagems of War*, 5.22.2.
Philip II's stratagem against the Byzantines is based on Polyaenus, *Stratagems of War*, 4.2.21.
The account of Dionysius fooling the Carthaginians into discharging the Greek mercenaries is from Polyaenus, *Stratagems of War*, 5.2.17.
Ventidius' defeat of the Parthians is from Florus, *Epitome of Roman History*, 2.19.
The account of the Numidian cavalry breaking the Ligures blockade is contained in Livy, *History of Rome*, 35.11.
Admiral Nicon's escape through disguising his ship is from Polyaenus, *Stratagems of War*, 5.34.
General Hermocrates' deceit of Athenian forces is based on Thucydides, *The Peloponnesian War*, 7.73–74.
Philip V's capture of Prinassus is described in Polyaenus, *Stratagems of War*, Book 4.18.1.
The description of the fake ambush by the retreating Greeks is from Xenophon, *Anabasis*, 5.2.
The account of Agesilaus' successful deception and campaign against Tissaphernes is based on Cornelius Nepos, *Lives of Eminent Commanders*, Agesilaus, 2–3.

Chapter 6: How Do You Minimize Surprise, Shock and Fear?
The quote 'Men are frightened … when foreseen' is from Vegetius, *The Military Institutions of the Romans*, 3.6.
The reference to Metellus warning his soldiers of an ambush from Frontinus, *The Stratagems*, 4.7.42.
The quote 'It is asserted… without loss' is from Vegetius, *The Military Institutions of the Romans*, 3.6.
The account of Iphicrates and associated quotes are taken from Polyaenus, *Stratagems of War*, 3.9.32, 3.9.16 and 3.9.17.
The quote on Appius Claudius, 'The rear was commanded… entire front to the enemy', is from Livy, *History of Rome*, 34.28.10.
The account of Gnaeus Fulvius recognizing the Etruscan ambush is at Livy, *History of Rome*, 10.4.8 and the quote 'tell them… conquered by arms' is from 10.4.10.
Accounts of the Roman reaction Hannibal's crossing the Alps, as well as Hannibal's own shock at Cornelius Scipio's rapid movement, are from Polybius, *The Histories*, 3.61.
The account of Clearchus and quote, 'had their turn…day of the battle' are from Xenophon, *Anabasis*, 2.2.

Chapter 7: How Do You Read the Situation and How Do You Adapt in Battle?
The statement of 'see, understand, act' is not an unusual description of any decision-making activity – the critical aspect for an ancient general was that it was not enough to see and understand, action was a ultimate requirement to impact the battle.

The account of Philopoemen at the Battle of Sellasia and associated quote is drawn from Polybius, *The Histories*, 2.67–68.
The observation that strategies developed by a general in response to the actual battle are at times preferable to existing plans and that a general might produce the best response by responding to the specific situation rather than experience is from Onasander, *Strategikos*, 32.9.
The quote 'He was very clever… likely to occur' is from Arrian, *The Anabasis of Alexander*, 7.28.
The account and associated quote on Scipio outside New Carthage are from Livy, *History of Rome*, 26.44.
The account of Democrates is from Xenophon, *Anabasis*, 4.4.
The account of Considius' mistaken report is from Julius Caesar, *The Gallic War*, 1.21–22.
The account of the Britons' attack on the Romans is based on Julius Caesar, *The Gallic War*, 5.15.
The account of Oppius and associated quote are from Livy, *History of Rome*, 31.2.7–9.
The account of the Battle of Philippi is based on Appian, *The Civil Wars*, 4.105–132, Plutarch, *Brutus*, 38–52, and Florus, *Epitome of Roman History*, with the associated quotes from Florus, *Epitome of Roman History*, 2.17.
Account of the Athenians attacking Megara is from Thucydides, *The Peloponnesian War*, 4.67–68.
The account of the Battle of Herdonia is from Livy, *History of Rome*, 27.1.
The account of Paetus and Vologeses and associated quote is contained in Tacitus, *The Annals*, 15.10–17.
The observations on Hannibal adapting his plans when faced with new information is based on Polybius, *The Histories*, 3.50.
The observation on Alexander adapting to the reality of the battlefield and associated quote 'he drew up his forces in the order which seemed to him especially adapted to his present circumstances' is based on Arrian, *The Anabasis of Alexander*, 5.22–24.
The quote 'Clearchus at the head… without opposition' is from Polyaenus, *Stratagems of War*, 2.2.1.
The account of Agrippa's change of tactics before the Battle of Actium is from Cassius Dio, *Dio's Rome*, 50.31.
The account of Chares is from Polyaenus, *Stratagems of War*, 3.13.1.
The account of Caesar's use of uncertainty to make his soldiers believe that the Pompeian forces were fleeing is from Florus, *Epitome of Roman History*, 2.13 and the account of the Battle of Munda is also drawn from Appian, *The Civil Wars*, 2.103–2.104.
Alcibiades' tactic of setting a fire so that smoke would hinder his enemies' view is from Polyaenus, *Stratagems of War*, 1.40.7.
Brasidas' order regarding the cutting down and burning of wood is in Polyaenus, *Stratagems of War*, 1.38.5.
The quote 'When the Roman generals… form their line again' quote is from Livy, *History of Rome*, 29.2.13.
The account of Phormio is at Polyaenus, *Stratagems of War*, 3.4.2. Recognition of Phormio as a commander who understood fighting at sea and the means of exploiting his opponent's inexperience draws upon Thucydides, *History of the Peloponnesian War*, 2.84.
Brasidas' guidance on recognizing and exploiting the enemy's mistakes is based on Thucydides, *History of the Peloponnesian War*, 5.9.
The quote 'Therefore the leader…of their commander' is from Polybius, *The Histories*, 3.81.
Accounts of the siege of Alesia and defeat and surrender of Vercingetorix are based on Julius Caesar, *The Gallic War*, 7.68–88; Plutarch, *Caesar*, 27; and Cassius Dio, *Dio's Rome*, 40.39–41.
The account of Xenophon's use of reserves is from Xenophon, *Anabasis*, 6.5. The suggestion that this is the first deliberate use of reserves in a battle is based on G. L. Cawkwell who makes this claim in his Introduction to the Penguin (1972) publication of Xenophon's *The Persian Expedition*.

Chapter 8: How Do You Exploit a Victory or Recover from a Defeat?

The quote 'He never defeated...rally their forces' is from Suetonius, *The Twelve Caesars,* Julius Caesar.60.

The account of Alexander capturing the multitude of Persians despite his own smaller numbers is from Curtius Rufus, *The History of Alexander*, 5.13.21–22.

The account of Tiberius' campaign against Illyricum is based on Suetonius, *The Twelve Caesars,* Tiberius.16.

The quote 'while success... to advantage' is from Polybius, *The Histories,* 10.36.

The claim about Cannae being one of the deadliest one-day battles in human history is based on the number of deaths. Polybius lists Roman deaths at 70,000 (*The Histories*, 3.117), with 5,700 of Hannibal's forces killed, while Livy puts the Roman deaths at more than 50,000 (*History of Rome*, 25.6.13) and 8,000 on the Carthaginian side (*History of Rome*, 22.52.6).

The quote 'After this immense success... do not know how to use one' is from Plutarch, *Fabius Maximus*, 17. Livy attributes the statement to Hannibal's commander Maharbal, Livy, *History of Rome*, 22.51.

Livy's conclusion 'That day's delay is firmly believed to have been the preservation of the city and the empire' is from Livy, *History of Rome*, 22.51.4.

The account of Hannibal departing Italy and quote 'he frequently looked back... to Rome' quote is from Livy, *History of Rome*, 30.20.7.

The account of Pompey's failure to pursue Caesar into his camp at the Battle of Dyrrachium and associated quote is from Plutarch, *Pompey*, 65.

The discussion on Caesar re-evaluating his strategy is from Plutarch, *Caesar*, 39.

The details of Pompeius' military life and his remaining on the defensive are from Appian, *The Civil Wars*, 5.143–144.

The account of the Samnite surrounding of the Roman armies, the debate over what to do with them, and the Romans' surrender and passing under the yoke are based on Livy, *History of Rome*, 9.1–9.6. This event is also captured by Appian, *The Foreign Wars*, 3.6–11.

The account of the Spartans allowing defeated enemies to escape or surrender unharmed, and the implication of such a tactic is based on Plutarch, *Plutarch's Moralia*, Lycurgus 30.

The description of Caesar offering Pompey's soldiers the opportunity to join him is based on Plutarch, *Caesar*, 46.

The account of Pyrrhus being approached to lead the Roman armies occurs in Hannibal's discussion with Scipio Africanus of great generals in Livy, *History of Rome*, 35.14.6–12.

The account of Pyrrhus' battles against the Romans and associated quote is from Plutarch, *Pyrrhus* 21.

The discussion on Caesar learning the right lessons is based on Plutarch, *Caesar*, 39.

The account of the Spartans' first naval battle against the Athenian navy is from Thucydides, *History of the Peloponnesian War*, 2.83–84 and the description of the Spartan commission is from 2.85.

The account of Xanthippus is at Polybius 1.32–1.36.

The account of Tiberius in Germany is based on Suetonius, *The Twelve Caesars*, Tiberius.18.

Account of the attack by Mithridates' cavalry and Xenophon's associated quote are from Xenophon, *Anabasis*, 3.3.

An example of the Byzantine guidance can be found at Maurice, *Strategikon*, 7. Points to be observed on the day of battle.11.

Account of Jason of Pherae's advice to the Spartans is based on Xenophon, *Hellenica*, 6.4.24.

Onasander's observation on the opportunity to counterattack a recently victorious army is from Onasander, *Strategikos*, 36.2.

The account of the Carthaginian attack in Sicily is from Polybius, *The Histories*, 1.24.

The quote, 'the conquerors were obliged to resign their victory to the conquered' is found at Polyaenus, *Stratagems of War*, 4.6.8.

The account of Marcius' leading the surviving Roman forces against Hasdrubal and Mago in Spain, and the associated quote 'Thus in a night and a day…' are from Livy, *History of Rome*, 25.37–25.39.

The account of Cerialis successfully defeating the surprise attack on the Roman camp and associated quote is from Tacitus, *The Histories*, 4.77.

The discussion on the aftermath of Cannae and quote, 'For though the Romans… masters of the whole world' is from Polybius, *The Histories*, 3.118.

Chapter 9: Why Is Speed of Action So Important?

Rufus' judgement that Alexander's speed of action was his greatest skill is from Curtius Rufus, *The History of Alexander*, 5.5.3.

Account of Alexander moving to engage the Mallians and Oxydracians and quote, 'with the express… confusion among them', is from Arrian, *The Anabasis of Alexander*, 6.4.

The quote, 'he arrived at the camp … safety by flight' is from Julius Caesar, *The Gallic War*, 4.14.

'Veni, vidi, vici' and the account of Caesar's Pontic triumph is based on Suetonius, *The Twelve Caesars*, Julius Caesar.37.

The account of Caesar's rapid movement with his 5,000 soldiers is based on Appian, *The Civil Wars*, 2.34.

The quote 'The die is cast' is from Suetonius, *The Twelve Caesars*, Julius Caesar.32. Quote is from Loeb edition (1914).

The statement on Caesar achieving control of Italy in sixty days comes from Plutarch, *Caesar*, 35.

The account of Pompey fleeing to Greece and putting his army into winter quarters and the related quote of Caesar moving swiftly to Brundusium to catch Pompey by surprise are from Appian, *The Civil Wars*, 2.52–53.

Hannibal's use of speed to deny the Romans time and to quickly implement a stratagem is based on Polybius, *The Histories*, 3.93.

The description of Caesar's rapid progress to Gaul and related quotation 'arrived there unexpectedly… the Roman people' are from Julius Caesar, *The Gallic War*, 2.3.

The account of King Artabanus' rapid march against Tiridates is based on Tacitus, *The Annals*, 6.44. Account of Jason of Pherae marching through Phocis is based on Xenophon, *Hellenica*, 6.4.21

Chapter 10: How Do You Avoid Hubris and Over-Confidence?

The quote 'So thoroughly had the present…with their hopes' is from Thucydides, *The Peloponnesian War*, 4.65.

The quotation 'In most cases men willingly believe what they wish' is from Julius Caesar, *The Gallic War*, 3.18.

The observation on human nature and reasoning is based on Thucydides, *The Peloponnesian War*, 4.108.

The account of Marcus Antonius' attack against Crete and related quote 'Marcus Antonius made… to their harbours' is from Florus, *Epitome of Roman History*, 1.42.

The quote 'going to the battle…Pontifex Maximus' is from Appian, *The Civil Wars*, 2.69.

The discussion on unwarranted feelings of superiority over an enemy is based on Thucydides, *The Peloponnesian War*, 1.122.

The account of the Gaius Duilius' Roman fleet's naval battle at Mylae, use of the ravens, and aftermath are based on Polybius, *The Histories*, 1.23–24.

The account and quote of Archidamus' advice to his son is from Plutarch, *Plutarch's Moralia*, Archidamus 8.

Archidamus' advice to the Spartans on not relying on the enemy's making mistakes but rather on their own planning and preparation is based on Thucydides, *The Peloponnesian War*, 1.84.

The account of Pericles' actions to keep the Athenians grounded is from Thucydides, *The Peloponnesian War*, 2.65 and the guidance on what Athens should do and Pericles' fear over the Athenians making mistakes is based on Thucydides, *The Peloponnesian War*, 1.144.

Vegetius' advice to generals, 'It is the duty… from the deliberation', is from Vegetius, *The Military Institutions of the Romans*, 3.9.

The account of Germanicus obtaining unguarded information from his soldiers and related quote is from Tacitus, *The Annals*, 2.12–13.

The account of Alexander's delay, incorrect interpretation by Darius and accepting flattering advice, then moving his army into a disadvantageous position, and related quotes, are from Arrian, *The Anabasis of Alexander*, 2.6.

Agrippa's advice to Augustus (Octavian) on flatterers is based on Cassius Dio, *Dio's Rome*, 52.10.

Gaius Marius' quote castigating the over-confident as 'traitors to their country' is from Plutarch, *Marius*, 16.

Account of Demaratus and reference to speaking with hatred is from Plutarch, *Plutarch's Moralia*, Demaratus 1.

Chapter 11: How Is Warfare Fundamentally Human and Why Does Psychology Matter?

Sallust's discussion on the importance of the mental state in warfare is based on Sallust, *The War with Catiline*, 2.

Polybius' observations on prolonged suspense and the relief of decisions is from Polybius, *The Histories*, 3.112.

Account of Clearchus deliberately delaying his response to the Persians is based on Xenophon, *Anabasis*, 2.3.

The observation from the Mytilenian Debate about people making decisions based on hope and then not being deterred from those decisions is based on Thucydides, *History of the Peloponnesian War*, 3.45. The point on the waking up to the reality of war is based on Thucydides, *History of the Peloponnesian War*, 3.82 and the account of the Romans' alarm over the potential sacking of Rome by Hannibal and their subsequent mobilization is from Polybius, *The Histories*, 2.23.

Octavian's quote 'it is a natural characteristic… what is to come' is from Cassius Dio, *Dio's Rome*, 50.30.

The quote 'conquered troops…never show the same courage' is from Tacitus, *The Histories*, 3.1.

Alexander's speech to his soldiers prior to the battle of Issus is from Arrian, *The Anabasis of Alexander*, 2.7.

Phormio's quote 'beaten men…same determination' is from Thucydides, *The Peloponnesian War*, 2.89.

The account of Masaesylians and associated quote are from Livy, *History of Rome*, 30.11.11.

The account of Xanthippus and associated quote is from Polybius, *The Histories*, 1.35.

The observation of the poor performance of Roman commanders in the field emboldening the Gauls and resulting in the sack of Rome is from Plutarch, *Caius Marius*, 11.

The accounts of the siege of Tyre are in Arrian, *The Anabasis of Alexander*, 2.23–24 and the siege of Gaza at 2.26–27.

Account of Alexander deliberately selecting strong points to attack is from Arrian, *The Anabasis of Alexander*, 2.26.

Account of the attack on Uspe and the related quote are from Tacitus, *The Annals*, 12.17.

The account of Paulus Aemilius determining to take the city of Dimale and subsequent psychological results are based on Polybius, *The Histories*, 3.18.

The account of Gylippus' observation and quote 'When men are once checked…with the Athenians' is from Thucydides, *History of the Peloponnesian War*, 7.66.

The account of the devastation of the Roman fleet in Germany and Germanicus' follow up attack and the demoralization evident in prisoners is based on Tacitus, *The Annals*, 2.23–2.25.

The account of Cleomenes offering battle to the Achaeans is from Plutarch, *Cleomenes*, 4.

The account of Caesar's confident movement and the impact on Ariovistus is based on Plutarch, *Caesar*, 19.

The quote 'Having thus marshalled ... cowed in spirit' is from Arrian, *The Anabasis of Alexander*, 2.10.

Numbers for the battle of Issus are from Arrian, *The Anabasis of Alexander*, 2.8 (Persians at Issus) & 3.12 (Macedonian figure provided later in Arrian's account).

The account of Pulcher's fleet surprising the Carthaginian naval force at Drepana and its aftermath are based on Polybius, *The Histories*, 1.50–52.

The account of the battle of Marathon is based on Herodotus, *The Histories*, 6.106–117 and the psychological significance of the Greek victory is from 6.112.

The contrast between Pompey and Caesar's views on static versus active soldiers is based on Appian, *The Civil Wars*, 2.79.

Suetonius' quote on Julius Caesar, 'He valued his soldiers...wind may blow them' is from Suetonius, *The Twelve Caesars*, Julius Caesar.65. Quote is from Loeb edition (1914).

The quotation 'all vain and imaginary fears are termed *panics*' is from Polyaenus, *Stratagems of War*, 1.2.2.

The account of Alexander's army taking control of the Rock of Sogdiana is from Arrian, *The Anabasis of Alexander*, 4.19.

The account of the Tyrians readily accepting unreliable information indicating the worst news because of their fears is from Curtius Rufus, *The History of Alexander*, 4.3.22.

The account of Alfenus Varus taking the fort with little opposition is based on Tacitus, *The Histories*, 3.61.

Rufus' point that in a disaster people usually blame each other is from Curtius Rufus, *The History of Alexander*, 4.3.7.

Appian's quote 'Having heard that an army...they blamed each other' is from Appian, *The Civil Wars*, 3.89.

The quote 'The result was... nobody obeyed them' is from Tacitus, *The Histories*, 3.73.

Tacitus quoted description of the Harii and the quoted material on how defeat in battle always begins with the eyes comes from Tacitus, *Germania*, 43.

Onasander's guidance on a general being accompanied to confer with the enemy by his finest and strongest looking soldiers, and the influence their appearance had on the enemy general is based on Onasander, *Strategikos*, 10.6.

Description of Clearchus marching his soldiers past the city of Opis is from Xenophon, *Anabasis*, 2.4

Hermocrates' quote 'We should also be reported...for the emergency' is from Thucydides, *History of the Peloponnesian War*, 6.34.

The account of Civilis fomenting a revolt and associated quote of displaying the standards of the defeated cohorts is from Tacitus, *The Histories*, 4.18.

The quote about Victorius and Atilius throwing the standards into the enemy ranks is from Livy, *History of Rome*, 34.46.12–13.

The account of the battle of Insubria and quote of Mago's wounding and being carried from the field is from Livy, *History of Rome*, 30.18.13.

The account of Ventidius' strategy and success against the Parthians at the battle of Mount Gindarus is from Florus, *Epitome of Rome*, 2.19.

Clearchus' deception of the Thracian envoys is from Frontinus, *The Stratagems*, 3.5.

Caesar's moment of doubt is reflected in Plutarch, *Caesar*, 39.

The account of Quinctius Flamininus' attack on Nabis at Sparta and Nabis' reactions is from Livy, *History of Rome*, 34.38–40.

The account of Pompey's at the battle of Pharsalus is based on Plutarch, *Caesar*, 45.

Chapter 12: Why Does Managing Politicians, Peers and Soldiers Matter?

The account of the Athenian ships supporting their Corcyrean allies is based on Thucydides, *History of the Peloponnesian War*, 1.49.

The account of Paetus fleeing Armenia, the success of Vologeses, Nero's response and Paetus' replacement by Corbulo, with associated quotes are from Tacitus, *The Annals*, 15.24–25.

The account of Fabius and quote 'kept away from… unskilfulness of the generals' is from Livy, *History of Rome*, 22.25.12.

The account of the Gaetulian War and quote on Augustus and Quirinius is from Florus, *Epitome of Roman History*, 2.31.

The account of Scipio Africanus' preparation of war games in Syracuse to reassure the Roman delegation reviewing his campaign preparations and associated quotes are from Livy, *History of Rome*, 29.22.1–6.

The quote 'land, money, and honours' is from Livy, *History of Rome*, 6.35.6.

The quote 'Caesar's power now… both of them' is from Florus, *Epitome of Roman History*, 2.13.

Tacitus' observation on credit for victory or blame for defeat in war is from Tacitus, *Agricola*, 27.

The account of the Greek commanders following the battle of Salamis, discussion of the aftermath and Spartan honour of Themistocles is based on Herodotus, *The Histories*, 8.123–124.

Discussion of the lead up to the battle at Trebia river, the battle itself, and the immediate aftermath are from Polybius, *The Histories*, 3.70–76.

The account of the war between Rome and the Veientines and quote 'For both Roman commanders… interest prejudiced each' are from Livy, *History of Rome*, 5.8.

The account of the rejected proposal to destroy crops, vegetation, and towns in the path of Alexander the Great's advance into Persia is based on Arrian, *The Anabasis of Alexander*, 1.13.

Carthaginian jealousies of Hannibal's success and the quote 'surpassed other commanders… against the ability of one' is from Cornelius Nepos, *The Lives of Eminent Commanders*, Hannibal, 1.

The accounts of the debate between Fabius and Scipio about launching a campaign in Africa or focussing solely on the war in Italy and associated quote is from Livy, *History of Rome*, 28.41.9, 28.44.15 and 28.43.7–8.

The account of Scipio comparing himself to Fabius and associated quote is from Polyaenus, *Stratagems of War*, 8.14.2.

The description of the meeting between Scipio Africanus and Hannibal and quote 'Alexander, king of Macedonia… as one of incomparable eminence' are from Livy, *History of Rome*, 35.14.6–12.

The account of Fabius fighting the Aequi and unable to make his infantry fight, with associated quote, is from Livy, *History of Rome*, 2.43.

Onasander's guidance to always ensure soldiers are occupied comes from Onasander, *Strategikos*, 9.1.

The description of Caesar keeping his army active 'Caesar, wishing to keep… experience in warfare' is from Velleius Paterculus, *The Roman History*, 2.78.

The observation that mutinies by soldiers with time on their hands, far away from Rome, and with communal military skills represented a real risk for Roman commanders particularly is supported by many accounts. For a detailed example refer to Livy, *History of Rome*, 28.24.

Fabius' advice to Lucius Paulus and associated quote 'For your own soldiers will desire the same thing as those of the enemy' are from Livy, *History of Rome*, 22.39.18.

The quote 'Fabius, keeping his attention… even at Rome' is from Livy, *History of Rome*, 22.15.1.

The quote concerning Primus Antonius 'courted the goodwill…of their caprices' is from Tacitus, *The Histories*, 3.49.

The account of Tiberius and associated quote that he 'saw that the soldiers…into three parts' is from Cassius Dio, *Dio's Rome*, 56.12.

The discussion of Xenophon's efforts to secure ships for the whole army and his recognition of the soldiers' refusal to face facts is based on Xenophon, *Anabasis*, 5.1.

The discussion of Alexander's soldiers determining to go no further is based on Arrian, *The Anabasis of Alexander*, 5.25.

Chapter 13: What Makes a Poor General?

The account and related quote 'Ships gone; Mindarus dead; the men starving; at our wits' end what to do' is from Xenophon, *Hellenica*, 1.1.23.

The description of the two Carthaginian losses (on land and at sea) and the blame being on the commanders is based on Polybius, *The Histories*, 1.31.

The discussion of Gnaeus Fulvius returning to Rome to report the defeat of his army, associated criticism from Senator Blaesus and quotes are from Livy, *History of Rome*, 26.2.8, 26.2.13–14, with the reference to Fulvius blaming his soldiers based on 26.3.1.

The description and quote on Vitellius 'He was ignorant... long run fatal' is from Tacitus, *The Histories*, 3.56.

The account of Sphodrias' failed attack on Piraeus is based on Plutarch, *Pelopidas*, 14.

Appian's criticism of the poor generalship of Scipio against Caesar and description of the events surrounding the battle of Thapsus are from Appian, *The Civil Wars*, 2.95–97.

Discussion of Gnaeus Cornelius Scipio and quote 'Scipio, though a wary... should meet him' are from Livy, *History of Rome*, 25.34.7.

Discussion of the Battle of Castulo, Battle of Ilorca and, collectively, the Battle of the Upper Baetis and aftermath are from Livy, *History of Rome*, 35.24-26

Vegetius' quote 'what is beneficial to you is detrimental to your enemy and what is of service to him always hurts you' is from Vegetius, *The Military Institutions of the Romans*, 3.26.

Discussion of the conflict with the Sabines is from Livy, *History of Rome*, 3.26 and the quotes are from Livy 3.26.3–4 and 3.26.4 respectively.

The description and details of Varus' defeat in the Teutoburg Forest are based on accounts and quotes by Velleius Paterculus, 2.117–120; Florus, *Epitome of Roman History*, 2.30; Cassius Dio, *Dio's Rome*, 56.18–56.24; Tacitus, *The Annals*, 1.61; and Suetonius, *The Twelve Caesars*, Augustus, 23. Paterculus' quote on Varus having 'lost his life and his magnificent army more through lack of judgement in the commander than of valour in his soldiers' is from Velleius Paterculus, *The Roman History*, 2.120.

The quote 'a man of character and of good intentions' is from Velleius Paterculus, *The Roman History*, 2.120.

Florus' quote 'the Germans had been defeated rather than subdued' and discussion on Varus assuming he could control them by his position and proclamations is from Florus, *Epitome of Roman History*, 2.30.

Paterculus' observations that Varus 'entered the heart of Germany as though he was going among a people enjoying the blessings of peace' and failed to pursue a summer campaign comes from Velleius Paterculus, *The Roman History*, 2.117.

The account of Varus making rapid changes to German society and treating them as slaves is based on Cassius Dio, *Dio's Rome*, 56.18.

The quote 'to such a complete degree of negligence ... heart of Germany' is from Velleius Paterculus, *The Roman History*, 2.118.

The accounts of the plot against Varus and his reaction, dispersing of soldiers, word of an uprising, Varus marching out and then the German chiefs leaving him are based on Cassius Dio, *Dio's History*, 56.19.

The description of the terrain, weather and lead up to the German attack is based on Cassius Dio, *Dio's History*, 56.20.

The quote 'but going along helter-skelter... no resistance at all' is from Cassius Dio, *Dio's Rome*, 56.20.

The description of the Romans struggling to form their lines and colliding with each other is based on Cassius Dio, *Dio's Rome*, 56.21.
The contrast of the impact on the storm on the Roman and German weapons and associated quotes are from Cassius Dio, *Dio's Rome*, 56.21.
The quote 'The general had more courage to die than to fight' is from Velleius Paterculus, *The Roman History*, 2.119.
The quote 'When this news was spread... without resistance' is from Cassius Dio, *Dio's Rome*, 56.22.
The quotation 'had always slaughtered like cattle... pity of the Romans' is from Velleius Paterculus, *The Roman History*, 2.119.
The quote 'Never was there slaughter... in the marshes and woods' and accounts of the torture of soldiers and digging up Varus' body are from Florus, *Epitome of Roman History*, 2.30 and the account of his body being desecrated, his head being cut off and sent back to Rome is from Velleius Paterculus, 2.119. Tacitus' description of what happened when Germanicus and his army returned to the site of the battle is from Tacitus, *The Annals*, 1.61.
Florus' description of the eagles still being held by the Germans and quote 'The result of the disaster... the banks of the Rhine' is from Florus, *Epitome of Roman History*, 2.30.
Account and quote of Emperor Augustus shouting 'Varus, give me back my legions!' is from Suetonius, *The Twelve Caesars,* Augustus, 23. Quote is from Loeb edition (1914).
The Germans and Gauls being sent from Rome, even those in the Pretorian Guard, and conscription to raise an army is from Cassius Dio, *Dio's Rome*, 56.23.
The quote 'unexcelled in bravery, the first of Roman armies in discipline, in energy, and in experience in the field' is from Velleius Paterculus, *The Roman History*, 2.119.

Chapter 14: What Makes a Good General?

The quote 'Iphicrates used to... it wanted everything' is from Polyaenus, *Stratagems of War*, 3.9.22.
The quote 'Philopoemen was possessed... devised was new to him' is from Livy, *History of Rome*, 38.25.1–7.
That Philopoemen's success was based on skill, his defeating the Cretans and Spartans, and the quote that his 'leadership made good soldiers' come from Plutarch, *Comparison of Philopoemen with Flaminius*, 2.
Florus' quote 'It is a true proverb which says that a general has the army he deserves' is from Florus, *Epitome of Roman History*, 1.34.
The discussion on Iphicrates and associated quote is from Cornelius Nepos, *Lives of Eminent Commanders*, Iphicrates, 1–2.
The quote 'nothing should be despised in war' is from Cornelius Nepos, *Lives of Eminent Commanders*, Thrasybulus, 2.
The account of Xenophon issuing orders and then ensuring they had been followed is based on Xenophon, *Anabasis*, 5.2.
Discussion on Alexander's presence and attentiveness at the Siege of Tyre is based on Arrian, *The Anabasis of Alexander*, 2.18.
The account of Sabinus is based on Tacitus, *The Annals*, 4.50.
Sallust's quote 'Catiline, during this time...a valiant soldier and a skilful general' is from Sallust, *The War with Catiline*, 60. The specific quote 'an eye to everything' is from Sallust, *Sallust*. Translated by J. C. Rolfe (1921). Loeb Classical Library, London: William Heinemann Ltd.
Marcellinus' advice 'And if it should... whether brave or timid' is from Ammianus Marcellinus, *The History of Ammianus Marcellinus*, 8.15.
The description of Scipio and quote 'Scipio took part...what was necessary' is from Polybius, *The Histories*, 10.13.
Florus' quote 'Spartacus himself fell, as became a general, fighting most bravely in the front rank' is from Florus, *Epitome of Roman History*, 2.8.

The account of Caesar urging his soldiers on to take Pompey's camp and finish the campaign is based on Appian, *The Civil Wars*, 2.81.

The discussion of Caesar at the Battle of Pharsalus and quote 'And if Caesar himself... the enemy!' are from Plutarch, *Caesar*, 52.

Suetonius' account of Caesar sending the horses away, including his own, to motivate his soldiers to fight is based on Suetonius, *The Twelve Caesars,* Julius Caesar.60.

The account of Alexander's actions which earned him the respect of his soldiers is based on Curtius Rufus, *The History of Alexander*, 3.6.19.

The account of Alexander tipping out the water and associated quote is from Arrian, *The Anabasis of Alexander*, 6.26.

The quote 'Never was a general... soldiers without reluctance' is from Livy, *History of Rome*, 7.33.

Xenophon's statement to his commanders that 'The soldiers outside...imitate you they will' is from Xenophon, *Anabasis*, 3.1.

The account of Marcus Centenius' elevation to general and associated quote is from Livy, *History of Rome*, 25.19.9–17.

The description of Antonius Primus' discussion with his soldiers over the differences between a soldier and a general and the quotes, 'But,' he said, 'an army and a general ...calculation and strategy' and 'The risks that face us... victory by force' are from Tacitus, *The Histories*, 3.19–20.

The observation from the Mytilenian debate on wisdom over unconsidered brute force is based on Thucydides, *The Peloponnesian War*, 3.48.

Livy's quote 'that the Roman commonwealth was more powerful by reason of its generals than its army' is from Livy, *History of Rome*, 2.39.2.

The discussion of Augustus' guidance on generalship and war is from Suetonius, *The Twelve Caesars,* Augustus. 25.

The reference to Augustus' advice *Festina lente* ('be active, but not rash') is from Polyaenus, *Stratagems of War*, 8.24.4.

The quote 'Nothing in the course... wisdom of its leader' is from Velleius Paterculus, *The Roman History*, 2.115.

The account of Tiberius' changed behaviour in Germany is from Suetonius, *The Twelve Caesars,* Tiberius.18.

The comparison and contrast of Julius Caesar's caution against his daring is based on Suetonius, *The Twelve Caesars,* Julius Caesar. 58 & 60.

The quote 'Actions speak louder than words' is from Sallust, *Histories,* 98.6, *Letter of Gnaeus Pompey to the Senate.* Quote is from Loeb edition (1921).

Teutiaplus' observation on what makes a successful general is based on Thucydides, *The Peloponnesian War*, 3.30.

Polybius' observation on Hannibal choosing unexpected options is based on from Polybius, *The Histories*, 3.78

Discussion on Hannibal's military genius being matched by Scipio Africanus is based on Polybius, *The Histories*, 18.28.

The quote on Scipio Africanus 'The fact was...most close calculation' is from Polybius, *The Histories*, 10.6.

Appian's comparison of Caesar and Alexander and associated quote 'men of the greatest ambition... military skill' is from Appian *The Civil Wars*, 2.149.

Arrian's reference to Alexander's uncontrollable passion for battle and glory is from Arrian, *The Anabasis of Alexander*, 6.13.

Account of Alexander against Bessus and quote 'was laying waste ... yet he persevered' is from Arrian, *The Anabasis of Alexander*, 3.28.

The observation of Alexander's determination and success in all his endeavours and associated quote is from Arrian, *The Anabasis of Alexander*, 7.15.

Bibliography

Ancient Texts

Ammianus Marcellinus, *The History of Ammianus Marcellinus.* Translated by C. D. Yonge (1911), London: G. Bell & Sons Ltd.

Ammianus Marcellinus, *The Later Roman Empire (AD 354–378).* Translated by Walter Hamilton (1986) with an introduction and notes by Andrew Wallace-Hadrill (1986), London: Penguin Books.

Appian, *The Roman History.* Translated by Horace White (1912). In four volumes (Vol.1). Loeb Classical Library, London: William Heinemann Ltd.

Appian, *The Roman History.* Translated by Horace White (1912). In four volumes (Vol.2). Loeb Classical Library, London: William Heinemann Ltd.

Appian, *The Roman History.* Translated by Horace White (1912). In four volumes (Vol.3). Loeb Classical Library, London: William Heinemann Ltd.

Appian, *The Roman History.* Translated by Horace White (1913). In four volumes (Vol.4). Loeb Classical Library, London: William Heinemann Ltd.

Appian, *The Civil Wars.* Translated with an introduction by John Carter (1996), London: Penguin Books.

Aristotle, *The Athenian Constitution.* Translated by Sir Frederic G. Kenyon (1914), London: G. Bell.

Aristotle, *Politics: A Treatise on Government.* Translated by William Ellis (1912), London: J. M. Dent & Sons Ltd.

Aristotle, *Politics* and *The Athenian Constitution.* Translated by John Warrington (1959), London: J. M. Dent & Sons Ltd.

Arrian, *The Anabasis of Alexander.* Translated by E. H. Chinnock (1884), London: Hodder & Stoughton.

Arrian, *The Campaigns of Alexander.* Translated by Aubrey De Selincourt (1958), revised with an introduction and notes by J. R. Hamilton (1971), London: Penguin Books.

Caesar, *'De Bello Gallico' and Other Commentaries.* Translated by W. A. McDevitte with an introduction by Thomas De Quincey (1915), Everyman's Library (702).

Caesar, *The Conquest of Gaul.* Translated by S. A. Handford (1951), revised with an introduction by Jane F. Gardner (1982), London: Penguin Books.

Cassius Dio, *Dio's Rome.* Translated by Herbert Baldwin Foster (1905). (Vols 1–6) New York: Pafraets Book Company.

Cassius Dio, *The Roman History: The Reign of Augustus.* Translated by Ian Scott Kilvert, with an introduction by John Carter (1987), London: Penguin Books.

Cornelius Nepos, [*Lives of Eminent Commanders*] in *Justin, Cornelius Nepos and Eutropius.* Translated by Rev. John Selby Watson, MA (1856), London: Henry G. Bohn.

Florus, *Epitome of Roman History.* Translated by E. S. Forster (1929), Loeb Classical Library 231, London: William Heinemann Ltd.

Frontinus, *The Stratagems and the Aqueducts of Rome.* Translated by Charles E. Bennett, edited and prepared for the press by Mary B. McElwain (1925), London: William Heinemann.

Herodotus, *The History of Herodotus*, Translated into English by G. C. Macaulay (1890). In two volumes (Vol.1) London: MacMillan and Co.
Herodotus, *The History of Herodotus*, Translated into English by G. C. Macaulay (1914), In two volumes (Vol.2) London: MacMillan and Co.
Herodotus, *The Histories*. Translated by Aubrey De Selincourt (1954), revised with an introduction and notes by John Marincola (1996, 2003), London: Penguin Books.
Homer, *The Odyssey*. Translated by E. V. Rieu (1946), London: Penguin Books.
Josephus, *The Jewish War*. Translated by G. A. Williamson (1959, 1970), revised with new introduction, notes and appendixes by Mary Smallwood (1981), London: Penguin Books.
Livy, *The History of Rome*. Translated by Daniel Spillan (1853). The first eight books. London: Henry G. Bohn.
Livy, *The History of Rome*. Translated by Daniel Spillan and Cyrus Edmonds (1858). Books nine to twenty-six. London: Henry G. Bohn.
Livy, *The History of Rome*. Translated by Cyrus Edmonds (1860). Books twenty-seven to thirty-six. London: Henry G. Bohn.
Livy, *The History of Rome*. Translated by William A. M'Devitte (1850). Books thirty-seven to the end.
Onasander, *Strategikos* (The General) in Aeneas Tacticus, Asclepiodotus, and Onasander. Translated by Illinois Greek Club (1923). Loeb Classical Library. London: William Heinemann Ltd.
Plato, *Dialogues of Plato (Laws)*. Translated by Benjamin Jowett (1892). In five volumes (Vol.5). New York: Charles Scribner's Sons.
Plutarch, *Plutarch's Moralia*, with an English translation by Frank Cole Babbitt, in 14 volumes, Vol.3. (1931) Loeb Classical Library, London: William Heinemann Ltd.
Plutarch, *Plutarch's Lives*. Translated by Aubrey Stewart and John Long (1894). In four volumes (Vol.1). London: George Bell & Sons.
Plutarch, *Plutarch's Lives*. Translated by Aubrey Stewart and John Long (1899). In four volumes (Vol.2). London: George Bell & Sons.
Plutarch, *Plutarch's Lives*. Translated by Aubrey Stewart and John Long (1892). In four volumes (Vol.3). London: George Bell & Sons.
Plutarch, *Plutarch's Lives*. Translated by Aubrey Stewart and John Long (1892). In four volumes (Vol.4). London: George Bell & Sons.
Plutarch, *The Lives of the Noble Grecians and Romans*. Translated by John Dryden and revised by Authur Hugh Clough (1979), New York: The Modern Library.
Plutarch, *Rome in Crisis*. Translated by Ian Scott Kilvert (1965) and Christopher Pelling, with notes and an introduction by Christopher Pelling (2010), London: Penguin Books.
Polyaenus, *Stratagems of War*. Translated by R. Shepherd (1793). Chicago: Ares Publishers Inc. (1974 print).
Polyaenus, *Stratagems of War*. Translated by R. Shepherd. Second edn (1796).
Polybius, *The Histories with an English Translation*, Translated by W. R. Paton (1922–1927). In six volumes (Vols 1–6). Loeb Classical Library, London: William Heinemann Ltd.
Polybius, *The Histories of Polybius*. Translated by Evelyn S. Shuckburgh (1889). In two volumes (Vol.1). London: MacMillan and Co.
Polybius, *The Histories of Polybius*. Translated by Evelyn S. Shuckburgh (1889). In two volumes (Vol.2). London: MacMillan and Co.
Polybius, *The Rise of the Roman Empire*. Translated by Ian Scott Kilvert, selected with an introduction by F. W. Walbank (1979), London: Penguin Books.
Quintus Curtius Rufus, *The History of Alexander*. Translated by John C. Rolfe (1946), Loeb Classical Library, London: William Heinemann Ltd.

Quintus Curtius Rufus, *The History of Alexander*. Translated by John Yardley (1984, 2001) with an introduction and notes by Waldemar Heckel (1984, 2001, 2004), London: Penguin Books.

Sallust, *Conspiracy of Catiline and the Jugurthine War*. Translated by J. S. Watson (1896). Philadelphia: David McKay.

Sallust, *Sallust*. Translated by J.C. Rolfe (1921). Loeb Classical Library, London: William Heinemann Ltd.

Sallust, *Catiline's War, The Jugurthine War, Histories*. Translated with an introduction and notes by A. J. Woodman (2007), London: Penguin Books.

Suetonius, *The Lives of the Twelve Caesars*. Translated by Alexander Thomson, revised and corrected by T. Forester (1909), London: George Bell & Sons.

Suetonius, *The Twelve Caesars*. Translated by J. C. Rolfe (1914). Loeb Classical Library, London: William Heinemann Ltd.

Suetonius, *The Twelve Caesars*. Translated by Robert Graves (1957), revised with an introduction and notes by James B. Rives (2007), London: Penguin Books.

Sun Tzu, *The Art of War*. Translated by Lionel Giles (1910), London: Luzac and Co.

Tacitus, *The Annals*. Translated by Alfred John Church and William Jackson Brodribb (1876 and 1884), Cambridge, MA: Hackett Publishing Company, Inc.

Tacitus, *The Annals of Imperial Rome*. Translated with an introduction by Michael Grant (1956, 1996), London: Penguin Books.

Tacitus, *The Histories*. Translated by W. H. Fyfe (1912), Oxford: Clarendon Press.

Tacitus, *The Histories*. Translated by Kenneth Wellesley (1964), revised with a new introduction by Rhiannon Ash (2009), London: Penguin Books.

Tacitus, *The Agricola and Germany of Tacitus*. Translated by Alfred John Church and William Jackson Brodribb (1868), London: MacMillan and Co.

Tacitus, *The Life and Death of Julius Agricola*. Translated by Alfred John Church and William Jackson Brodribb (1876), London: MacMillan and Co.

Tacitus, *Agricola* and *Germania*, Translated by Harold Mattingly (1948), revised with a new introduction and notes by J. B. Rives (2009), London: Penguin Books.

Thucydides, *The History of the Peloponnesian War*. Translated by Richard Crawley (1903), London: J. M. Dent & Sons.

Thucydides, *History of the Peloponnesian War*. Translated by Rex Warner (1954) with an introduction and notes by M. I. Finley (1972), London: Penguin Books.

Vegetius Renatus (Flavius), *The Military Institutions of the Romans*. Translated by John Clarke (1944), Harrisburg, PA: The Military-Services Publishing Company.

Vegetius Renatus (Flavius), *The Military Institutions of the Romans*. Translated by John Clarke (1767).

Velleius Paterculus, *Compendium of Roman History*. Translated by F. W. Shipley (1924), Loeb Classical Library 152, London: William Heinemann Ltd.

Virgil, *The Aeneid*. Translated by C. Day Lewis (1952) with notes and an introduction by Jasper Griffin (1986), Oxford: Oxford University Press.

Xenophon, *The Works of Xenophon*. Translated by H. G. Dakyns (1890). In four volumes (Vol.1), London: MacMillan and Co.

Xenophon, *The Works of Xenophon*. Translated by H. G. Dakyns (1892). In four volumes (Vol.2), London: MacMillan and Co.

Xenophon, *A History of My Times*. Translated by Rex Warner (1966) with an introduction by George Cawkwell (1979), London: Penguin Books.

Xenophon, *The Persian Expedition*. Translated by Rex Warner (1949) with an introduction by George Cawkwell (1972), London: Penguin Books.

Modern Texts
Andrewes, Antony (1967) *Greek Society*, Harmondsworth: Penguin Books Ltd.
Arnheim, M. T. W. (1977) *Aristocracy in Greek Society*, Thames and Hudson.
von Clausewitz, Carl (1982) *On War*. Edited with an introduction by Anatol Rapoport, London: Penguin Books.
Eisenhower, Dwight D. (1948) *Crusade in Europe*, New York: Doubleday & Co. Inc.
Keegan, John (1988) *The Face of Battle*, London: Barrie & Jenkins Ltd.
Liddell Hart, B. H. (1944) *Thoughts on War*, London: Faber & Faber.
Payne, Robert (1962), *The Roman Triumph*, London: Pan Books Ltd.

Index